The Seventeen Solutions

Ralph Nader

The Seventeen Solutions

BOLD IDEAS FOR OUR AMERICAN FUTURE

HARPER

NEW YORK · LONDON · TORONTO · SYDNEY

HARPER

THE SEVENTEEN SOLUTIONS. Copyright © 2012 by Ralph
Nader. All rights reserved. Printed in the United States of
America. No part of this book may be used or reproduced in
any manner whatsoever without written permission except
in the case of brief quotations embodied in critical articles
and reviews. For information address HarperCollins Publishers, 10 East 53rd Street, New York, NY 10022.

HarperCollins books may be purchased for educational,
business, or sales promotional use. For information please
write: Special Markets Department, HarperCollins
Publishers, 10 East 53rd Street, New York, NY 10022.

FIRST EDITION

Designed by Fritz Metsch

Library of Congress Cataloging-in-Publication Data is
available upon request.

ISBN 978-0-06-208353-1

12 13 14 15 16   OV/RRD   10 9 8 7 6 5 4 3 2 1

*To Allan Nairn, who has bravely, humbly,
and methodically exposed human rights abuses
from East Timor to Guatemala.*

Acknowledgments

First, I am grateful for the many citizens who have urged or worked on many of these solutions at one time or in one or more places in the United States. Without them, the linkages of concepts to practices would have not been possible.

I also thank my editor, Cal Morgan of HarperCollins, whose eye and pen few peers can match, and the incomparable John Richard for keeping this effort on track in all its details. The late-stage assistance of Katherine Raymond, Jeff Musto, Monica Giannone, and Matthew Marran kept the train moving toward its destination. Last, thanks to Marlene Thorpe and Lois Riley, who year after year kept me supplied with the contemporary material that informed this book.

Finally, I look forward to acknowledging those readers and doers who find any of these solutions sufficiently motivating to expand the number of public citizens pursuing their realization for the generations of today and tomorrow. Together we can overcome the institutional ravaging of social justice and the good life.

Ralph Nader

Contents

Introduction

Since the mid-eighteenth century, American society has been known for its ability to solve problems through innovation. Yet in recent years it has become solution-averse. In an era when the American people are experiencing major deprivation, the powers that be are devoted to the status quo—as long as their share of the pie keeps getting bigger, which it does—and they have the means and propaganda to keep it that way. More than ever, our nation needs change: stronger social safety nets; more effective electoral reforms; greater accountability for corporations; a shift of power away from the few toward the many; a return to communal self-reliance. Yet the public's expectations about what kind of country we can become are at a low tide.

Despite the stunning technological innovations that have marked our world for more than half a century, these conditions are only getting worse. Our country has far more problems than we deserve . . . and far more solutions than we apply. That gap is the democracy gap, and it underlies the paralyzing feeling of powerlessness shared by too many Americans—a feeling easily mistaken for apathy.

This sense of powerlessness is surprising, given how deeply we are steeped in information. There is no exposé gap in the United States. We are living in a golden age of investigative research: every year we are confronted by new documentary films, new

TV reports, new online journalists and bloggers, new newspaper and magazine articles, and new books detailing abuses of power throughout our society—from Pentagon contractors cozying up to politicians for exorbitantly unneeded or fraudulent deals; to perpetrating illegal wars and tax shelters; to critically contaminating land, air, and water; to the looting or draining of trillions of dollars of other people's money; to the impoverishment of political dialogue within a rigged political system; to the entrenchment of a corporate state of privileges, immunities, and bailouts; to the exacerbation of deepening poverty and casualties brought about by our corporate system—American-style.

Even the mainstream corporate media offer their share of exposés: *Bloomberg BusinessWeek, Fortune, 60 Minutes,* ABC's *It's Your Money,* the *Wall Street Journal*—all routinely publish probing journalistic investigations that far outstrip our undeveloped democracy's ability, or willingness, to correct the injustices they expose. With few exceptions, the mainstream media pays far less attention to the civic actions that strive to do something with that information. Which is why we cannot claim to enjoy a truly democratic society until we also have a truly democratic, noncommercial media that is owned and controlled by the audience it serves.

Progress is supposed to be America's trademark. And yet the reality is that, since 1972—the peak year of real wages in our country—80 percent of U.S. households have been sliding downward in standard of living. In the past three years, despite working longer hours, that slide has accelerated. Unemployment and underemployment as of this writing were at 8.2 percent and 15.7 percent (www.bls.gov/cps/), respectively. That is a blot on the face of the world's largest and richest economy. Fifty million people should not have to fear illness without health insurance. Every year forty-five thousand Americans die because they cannot afford insurance for diagnosis and treatment. One of every three workers earns Walmart-level wages—from $7.25 to $10.50

gross per hour. Even two such workers, many without health insurance, can't support a household of four on that income.

By any measure, more Americans are poorer today than in 1972. What do we mean by poor? Look at the Department of Labor's ridiculous definition of poverty: a family of four is not considered poor if it earns $23,050 a year before deductions. Economists have figured that to afford the bare necessities of life for four people would require an annual income of just over $40,000. By that yardstick, half of American households are poor. And statistics cannot begin to capture the sufferings, the impoverishment, the fear and insecurity of tens of millions of our fellow citizens who pick up after us, harvest and serve our food, care for our children, care for our elderly, and, disproportionately, fight our wars.

The poor pay more, often in unexpected ways. Impoverished Americans are especially vulnerable to consumer fraud, shoddy merchandise, and other marketing rackets involving fine-print contracts. For those who live in areas where public transportation is woeful—which means much of the country—just getting to work takes up precious unpaid hours. Many domestic workers leave the inner city at dawn and make two or more connections to reach their employers' well-appointed suburban homes by nine A.M., then spend much of the evening returning home. Millions of single mothers with long commutes have to send their children to day care centers that can cost around $500 a month.

Those commuters depend on the nation's public works, which are in great need of repair. The American Society of Civil Engineers (ASCE) tells us every year what it estimates it will cost to maintain and repair our public works—highways and roads, schools, clinics, water and sewage systems, public transit, dams, public buildings, and so on. Last year ASCE put the figure at $2 trillion. What they cannot estimate is how decrepit public services inconvenience, deny, and sometimes endanger those who use them day after day, rain, shine, snow, or sleet.

Millions of Americans are shackled to chronic high-interest debt, without any light at the end of the tunnel. We are in a period of record consumer debt, record bankruptcies, and record home foreclosures. To rub salt in the wound, the federal minimum wage has far less in purchasing power than it did in 1968. After accounting for inflation, our current minimum wage of $7.25 would have to be $10 to equal the rate forty-four years ago—even though worker productivity was half of what it is today. The gains from that productivity have gone overwhelmingly to the wealthiest 5 percent of Americans—and especially to the top 1 percent, who own 40 percent of the nation's private wealth and receive 25 percent of its income.

Five years ago, I published a book called *The Seventeen Traditions*. In that book, I reached back to my childhood to share seventeen lessons I learned from my family, our heritage, and the small-town New England civic community in which I was raised.

In the decades since then, the world has become a very different place. Corporate globalization has produced a massive exodus of American industries and jobs to repressive regimes abroad that know how to keep their workers in dire straits. Our traditional economy has been "financialized" to the point where it is now fueled by speculators bent on making money from money—enlarging the paper economy at the expense of a real economy that makes goods and services for the necessities of life. Despite the overall expansion of the GDP, poverty and near poverty *in our country* have grown and become more entrenched for tens of millions of people. The twin forces of militarism and commercialism have distracted money and effort away from civic and community values. Power is more concentrated than ever in fewer corporate and governmental hands—transforming us from a democratic society into a corporate state.

Polls show that between 70 and 80 percent of Americans

believe our country is going in the wrong direction—and that corporations have too much control over American lives. Most people have lost faith that those who work hard will be rewarded. Broken political promises, Wall Street bailouts of big-time crooks, and other betrayals have made us cynical and suspicious as a people—a cynicism that usually leads to withdrawal from civic and political engagement. Even the grassroots Occupy initiative, which showed promise in the fall of 2011, has yet to achieve the momentum of a united change agent.

Any working American during these years has felt the need for serious change in the fabric of our society. That appetite for change is what drove the election of Barack Obama, and today it drives the persistent undercurrent of dissatisfaction with both the president and his opposition. It is behind the cries of "We are the 99 percent," the disgust over our political discourse, even the contradictions of the Tea Party protestors and their allies in the Republican Party.

Much of the debate engendered by these groups is simplistic at best, poisonous at worst. But the need for change is real. And change cannot happen until we, as Americans, decide to expect more from our country.

Change has always started with people elevating their expectation levels—from the antislavery, women's suffrage, farmers' and workers' revolts of the nineteenth century to the civil rights, consumer, and environmental movements of more recent times. It begins when we, as citizens, look beyond our own fears and prejudices and, in a tone of mutual respect with our friends and neighbors, engage in a vigorous, challenging conversation over the future of our nation.

The Seventeen Solutions is my effort to start a new conversation about our problems.

In these seventeen chapters, I offer fresh ideas on how to solve some of the deepest problems affecting our society today. Some of these ideas, like cracking down on corporate crime and ending corporate welfare, point to changing conditions on the ground. Others, like electoral reforms, call for consumers, workers, and small taxpayers to come together and use the available forums of justice to enact solid change. Still others respond to the assault on our earth's fragile biosphere—the thin slice of soil, water, and air that sustains living beings on the planet.

These seventeen solutions are in no way an exclusive list. They are merely a jumping-off point for activists. Each solution invites you to participate at whatever level of talent, energy, and resources you are willing and able to devote. No power can stop you from at least taking that first crucial, galvanizing step. For the future, it must be declared, is up to us to organize. As the great freeman and abolitionist Frederick Douglass exclaimed in lecture after lecture: "Power concedes nothing without a demand."

In the Depression-racked 1930s, the famous British economist John Maynard Keynes wrote an essay entitled "Economic Possibilities for Our Grandchildren." In that piece, he made a prophecy that we have shamelessly failed to fulfill. At the time of his writing, the world economy had reached a level of productivity that would enable society to eliminate the "economic problem"— that is, the persistence of abject poverty. "The *economic problem* may be solved, or be at least within sight of solution, within a hundred years," he wrote. "This means that the economic problem is not—if we look into the *future—the permanent problem of the human race.*" Keynes argued that there was no economic excuse for not abolishing poverty and for providing everyone with the necessities of life, including retirement security.

I say "shamelessly failed to fulfill" because everyone knows that Keynes was right—that our economy is hugely more productive but also unjustly distributed in its gains and misdirected in its investments. Our wisest voices have historically had an honest disagreement over the best ways to fix this imbalance.

But those honest arguments tend to be drowned out by dishonest opposition from the powerful few, who want to decide for the many how the economic pie is to be divided, invested, applied, and inherited.

The Seventeen Solutions I offer here are designed to diminish these worsening injustices. The growing disconnect between GDP figures and corporate profits on one hand, and the conditions of the great majority of American workers and families on the other, represents the expanding failure of corporate capitalism—and the corporate state in Washington, D.C., that protects it—to deliver the goods for the working families of America.

American workers labor longer than any of their counterparts in the Western world. But they are also worse off than any of those counterparts. They are not receiving their just deserts.

Now let's do something *together* about this abomination.

The Seventeen Solutions

1

Fundamental Tax Reform

"Taxes are what we pay for civilization," remarked Justice Oliver Wendell Holmes.

Today, however, the taxes we pay are used not just to foster civilization but also to support the tax-free existence of countless massive corporations.

Want to brag? If you paid a dollar or more in federal income taxes in 2010, or the two years before that, you paid more in taxes than many large corporations. U.S. chartered companies like Bank of America, Verizon, General Electric (GE), Boeing, Citigroup, and Honeywell report big profits every year, but they often pay zero in federal income tax. These corporations have legions of specialized tax attorneys and accountants who view their departments as profit centers. By manipulating the tax code and playing one nation against another, they can and do bring down their tax obligations to Uncle Sam to zero and sometimes even get a tax benefit or credit from the U.S. Treasury.

The U.S. tax code—7,500 pages long, plus thousands more pages' worth of interpretations—is the product of many years of corporate lobbying, low IRS enforcement budgets, and eager senators and representatives craving campaign contributions.

Corporations truly are different from you and me. As humans, we cannot create hundreds of subsidiaries (children) abroad to reduce our taxes. But there seems no limit to the number of offspring these artificial entities called corporations can create. The disgraced Enron alone created 881 subsidiary companies, parking 692 in the Cayman Islands, 119 in the Turks and Caicos Islands, 43 in Mauritius, and 8 in Bermuda. These corporate entities are fictitious, but they produce real facts that affect you. Even as they receive all the public services and protections due to a U.S. corporation, these companies shift their profits and royalties to these tax havens and use all the domestic loopholes they have driven through Congress for their self-serving privileges and immunities. The result? Your taxes are higher, public services are reduced, and the government goes into greater debt.

These tax escapees use many offshore havens to game the tax code, but none is more dramatic than the overpopulated Ugland House in the Cayman Islands. Nearly twenty thousand companies have the legal addresses of their many overseas corporate subsidiaries in this one building for the sole purpose of avoiding taxes.

These clever tax lawyers for these global companies must be delirious with their successes. Imagine their celebratory parties, full of jokes about how their company pays its CEO more money than the entire corporation pays into the U.S. Treasury. Imagine the lawyers for gigantic GE, looking back on their year's work—a year in which they not only protected GE from paying any taxes but got the Treasury to send *them* a multibillion-dollar check. In the three years from 2008 to 2010, GE made $7.722 billion in profit in the United States, paid no federal income tax, *and* got $4.737 billion back from the U.S. Treasury—while paying its CEO, Jeff Immelt, a total of nearly $25.58 million in executive pay.

All these tax maneuvers are "perfectly legal," say the corporate attorneys, who cloak them with the euphemism "tax avoidance." That means they believe their companies are complying with the tax code, whose perforations their corporate lobbyists got through Congress. "Tax evasion," on the other hand, is illegal. The line between the two is increasingly blurred as the tax laws become more complex and the global corporations learn how to work different nations' tax laws to perfection. The nation's leading tax reporter, David Cay Johnston, who won a Pulitzer Prize for his writing for the *New York Times*, has noted that these giant corporations can now decide how much to pay in taxes, where to pay them, and when to pay them.

The tax escapees work from a long and lucrative playbook. Their tactics include finding ways to avoid reporting income from their companies and partnerships; soliciting huge technology and natural resource gifts from the government; and devising countless ways to inflate expenses and defer income indefinitely into the future.

The more complex the laws are, the more shenanigans the corporations are likely to attempt. True, we have a complex economy, but so does Canada, whose tax code is much simpler. Our modern tax code is designed to benefit the rich and influential, with only a tiny number of outside people knowing how they are getting away with it. Its complexity, enacted without public hearings, camouflages their endless and varied tax escapades. And the IRS is hopelessly understaffed, in need of auditors skilled enough to monitor these giant companies.

Notwithstanding the economic meltdown of 2008, these corporations continue to earn massive profits: $1.678 trillion in 2010 alone. Yet the share of federal tax revenue contributed by effective corporate income taxes has shrunken from close to 30 percent in the 1950s to roughly 10 percent today.[1]

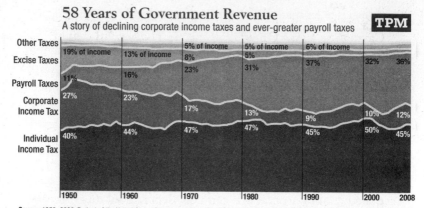

58 Years of Government Revenue
A story of declining corporate income taxes and ever-greater payroll taxes

Source: 1950–2006: Budget of the United States Government, Fiscal Year 2008, HISTORICAL TABLES, Table 2.1. Receipts by Source: 1934–2012

This graph depicts fifty-eight years of taxes levied by the government. As Brian Beutler pointed out in Talking Points Memo: "Since 1950, regressive payroll taxes have grown to comprise over one-third of federal revenues—they used to comprise about one-tenth. For corporate income taxes, it's just the opposite—what used to provide the Treasury over a quarter of its revenue now provides just over 10 percent." Source: Talking Points Memo.com, Brian Beutler.[2]

Chuck Collins, a leading tax reformer who teamed with William Gates, Sr., years ago to organize roughly one thousand wealthy Americans to oppose the proposed congressional repeal of the estate tax, has expressed exactly how these corporations affect the American landscape:

> See that FedEx delivery van go by on the roads you paid for? Pay up FedEx! Don't pretend you're not making billions in the U.S. Don't lie and tell us you made all those profits on some island with more palm trees than people. We know the demand for coconut delivery isn't that big. . . .
>
> So, ExxonMobil: the next time your gas station erupts

in flames, why don't you call the fire department on the Cayman Islands? Or when someone holds up the joint, how about calling the Luxembourg police, since that's where you claim your profits so you don't have to pay the taxes you owe Uncle Sam.

Hey, Pfizer: without our remarkable taxpayer-funded system of patents and intellectual property rights protections, everyone and his brother would be making Viagra and undercutting your sales of little blue pills. Pay up!

Boeing, you want another contract for a taxpayer-funded military jet? Well, pay up! Pay up General Electric, Mattel, Dow Chemical, Hewlett-Packard, and Cisco. Yes, we know you pay some taxes. But look these children who are losing their health insurance and teaching aides in the eye. Tell them you're paying your fair share.[3]

Collins could have said much of the same for the wealthy, whose returns on capital—capital gains and dividends—are taxed at a maximum of 15 percent, a lower rate than the taxes on labor. This has been true for years: the return on capital has been outpacing the return on labor. For the past few decades, tax cuts for the rich have been followed by more demands from many members of Congress for still more tax cuts on corporate firms and wealthy individuals. The tax laws have become more regressive, especially when payroll and sales taxes are included as a percentage of individual income paid in taxes.

Collins also noted: "Those of us who pay sales taxes and have income taxes withheld from our paychecks will bear the brunt of state and federal budget cuts in schools, public transportation, and recreational facilities. Our most vulnerable family members and neighbors will suffer thanks to cuts in mental health services, elder care, and Medicaid. . . ."[4]

When it comes to tax policy, Congress is an endemic mess. Avaricious lobbyists swarm its members daily, campaign checks in hand, demanding special provisions for corporate jets, drilling equipment, consumables like alcoholic beverages used for business entertainment—even credits to the corporations for doing what they should be doing anyway, such as investing in research and development (R&D). Sometimes surreptitiously inserting just a small paragraph can mean a reduction of hundreds of millions or even billions of dollars for the companies or industries quietly behind them. In years gone by, our tax reform group launched a campaign to expose the sudden moves corporations use to get a tax loophole included in a bill late in a congressional session. Nicknamed "Christmas tree insertions," these provisions are inserted into gigantic tax bills so deftly that few know who is behind them and almost no one truly understands them. The *New York Times* often reported our findings, and under the embarrassing glare of publicity the provisions would be dropped by the House Ways and Means Committee or the Senate Finance Committee. Yet the media (with some exceptions) have eventually stopped this kind of watchdog service, and the tidal wave keeps getting larger.

To this point, even the most vigorous tax reform efforts have barely put a dent in the corporations' massive abuse of the system. Narrow, topical reforms have quickly disappeared into the trees, and the reformers and media alike have proven unable to see the forest. If we are to have any hope of eradicating corporate abuse of the tax system, we must start by looking at the principles that are supposed to characterize the entire forest of tax policy in order to arrive at a consensus opinion about how a fair, productive, and *comprehensible* tax system should work.

The basic purpose of taxation is to raise revenue needed for public services. A second, ancillary purpose is to encourage or discourage various social and economic behaviors—by producers, vendors, or consumers—such as through "sin taxes" on things like cigarettes and gambling.

In my lectures around the country, I often open up the

conversation about taxes by proposing that, before we tax gainful labor, we should tax first that which society likes the least or dislikes the most. For instance, we should tax Wall Street speculation, which currently is subject to zero sales tax on its trillions of dollars of annual transactions—while daily, consumers have to pay sales taxes even on necessities. Wall Street speculation has long since become a house of cards, a game of computer-driven bets on bets on bets, far removed from real-world investments in real economic activity. Now-infamous Wall Street gambits such as credit default swaps and collateralized debt obligations, which attracted billions of investment dollars, have directly or eventually put entire national economies at risk. Shouldn't we want to dampen this kind of rampant speculation with other people's money—often called "casino capitalism"—that is clearly unproductive for the real economy?

We should tax pollution—through, for instance, a carbon tax—both to collect revenue and to reduce pollution by making polluters pay for their damage. Even ExxonMobil favors this kind of tax over cap-and-trade alternatives, which would result in mandatory limits on emissions, albeit with the option for companies to buy or trade for more "credits" if it cannot reduce its pollution below the cap. The Carbon Tax Center (CTC) has called for a tax that would grow at an annual rate equivalent to 5 to 10 percent of the baseline cost of fossil fuels. This amounts to a "starter tax" of approximately $37 per ton of carbon or roughly 10 cents per gallon of gasoline. The CTC estimates that a federal starter tax applied to U.S. fossil fuel burning, equaling about 10 cents per gallon of gasoline (but paid by corporations, not individuals), would initially generate about $55 billion per year.[5]

We should tax the addictive industries—not just alcohol, tobacco, and gambling, but also junk food and drinks, which account for so many illnesses, including our epidemic of childhood obesity. Don't we want to diminish these painful or harmful human conditions?

And we should tax corporate crime—far more than the trivial penalties levied today when corporate criminals are convicted (or settle out of court). Don't we want to reduce corporate crime by changing the cost-benefit calculation of those who commit them?

The Canadians came up with a phrase describing this kind of policy: "Tax what you burn, not what you earn." I would add, "Tax first what you bet, not what you net."

Obviously this strategy alone would not produce all the revenue our nation needs. But it would greatly lighten the burden on what we like the most—such as remunerative work—and in ways that are much harder to game or evade than occurs presently with the income tax. Moreover, diminishing harmful or reckless activities provide tangible and intangible savings in their own right that do not have to be paid by society.

For almost thirty years, one of our former public interest lawyers, Robert McIntyre, has been running Citizens for Tax Justice, a respected nonprofit group that documents exactly how, when, and why taxpayers fill—or avoid filling—the coffers of the U.S. Treasury. Even McIntyre's opponents recognize the accuracy of his team's work.

A few years ago, the Institute on Taxation and Economic Policy (ITEP) published a concise two-page brief offering an overview of five commonly cited principles of sound tax policy: *equity, adequacy, simplicity, exportability,* and *efficiency.* ITEP recognizes that these are not the only criteria policymakers can use in enacting tax changes but argues that tax reform advocates should remain mindful of each of these principles in proposing new reforms.

Here are some reforms that undergird these principles:

Equity comes in two varieties: vertical and horizontal. *Vertical equity* is violated by regressive tax systems—such as consumer sales taxes, excise taxes, and property taxes—which take a bigger chunk out of lower incomes than wealthy incomes. Progressive taxes, on the other hand, apply horizontal higher tax rates to the wealthiest taxpayers. Tax experts usually justify this on the simple grounds that the wealthiest Americans are able to pay a higher percentage on their millions of dollars in income without feeling any pinch. But there are two other less frequently mentioned reasons for taxing the wealthy at higher rates. One is that wealthy corporate power players have greater economic power to keep workers' income down. Think of the disparity between the huge annual income of CEOs at companies like McDonald's, the Walt Disney Company, Walmart, Kmart, and Home Depot—many of whom make from $5,000 to $15,000 per hour—and the frozen $7.25 federal minimum wage earned by millions of their workers. A second reason is that the wealthy classes have *political* power, which they use to rig governmental systems to favor their accumulation of wealth—through corporate subsidies, free technology transfers, inflated noncompetitive government contracts, and other tactics. Real estate and communications moguls benefit from amazing tax advantages and free licenses; mineral and timber bosses feast off giveaways, bargain-basement leaseholds, and other lucrative tax benefits. And when these power brokers profit, their large shareholders do too.

Horizontal equity is violated when different forms of income are treated with different tax rates—a tactic that, once again, usually favors the wealthy. In our current system, income from dividends and capital gains is taxed at 15 percent, while income from daily labor can be taxed as high as 35 percent. President Reagan raised the tax on capital gains to 28 percent. President Clinton reduced it to 20 percent, setting the stage for President George W. Bush to diminish it further to 15 percent.

Adequacy refers to the fact that, as taxpaying citizens, we expect the federal government to have a stable and sufficient source of revenue to fund the public services we need. No one would support a system in which taxes decline as the economy grows and demand for public services increases. Nor would one support a system that collects more taxes when the economy is in recession unless they were invested in public works projects and jobs. In principle, the personal income tax system usually meets this test: When everyday Americans are making more, they can afford to pay more. When they make less, the government collects less.

Simplicity, of course, may be the word least likely to be associated with today's tax system. The complexity of our tax code seriously hampers the government's ability to enforce its basic principles. Years ago, over lunch with the Internal Revenue commissioner, I noted that the insurance section of the tax code was so complex that fewer people probably understood it than understand Einstein's theory of relativity. He did not disagree.

The tax code's complexity also increases the cost of enforcement. Our current tax code is marked by imprecise language and dense levels of ambiguity, offering a field day for corporate tax attorneys with their strategies of attrition and delay on the overburdened Internal Revenue Service. Global corporations such as Merck, Citigroup, and ExxonMobil should require the IRS to employ enough auditors year-round just to perform minimal scrutiny on their activities in scores of different nations and jurisdictions. Instead, the IRS assigns considerable resources to police petty violations by middle-class and even low-income taxpayers, who use the Reagan-approved earned income tax credit (EITC).

Exportability is the principle that prevents people from enjoying a free lunch at other people's expense by traveling across state lines to avoid taxes. Tourists who use a given state's public transit, for instance, have to pay that state's sales taxes; multinational corporations based in a specific state or country are taxed by a formula that reflects their sales in other states.

Efficiency is a term for tax systems that limit the risk of corporations making business decisions based on tax avoidance considerations rather than pure business reasons. Back in the 1970s, for example, Chrysler created a real estate investment subsidiary purely to take advantage of tax avoidance opportunities. As Robert McIntyre notes, "The big tax breaks that the Reagan administration provided for commercial real estate in the early 1980s [also] led to far too much office construction and the phenomenon of 'see-through office buildings' that nobody wanted to rent. These wasteful investment scams, of course, come at the expense of more productive investments—and were paid for by all other taxpayers."[6]

These principles, of course, can conflict with one another. For instance, it may well be advisable for the tax code to be used to further energy independence and a shift from fossil fuels and nuclear to energy efficiency (conservation) and renewable energy (solar, wind, and geothermal). Locating more jobs in retrofitting buildings throughout America to conserve energy may be another purpose of a tax preference policy.

Within these guidelines, deductions can be adjusted or eliminated. Business entertainment, for example, involving very expensive shows and high-priced celebrities at posh resorts, are suitable candidates for curtailment to give small taxpayers some relief. If these taxpayers ever got a glimpse of what corporations deduct as "ordinary and necessary" business expenses for their executives and their firms, they would be outraged.

In more prosperous times, the U.S. tax code was much more progressive. During the Eisenhower administration, the largest earners paid roughly 90 percent after deductions. Under Ronald Reagan, that number started at 70 percent but was whittled down to 28 percent when he left office. By the end of Bill Clinton's administration, that number had increased to 39.6 percent.[7] Given that 3.1 million people have more than $1 million in investable finance (assets not including primary residence)[8], and that there are more billionaires and megabillionaires than ever, we must raise the highest tax rates—and/or eliminate the many tax shelters for the wealthy, legal and otherwise—if we are to have a fair and just tax system.

We must also address the massive matter of uncollected taxes, currently estimated at nearly $400 billion by the IRS. Rather than going after the small-fry—which would likely not be cost-effective—the government could collect billions of dollars simply by requiring brokerage accounts to withhold taxes on savings interest and stock dividends, including those of foreign investors. Once the government begins collecting this category of uncollected revenue, it would find remarkable opportunities for fairness to those who do pay. As David Cay Johnston reported in his book *Perfectly Legal: The Covert Campaign to Rig Our Tax System to Benefit the Super Rich—and Cheat Everybody Else*, IRS commissioner Charles O. Rossotti told the Senate Finance Committee in 2001 that "perhaps one in every five dollars of K-1 income ['partner reports' detailing how much money each partner made or lost and whether it should be taxed as capital gains or ordinary income] was not showing up on income tax returns. The cost in lost tax revenue was perhaps $30 billion each year. What Rossotti's reports revealed was the utter misallocation of law enforcement resources."[9]

In the early days of the Clinton administration, the Pulitzer Prize–winning investigative reporters Donald L. Barlett and James B. Steele published the bestselling book *America: Who Really Pays the Taxes?* In it, they called for the IRS to devote more budgetary resources to enforcement and to use electronic tools more aggressively "for tracking financial transactions in a global economy."[10] They argued that Americans live under "two tax systems, in which enforcement efforts are more heavily concentrated in the middle-income brackets than at the top," and note that replacing "the current system of criminal penalties for tax crimes" with severe economic penalties would remove "the profit motive from tax evasion."

Barlett and Steele write that a simplified tax system would nearly end what they call "the tax industry," in which lawyers, accountants, and consulting businesses thrive off the complexity of the current system. They point out that such specialists, and their auxiliaries in government and commerce, have a vested interest "in preserving two tax laws—one for the privileged person, whom they represent, and another for the common person, who has no representation."

After more than a year traveling across the country observing the tax system's consequences on the economy—including the plight of workers afflicted by wasteful, inequitable, and unproductive tax laws—Barlett and Steele encountered one question posed over and over again by people from Cherry Hill, New Jersey, to Portland, Oregon; from Boston to Miami. The question was asked not by radical students but by grandmothers and professionals and blue-collar workers and a white man from Philadelphia in a three-piece suit, who stated it most bluntly: "Do you really believe these problems can be solved without people taking to the streets?"

Seventeen years later, the Occupy Wall Street movement answered his question.

For all the time Americans spend grumbling about taxes—far more than in Western European countries—we devote remarkably little serious *public* discussion to the tax code, beyond the general condemnations uttered by pandering politicians. What little discussion there is tends to focus on income, property, and capital gains taxes, plus an occasional call for sin taxes when things get desperate. Sheldon Cohen, a former IRS commissioner under President Jimmy Carter, wrote: "If you know the position a person takes on taxes, you can tell their whole philosophy. The tax code, once you get to know it, embodies all the essence of life: greed, politics, power, goodness, charity." Former senator Russell B. Long said, "[A tax loophole] is something that benefits the other guy. If it benefits you, it is tax reform."

Why such cynicism about a system in such urgent need of reform?

One answer may be the lack of leadership from labor unions, citizen groups, and other foundations, which should be taking the initiative and calling for fundamental changes in the ways taxes are imposed. Another explanation is that Americans have come to view their take-home pay as the true measure of their salaries, forswearing any claim on the portion of their income that is withheld for taxes. The withholding system has led to a fatalistic attitude among many taxpayers. Finally, beyond the most basic public services—maintaining roads and bridges, providing police and fire services—the American public has lost sight of the potential benefits we might enjoy if we were to enact a system of fairer progressive taxation.

Consider the difference in Western Europe. In some categories, Europeans do pay higher taxes. But in return they receive an unmistakable array of public services: complete coverage health insurance for all; tuition-free higher education; paid day care, maternity leave, and family sick leave; higher wages for lower-level jobs; universal pensions; and better unemployment benefits—not to mention well-funded arts programs, more parks, and better public transit. Most Europeans enjoy an annual minimum of four weeks' paid vacation—in Sweden the average is five weeks, up to seven in certain cases—while benefiting from more extensive union protection.

The one obvious analog in American history is the Social Security system, which has become our most universally valued entitlement. Social Security has earned the faith of the American people, largely because they recognize that paying into the system now will pay off later, after retirement, in the form of tangible monthly checks. Especially among the elderly, the same is true of Medicare: this sense of receiving something back from a fund they helped build with their taxes is a very personal one.

In deliberating new tax policy, Congress rarely focuses on linking new taxes to these kinds of material returns. But any basic changes to our tax laws should involve a clear link between new revenue and significant tangible rewards—as well as a real effort to communicate what those new tax dollars are funding. American taxpayers are conditioned, not unreasonably, to expect their tax contribution to disappear into a bottomless well of wasteful spending, while they suffer under crippling fiscal obligations. In contrast to Western Europe, for instance, where university education has been mostly tuition-free, American students assume very large debts with high interest rates and onerous fine-print contracts that they must start paying off right after graduation. Taxpayers who enter the workforce under such a burden are not likely to view their tax obligation with much expectation of reciprocal reward.

This cynicism helps explain how even a Bob Riley, a former antitax congressman turned Alabama governor, lost a state referendum in 2003 to make state taxes less burdensome on the poor—who earned less than $13,000 yet paid almost 11 percent of their income in state and local taxes in that year, while Alabamans who made more than $229,000 paid about 4 percent. Despite campaigning eloquently around the state—"If the New Testament teaches me anything," he said, "it teaches me not only to love thy neighbor but also to help those who are the least among us"—Riley saw his referendum rejected by poor and rich voters alike, assuring that the state's abysmally low level of public services, including education, would continue. In 2010, a similar measure to raise taxes on the wealthy, championed by William Gates Sr., in Washington State failed at the polls as well. Voters are eternally suspicious that any new tax reform measure is really a malicious "tax scheme," skewed for the rich and corporate like so many that have come before.

As David Cay Johnston notes, "If people look around and see that they are being taxed on their labor while those who started out with capital [from wealthy estates] are not, then they are likely to demand more direct benefits for their taxes."

Ultimately, however, any call for tax reform must begin at the doors of Congress, which should vote only on tax bills and amendments that have been aired at public hearings and that have the names of the sponsors disclosed for each change. Our congressional elections have become wholly corporatized, offering candidates slush funds in exchange for commercial tax breaks, deferrals, credits, and exemptions. Changing this system is a precondition of fundamental tax reform and enforcement.

2

Make Our Communities More Self-Reliant

Growing up in the 1940s in Winsted, Connecticut—a typical New England factory town—I always knew when my father was making ice cream at his restaurant on Main Street. Almost before I could place my order, it was pouring right out of the machine into my cup—just delicious. The milk and cream he bought from local dairy farmers, whose cows could be heard mooing in the morning on the neighboring hillsides; nearby residents received freshly filled bottles delivered directly to their front doors.

Today, the ice cream we buy in stores and restaurants comes from large national producers. The local dairy farms are mostly gone. We can only wonder what additives are in the ice cream and milk we buy—including bovine growth hormone, which many Western countries have banned—and such questions are not easily answered. The degree of tampering with our dairy and other foods, for the profit and convenience of the sellers, grows more complex and unknowable each year.

At one time, the community of Winsted, home to ten thousand people, also harbored about one hundred factories and fabrication shops, manufacturing everything from appliances to textiles, pins, electrical equipment, clocks, and wire. They're long gone too. Today Winsted is largely a bedroom community, with most of the dwindling good jobs an hour's commute away in the Hartford/Waterbury/New Britain area. It's been decades since the great New England factories went south for cheaper labor, or were merged and shut down, or (more recently) have been displaced by China.

On Route 44 to Hartford, twenty-six miles away, scores of businesses line the highway. Most of the money spent along this motorway goes to the national chains, with their familiar logos hoisted on backlit signs along the roadside. Few family-owned businesses remain.

This local economy has largely been replaced by regional outposts of national companies, whose leaders make decisions that are far removed from the interests of local residents but which affect their lives every day. Big banks have replaced many smaller community banks; big supermarket chains have pushed aside grocery stores. In area after area, the big guys have taken over—either directly or through franchise arrangements that amount to fine-print contract servitude.

For years, the old debates about this kind of displacement have raged back and forth. Now, however, the terms of the debate have changed dramatically. There are several reasons.

For one thing, more and more Americans recognize how the big multinationals have abandoned America, facilitated by trade agreements of their own making. The evidence—empty factories, hollowed-out communities, unemployed workers, looted pensions—is everywhere. Lately, white-collar jobs have been outsourced to India and other English-speaking countries as thoroughly as they once shipped our blue-collar jobs overseas.

For another, the large producer companies have begun exacting heavier and heavier tolls on local communities, especially when it comes to environmental health issues. Hydrofracking for natural gas in the mid-Atlantic states is just the latest peril to our land, water, and other natural resources. Local consumers are being whipsawed by price manipulation and speculation by faraway entities with no stake in their communities. Exhibit A

is the price of gasoline and heating oil, manipulated by speculators at the New York Mercantile Exchange. As health care and
pharmaceuticals become more corporatized and centralized,
costs are also rising sharply, leaving millions more Americans
uninsured and at serious risk each decade.

These discomforts can lead to positive popular responses.
Our growing awareness of nutritional issues has led consumers
to reject the plastic, processed foods sold in supermarket and fast-
food chains. For more consumers, processed white bread is out,
farmers' markets are in. As banks have heaped more and more
burdens on their customers in the form of fees, penalties, and
other fine-print costs—and as the subprime mortgage–assisted
crash of Wall Street and the economy revealed the outrageous
practices of many of our largest lenders—Americans have been
learning to expect more from our vendors.

Old and new technologies, and a greater appreciation for the
importance of sustainable economic activity, are leading more
and more Americans to go local. Communities are harnessing
their assets—sun, wind, water, money, and unused fertile land—
and putting them to work. Community and backyard gardens
are providing fresh produce for increasing numbers of American
shoppers. Cleaned-up rivers and ponds are allowing recreation
and tourism to thrive in areas that may have been neglected for
decades. Long-dormant factory buildings and storefronts are being repurposed by local arts and crafts centers. Farmers' markets,
cooperatives, and recycling centers are fostering greater social
interaction and neighborhood spending. Bicycle pathways, often
replacing disused train tracks or other rights-of-way, have flourished. The results are bearing out the argument of E. F. Schumacher's classic bestseller *Small Is Beautiful: Economics as if People
Mattered*—that a grassroots effort to harness alternative models,
designed to serve local residents and their traditional rhythms,
can benefit a community far more than an economic landscape
imposed unilaterally by absentee multinational corporations.

Even though these alternative models are working on the ground here and there throughout America, they are not yet on a fast track to spread fully throughout the nation. They confront many kinds of obstacles, chief among them the big companies' dominant control of our political institutions—legislative, executive, and judicial; at the national and state levels. But if the American people are to turn around our declining standard of living, we must start by reversing our dependence on global corporations and shifting our spending to community businesses that interact face-to-face with their customers and are rooted deeply enough in their communities that they will not threaten to leave. (None of which is to idealize local communities, of course; it's not uncommon in small towns for one or two wealthy families to rule the community's fiscal and political fortunes. But even a powerful small-town family is more likely to serve its community's interest than a distant, profiteering corporation.)

Opportunities for sustainable community economies may be more apparent in towns and villages than they are in larger urban and suburban areas. Population density does tend to foster the ability of certain services, such as credit unions, to develop and thrive. But the opportunities are everywhere. As Gar Alperovitz and his associates at the Democracy Collaborative at the University of Maryland have noted:

> Restraining corporate power requires changing the way we think about business. This means changing who owns, controls, and benefits from it. Profits, for instance, can flow to workers, consumers, or the community—not just to outside investors. And these [community] businesses succeed.[1]

Alperovitz has called attention to seven "cool companies" as alternatives to corporate power:

W. L. Gore in Newark, Delaware, with forty-five locations

worldwide, produces Gore-Tex fabrics, heart patches, and synthetic blood vessels. It has 7,500 employees who own the company and tallies $1.84 billion in annual sales.

Pioneer Human Services, a Seattle nonprofit organization, offers recovering alcoholics and drug addicts assistance via drug- and alcohol-free housing, employment, job training, counseling, and education. With a thousand workers, it finances 99 percent of its $60 million annual budget through fees for services and earnings from manufacturing, distributing, and selling products, businesses that range from sheet metal fabrication to wholesale food distribution.

As a cooperative owned by approximately ten thousand consumer-owners and ninety worker-owners, the Weaver Street Market in Carrboro, North Carolina, draws on local food to supply its restaurants and stores, has several community events a week, and invests in local suppliers. According to the company, 50 cents on every dollar spent at the co-op remains in the community—compared to 15 cents at chain stores.

Another alternative model is exemplified by ONE DC, which stands for "Organizing Neighborhood Equity DC," in the nation's capital. As one of 4,600 nonprofit community development corporations (CDCs), ONE DC focuses on developing local business while promoting affordable housing, living-wage jobs, and community control over development.

In Burlington, Vermont, a community land trust known as Champlain Housing Trust, with five thousand members and annual revenues of $5.9 million, provides affordable housing for more than two thousand households. Its volunteer board of directors includes residents in this housing community along with representatives from four towns. Land trusts stem gentrification by holding land in trust and off the market. The trust then sells houses with restricted deeds that keep title to the land, thereby allowing lower-income people to buy homes at lower prices. In return, the homeowner agrees to limit the resale price and share any profit with the trust, which ensures that the homes remain affordable for future buyers.

California's Public Employees' Retirement System (Cal-PERS), with almost $250 billion in assets, uses its leverage as a large shareholder in certain companies to push them for more information disclosure, better environmental practices, and stronger human rights in emerging nations. It invests some of its funds in California's low-income communities to stimulate businesses there.

None of these organizations was founded by huge groups of people. Rather, a few people with cultivated imaginations and visions who sensed unfulfilled needs and, understanding why they were unfulfilled, were able to enlist broader community support from residents who were willing to purchase their goods and services. The more such efforts reach critical mass, the more this community movement will spread.

In 2006, the Seattle Local Economies Mapping Project (www.seattlemap.org) collected, according to *Yes!* Magazine writer Ethan Miller, "inventories of alternative economic initiatives, from cooperatives and local currencies to volunteer fire companies and community food banks. Inspired by what is sometimes called 'asset-based community development,' other groups are cataloging forms of wealth left out of the dominant economic equation, such as subsistence skills, traditional arts and crafts, local stories and lore, and natural landscapes."[2]

Making the transition to community-based economies is a tough challenge when large corporations—with their massive daily advertising budgets—have spent decades lulling the American people into caged routines and dependencies. We are reluctant to look beyond our habits, to envision a radical shift in the way our economy works.

For example, we have become so reliant on centralized energy sources—oil, coal, gas, and nuclear—that we have ignored other solutions that have been available for decades. Consider

this September 2011 report on solar energy from Renewable
EnergyWorld.com:

> A recently released solar map of New York City found
> enough room on building rooftops for solar panels to
> power half the city during hours of peak electricity use. . . .
> and create tens thousands of jobs. . . . Almost 60 million
> Americans live in areas where solar prices are competitive
> with retail electricity costs, but this opportunity is often
> kept out of reach by utilities and the antiquated rules of the
> U.S. electricity system.[3]

Physicist and energy conservation expert Art Rosenfeld has
argued that simply painting roofs white "over the next 20 years
could save the equivalent of 24 billion metric tons in carbon dioxide emissions," the *New York Times* reported in 2009.[4]

Once we start investigating alternatives to the global corporate model, our common sense and spirit of discovery may
start liberating our thinking. Consider, for instance, the fact that
there is often a fundamental conflict of interest between buyers
(consumers) and large sellers. When buyers lack the information they need to make smart decisions, they become vulnerable
to higher prices, misleading sales pitches, and outright fraud.
When we buy fuel (such as gas and heating oil), for instance,
it's in our interest to get more for our dollars through efficient
cars, furnaces, and air-conditioning and lighting systems. When
companies sell us their product, on the other hand, it's in their
interest that our cars, trucks, and HVAC systems are *inefficient*,
because that inefficiency forces us to consume more fuel, leading
to greater sales and profits for the fuel companies. For a century,
the wastefulness of our technologies was basically unchallenged.
But in recent years that has started to change, as public pressure led the government to tighten its efficiency standards. Even
the Pentagon is moving into renewable energy for economic and

security reasons. The Department of Defense is pledging to obtain 25 percent of its huge energy needs from renewable sources by 2025.

Such conflicts of interest may seem endemic to a market-based culture like ours. But there are other, perhaps even more troubling conflicts between the interests of global corporations and those of the American people.

For decades, our corporate economy has been shifting its focus from fulfilling basic human needs (food, shelter, warmth) to fulfilling (and creating!) more trivial wants and whims. From commercial entertainment, video games, and spectator sports, to stylized snack foods, communication gadgets, and even redundant weapon systems, corporations have invested billions of dollars into research and development (R&D) on items that rob consumers of endless amounts of their not-so-disposable income. And this continues even though large segments of the population are suffering from inadequate nutrition, employment, capital ownership, shelter, transportation, and health care coverage.

Entrepreneurs who develop businesses that serve civic interests as well as their own often discover that our inner cities, and lower-income rural families, can offer fertile and sustainable markets. As economist Paul Davidson has written: "These institutions, when properly designed, protect civic values from the corrosive effects of self-interest. At the same time, institutions make use of productive forms of self-interest, enabling people to enjoy the products of both."[5]

Increasingly, progressive voices in the media are shining a spotlight on the need for new businesses that serve both entrepreneurs and local communities. *Yes!* Magazine is a leading chronicler of independence from the global economy, with features such as "31 Ways to Jump Start the Local Economy," "Wendell Berry's 17 Rules for a Sustainable Economy," "A Resilient Community," "Small Banks, Radical Vision," and other numerous stories on how consumers and householders can become producers of energy and food. Epidemiologist Richard Wilkinson, in his bestseller *The Impact of Inequality: How to Make Sick Societies Healthier*, offered both a survey of our nation's growing economic inequalities and an eloquent argument that such inequalities will lead to increased anxiety, fear, isolation, health failures, and chronic insecurity.

One voice that has been fighting for change for seven decades is the great folk singer Pete Seeger, who has brought thousands of people and children together for community songs and good deeds. At the age of ninety-two, he told *YES! Magazine* that "If there's a world here in a hundred years, it's going to be saved by tens of millions of little things. The powers-that-be can break up any big thing they want. They can corrupt it or co-opt it from the inside, or they can attack it from the outside. But what are they going to do about 10 million little things?"[6] Seeger's words echo perhaps the most-quoted aphorism of anthropologist Margaret Mead's: "Never doubt that a small group of people can change the world, indeed it is the only thing that ever has."

It was the renowned biologist René Dubos who said "think globally, act locally." This is just what Native American leader Winona LaDuke has been doing in the northern Great Plains, where her tribe, the Chippewa, has embarked on a wind power initiative to bring other tribes to recognize their potential to harness this huge natural resource on their sovereign lands. As LaDuke has pointed out, native peoples all over the world have historically shared an understanding that working *with* nature, instead of conquering it, provides greater self-sufficiency while preserving the planet's life-sustaining ecology. Her wind power project marries that timeless wisdom with twenty-first-century technology.

Community economies, by definition, create or strengthen neighborhoods by encouraging neighbors to interact in socially constructive ways. This interaction can foster cultural activities and gift relationships (such as sharing garden produce, exchanging child care services, and tutoring). Edgar Cahn's Time Dollar movement is one way that community leaders are trying to formalize such relationships. The Time Dollar is just as it sounds: a time-based currency that is bartered through an exchange bank, which can be operated by a community college, church, or local service club. If an elderly couple tutors a teenager for twenty hours, for instance, that teen, or someone else in the exchange, then gives twenty hours to mow the couple's lawn or shovel their sidewalk. A Time Dollar can be reimbursed in many ways, but the basic idea of equal, reciprocal service underlies the entire project. A lawyer's time dollar is worth the same as a homeless person's time dollar. When a community starts to see the value in such equal reciprocity, its residents must soon start to wonder what they're getting in exchange for giving corporations free rein over the people's commons—mining resources from public lands, using public airwaves for commercial purposes, giving tax breaks to corporations ostensibly in return for creating jobs. This is the essence of reciprocity in which powerless people find it an awakening principle of moral or ethical equality as well as one of economic value. Such a revelation can have moral, not just economic, weight.

It was just that principle of reciprocity that jolted the late Ray Anderson, who, as CEO of Interface corporation, started transforming his company into a zero pollution, 100 percent recycling enterprise by 2020. As the largest carpet tile manufacturer in the world with factories here and abroad, he launched a plan in 1994 to reduce the company's output of waste and pollution—a process that also reduced the company's expenses, increased its sales and profits, and made it a preferred place to work. Anderson said he saw himself as a "recovering plunderer of the planet" who had resolved that Interface should give back no less than what it took from the environment—a standard far beyond any existing government regulations.

And such movements aren't limited to businesses. Communities of any size, from the local to the national level, can start initiatives that dramatically enhance their own economic well-being. Perhaps the most dramatic example in the past century was the revival of the nations of Western Europe after World War II, taking them from destitution to the highest living standards in the world through the principles of social democracy—combining self-interest with civic values. Working through their trade unions, cooperatives, and multiparty systems, the citizens of Western Europe responded to the rebound of their economies by raising their expectations. During the decade after 1945, these countries embraced their citizens' demands for universal health care, decent pensions, cheap and accessible public transit, tuition-free university education, at least one month of annual paid vacation, free child care, paid family sick leave and maternity leave—to name only a few of the amenities fostered by this collaboration between local and national.

Sixty-seven years after 1945, however, the United States—the victor in World War II and long touted as the richest nation in the world—offers none of these civilized services for all of its people. Not one. We do not have a multiparty system in which smaller parties with pioneering agendas can be part of governing coalitions. Instead, we have a winner-take-all two-party dictatorship, its voting blocs broken into gerrymandered districts largely dominated by one party or the other. We have the weakest, most obstructionist labor laws among industrialized nations, which have led to the lowest percentage of labor union members in the Western world. A much smaller segment of our economy is devoted to consumer cooperatives. In short, the institutional flaws of our government have allowed powerful corporate interests to drive the American standard of living downward for the past thirty-nine years.

Consider what a century ago was widely seen by reformers as the alternative model to the larger stock-held commercial corporation—namely the producer and the cooperative. Under cooperatively-owned forms of business activity, consumers band together to start their own business that they own and control. Thus combined, consumers cannot only greatly expand their bargaining power vis-à-vis manufacturers and wholesalers, but they can also determine what they want to sell to themselves and under what standards. They can condition the terms of purchase from suppliers, well beyond price, to include quality, safety, nutrition, warranty, durability, and sustainability (as with solar power). They can refuse to stock products like tobacco, pesticides, or drugs and foods with harmful ingredients. They can federate into larger cooperative networks to move into the wholesaling and even the manufacturing sectors. They can use their cash flow to add ancillary services and leverage their membership into their own insurance, media, travel, and adult education enterprises. They can form ad hoc buying groups for specialized goods and services not available in their stores but available locally. When economic and environmental policies are shaped by political decisions, cooperatives can inform and organize their membership to participate in a highly informed and persistent manner.

Two horizons present themselves. One is for the emergence of cooperative subeconomies, providing a network of multiple benefits to the bulk of consumer purchases so that membership increases. Imagine, for example, entire cooperative shopping malls or streets providing food, clothing, banking, insurance, fuel, appliances, reading materials, children's products, patient health care, adult education, communications, repairs, and other services.

The other is for cooperative institutions to strive toward a steady transformation of the political economy away from waste, inefficiency, environmental damage, price gouging, multinational absentee corporate control, and regulatory obeisance toward an organized, informed, and consumer-driven political economy. It would involve a faster transition from fossil fuels and nuclear to solar energy; from obesity-promoting junk food to nutritious food; from corporatized medicine to cooperative preventative medicine; from massive waste of land, water, and other natural resources that increase global climate change to a conserver economy that safeguards the environment for our descendants; from governments and elections for sale to governments of, by, and for the people.

What America needs is to reengage with the promise of a society controlled by citizens/consumers, not corporations. Today, our universities specialize in teaching seller-side skills (business management, marketing, and so on) to aspiring businesspeople. Tomorrow, our schools—from the elementary and secondary level up—should start teaching *buying* skills, individual and organized, which include choosing *not* to buy. When complete amateurs buy stocks, insurance, motor vehicles, homes, and health care—bargaining with expert sellers who are motivated to get the most money for the least return—our nation's economic welfare suffers as a result.

The fate of community economies in the United States comes down to a basic question: Are consumers willing to step away from the creeping corporatization of their lives and take the time to empower their dollars by joining economic institutions that will endure and outlast their originators? The internet offers infinite new promise for consumer cooperatives, giving consumers much greater power through group purchasing, terms-of-sale negotiation, and complaint handling. Yet it will take more than just technology to interest the American people at large in the potential of community-based cooperatives; it will take a new awakening of interest in our shared standard of living. We will have to raise our expectations.

"We need a 'new economy' . . . if critical economic, social and environmental goals are to be met. . . . by activists, economists and socially minded business leaders," argues Gar Alperovitz, who has written extensively on cooperative experimentation.[7] He speaks highly of the growing network of Evergreen Cooperative businesses—such as the Evergreen Cooperative Laundry—in the low-income neighborhoods of Cleveland, which are designed to create good jobs and sweat equity by serving the buying needs of "anchor institutions" such as the local universities and hospitals that have made a long-term commitment to the city.

Social entrepreneurs are among the most dynamic engines of the cooperative movement. Where corporate moguls work for personal enrichment, these civic-minded business leaders work for the cooperative equivalent, which is a desire to generate community self-reliance, abolish poverty, and enhance community economic well-being by improving housing, food, transportation, energy, health, finance, and a host of other products and services. Their motivations are not selfishly financial; they are far deeper, rooted in both the human spirit and the pervasive sense of community that human beings have striven to express throughout history.

As the economist Jean Monnet once said, "Without community, there is crisis."

Any social community owns assets—assets that are controlled by them, not by corporations. These are called the "commons"—property and rights that are everywhere but nowhere—and they should be high on any list of what We the People must work to preserve in a new economy. Children today do not study the commons in school, nor do our politicians debate them in their campaigns, other than to demand that they are privatized or exploited for profiteers without any returns to We the People who own them.

If you were asked to make a list of everything you own, chances are you wouldn't answer: "Well, I own part of the public airwaves; part of the one-third of America that is public land;

part of the national parks and the national forests." Once you become conscious of your share in these public holdings, however, it's impossible not to start asking questions that the corporatists and their politician sponsors find very uncomfortable.

For instance: If the people are the landlords of the public airwaves and the television and radio stations are the tenants, why don't the tenants pay rent? In fact, they pay nothing. Broadcast airwaves are licensed for free on a term of nearly eighty years, allowing the licensees to decide who says what at any time on the part of our spectrum that they exploit for their profit. If those airwaves are our property, you might further ask, why don't we have access to them for our own television and radio programs? Why can't we devote an hour or two a day to our own audience network? Why shouldn't we collect the rent they should be paying us and use it to open studios and hire reporters, editors, programmers, and managers who air the content we want to see—from serious political debate to local culture and humor, very little of which gets on the air now—without corporate manipulation or advertisement?

Our public lands contain a wealth of natural resources— trees, oil, gas, coal, gold, silver, copper, iron, zinc, and many other minerals, onshore and off. We own these lands. Yet under current law the corporations control their extraction and pay very little to Uncle Sam for what revenues and profits they reap. Sometimes, in fact, they pay just about nothing. The 1872 General Mining Act, if you can believe, allows any foreign or domestic company to come onto our land with its geologists; discover hard-rock minerals like gold, silver, and molybdenum; and gain ownership of them to sell, without any royalties back to us, for no more than $5 an acre—a figure presumably based on 1872 land prices! As a result, when the Barrick Gold Corporation, a large Canadian company, discovered $9 billion of gold on federal land in Nevada, it was able to take ownership for less than $30,000—enabling it to sell its freely gotten gold for an immense profit, with no obligation to pay royalties on the profits, as any corporate landowner would charge if the shoe were on the other foot.

There have been some exceptions. When big oil was found on the Alaska North Slope, the state government created a royalty trust fund for the people there. As a result, every woman, man, and child in that state receives an annual royalty check as compensation—checks that can range from $1,000 to $2,000.

One of the largest commons is the trillions of dollars in taxpayer-funded R&D that federal agencies such as the Pentagon, the National Institutes of Health (NIH), the National Aeronautics and Space Administration (NASA), and the Department of Agriculture have transferred, virtually free, to private industry. The aerospace, defense, biotechnology, agribusiness, semiconductor, pharmaceutical, and containerization industries—among many other corporate enterprises—all grew out of taxpayer-funded R&D initiatives. In addition, many of these industries receive annual tax credits from the U.S. Treasury to subsidize the kind of research they would certainly be doing anyway. Imagine: every year, your tax dollars go—in the form of large credit checks—to massively profitable companies such as Cisco, Intel, Microsoft, and the drug corporations. These businesses are built on a vast body of discovered knowledge that was originated by your "commons" and was given away, without your consent or even knowledge, for bargain-basement prices. The companies involved then sell you their products—based on the technology you paid to develop—for huge markups. Even such breakthroughs as the medicines Taxol and AZT, discovered and clinically tested by the National Cancer Institute before the giveaway to drug companies, were developed via taxpayer money.

Suppose you and other citizens prevailed upon your senators and representatives to require a better deal in exchange for the use of such common property—the kind of paycheck any private business would demand. Suppose, further, that the money was invested in community jobs through responsibly run local economic institutions. Suppose, that is, you got something for your taxpayer dollars—that they were paid back into the community where you live, work, play and where you raise your family.

Two former postgraduate associates of mine, David Bollier and Jonathan Rowe, have become eloquent scholars and champions of "reclaiming the commons." In an address called "The Marginalization of the Commons and What to Do About It," Bollier had this to say:

> Paradoxically, the commons does all sorts of work that markets depend upon—but this work usually goes unacknowledged. The "caring economy" and other so-called "women's work" is part of the vast, off-the-books shadow economy that invisibly props up the formal market economy. Nature is also part of this shadow economy. So is the public domain of information and culture. It tells you something about the vaunted "productivity" of the formal economy that quietly relies upon so many invisible commons-based subsidies![8]

As Bollier has noted, the commons are what we share and pass on to future generations: the rivers, lakes, earth's atmosphere, wildlife; our genetic heritage; and much more. Without legal protection and enforcement, however, the commons can all too easily become a "free" dumping ground for corporate and governmental contamination. Cannibalizing the commons is big business and getting bigger. Corporations now hold monopoly patents on one-fifth of the human genome—our genetic inheritance—and more such patents on flora seeds and fauna. This may be the ultimate instance of nature's commons being co-opted for private profit. Way out of public sight, nanotechnology companies and synthetic biology firms are moving to patent synthetic versions of the basic elements of nature. The results are potentially catastrophic—from loss of biodiversity and the exhaustion of ocean fisheries, to groundwater depletion, species extinctions, permanent genetic damage, and downward-spiraling ecosystems. But these costs appear nowhere on any corporate ledger. Nor are they subtracted from the absurdly one-sided GDP, a figure long determined and defined by corporate interests.

The phrase "public commons" once referred to a literal place: a public gathering space, such as the area that emerged in Boston when Peter Faneuil built Faneuil Hall in 1742, giving rise to some of the most momentous gatherings in American history. From Samuel Adams and his allies stirring the spirit of liberty before 1776, to the great orations of William Lloyd Garrison, Frederick Douglass, and Lucy Stone against the evils of slavery, that public space was a breeding ground for community. Next door, a sprawling open market sold food and goods of all kinds while people interacted socially and sometimes civically as part of daily life. Even while I was attending Harvard Law School, I saw this kind of community spirit in action.

Now, though, these open-air markets are gone from most of our communities. Today's giant malls are privately owned spaces, controlled by owners who refuse even to allow people to gather petitions there. No forms of civic engagement need apply.

Yet the hunger for such social experiences remains, and it is feeding the expansion of more than four thousand farmers' markets across the country. In Washington, D.C., one such market sprawls over the parking lot of a major bank—which donates the lot for the public relations reward. The same desire for social interaction is built into the expansion of the urban community garden movement, of which there is about seven hundred in New York City.

The corporate world will never voluntarily value civic engagement. On the contrary, companies like Walmart, as Jonathan

Rowe notes, "have sucked commerce out of traditional market settings, [and] they also have cannibalized the attendant social and civic functions—the commons productivity—that were a part of the purpose of markets in the first place."⁹ This sucking process is hollowing out our post offices—one of our original commons—around the country. By order of the U.S. Postal Service—governed by a board of directors dominated for years by corporate executives and corporatist dogma—small post offices are being replaced across the country by kiosks in Walmarts, Kmarts, and large shopping malls. Other branches are seeing their revenue so depleted as to set them up for closing. There are now more kiosks than the thirty-two thousand post offices in the land.

The history of McDonald's offers an example of how corporate mandates can reduce the role of an ostensibly public experience like eating out to the lowest common denominator. Founder Ray Kroc imposed an iron-willed dictum on his franchisees—including instructions not to trust "people who are nonconformists, you cannot give them an inch. . . . The organization cannot trust the individual; the individual must trust the organization."¹⁰ Kroc demanded that portion and content control must be exact whether in Pasadena or Peoria, Augusta or Albuquerque, so that a hamburger in one locale would be an advertisement for one in another locale. While this approach made billions of dollars for Kroc and his family, it also ushered in a permanent low-wage subeconomy—and a high-fat diet that contributed overwhelmingly to today's obesity epidemic.

Every major religion in the world has warned its adherents not to give too much power to the merchant class—for example, the moneylenders. This common tendency did not arise from divine revelation; rather, it came from the community's daily experience. Leaders observed how the single-minded monetized mentality could run roughshod over civic and spiritual values.

Community economies—by their nature decentralized, intimate with people, and locally rooted—are simply in a better position than corporations to mix the mundane with the humane, the formal with the informal, the prudential with the discretionary features that bring people together in their proximate reality where they live, rather than leave them immersed in a lonely crowd watching TV or other screens in virtual reality. A skeptic once said, "but people like humor and entertainment," not knowing that he had unintentionally made my point. I replied: "Tell me, when have you laughed the most, from deep inside you? Watching a sitcom on TV or from funny interactions with your friends and relatives?" There's no comparison. Also, do you think children would rather watch a play on TV if they had the chance to perform in a play at school or in the neighborhood? The answer for most kids, except perhaps the shy ones, would be participating in the play.

From the conventional economy there are assets and collaborations to be pursued. When the Pentagon goes big-time into installing or purchasing various kinds of solar energy, the result is a larger market for such technologies and probably a reduction in per-unit cost from mass production. Originally suggested to the Pentagon by Professor Barry Commoner more than thirty years ago, this energy shift can only redound to the benefit of self-sufficient community energy production in this "new economy." Community health clinics many years ago benefited when the U.S. Army decided to buy generic drugs for large cost savings and thereby rebutted Big Pharma's specious claim that generics were not safe.

But there are good stories too. Many communities are still served by sole-proprietorship businesses—restaurants and bookstores come to mind—that were created to mix profit and community values. One outstanding example is the restaurant enterprise of Andy Shallal, who immigrated to the United States from Iraq as a youngster. His small chain of Washington, D.C., restaurants, known as Busboys and Poets (for the poet Langston Hughes, who was also a busboy at what is now the Wardman Park Hotel), offers an ethnically diverse clientele an elegant restaurant, bookstore, and community event space where authors, advocates, artists, and politicians come together. Shallal attributes his restaurants' popularity not just to their good, reasonably priced food and unique decor, but to his customers' hunger for community. The city's many fancy expense-account restaurants don't fill that need. At Busboys and Poets, no topic is too controversial, no presenter is taboo, and no debates are avoided. I call Andy Shallal "Democracy's Restaurateur."

And yet Shallal has only a handful of restaurants, while McDonald's has tens of thousands around the world. How can community-minded enterprises overcome our deeply ingrained dependence on corporate services? As Harvard lecturer Lisbeth B. Schorr notes in her book *Common Purpose: Strengthening Families and Neighborhoods to Rebuild America*:

> All over this country, right now, some program or some institution is succeeding in combating such serious problems as high rates of single parenthood, child abuse, youth violence, school failure, and intergenerational poverty. Yes, successful programs exist, but they have, in the main, been small and scarce. Why? . . .
>
> What makes the difference in whether your wonderful demonstration can thrive outside the hothouse? Is it money? Is it one leader's charisma? Is it luck?[11]

What matters most, Schorr argues, is being able to beat or manipulate "the system." "The problems," she continues, "arise when the successful pilot program is to expand and thereby threatens the basic political and bureaucratic arrangements that have held sway over the decades. . . . When effective programs aiming to reach large numbers encounter the pressures exercised by prevailing attitudes and systems, the resulting collision is almost always lethal to the effective programs. Their demise can be prevented only by changing systems and public perceptions to make them more hospitable to effective efforts to change lives and communities."

There is an important lesson here: Taking such initiatives to a wider audience does require a concerted effort to educate the people on the benefits of local economic self-reliance—to show how much more secure, enjoyable, safe, and happy their lives can be when they participate in and reap the benefits of decisions about their own communities—decisions that are now being made thousands of miles away by a few powerbrokers who view them as mere subentries on an income statement.

Teaching people about this new economy (with old roots) and conveying what it takes to get such programs under way in their own communities is a lot of work—though the internet and other modern communications technologies can speed the plow. The goal of such a campaign should be to give people appropriate yardsticks—what David Korten, a prominent critic of globalization, calls "life indicators"—to use in measuring their community's economic progress. It should demonstrate to them that a shift in power from the few to the many will lead to increased fairness, justice, and economic stability. When this message finally takes hold—especially among average Americans, who are inflicted daily by small and large injustices—the result should be a new American way of life, one that will ensure our economic future while remaining consonant with age-old rhythms of local culture.

3

Give Science and Technology
Back to the People

Hardly a day goes by without the media reporting some new scientific or technological discovery—the kind of breakthroughs routinely referred to as "game-changers," "life-changers," or "lifesavers." To be sure, researchers today are making exponential advances in scientific knowledge. These breakthroughs, in turn, have led to the development of impressive new tools and technologies. But these advances are heavily skewed toward the needs of military and corporate interests and away from the necessities for human betterment.

Compare the changes in our daily lives in the past sixty years with changes in the corporate and military arenas.

Our heavy industries are driven by stunningly automated, futuristic production lines and drilling and oil refining techniques, yet the motor vehicles and energy resources they produce are not all that different from what our parents used. Our food and beverage industry has seen the development of supermodern food processing and packaging plants, yet the foods they produce have fewer nutrients and more additives. Our hospitals are filled with dazzling new medical technologies, yet they can't seem to stem the tide of deaths through medical error, malpractice, and hospital-induced infections. We have seen dramatic advances in molecular biology, yet infectious diseases still claim millions of lives.

There is a huge imbalance between the benefits reaped by corporate and military interests from R&D and the benefits that trickle down to civilian life. For weapons of mass destruction and the ongoing "war on terror," the public budget has been limitless, the agenda served by the best scientists and engineers. Columbia University industrial engineering professor Seymour Melman wrote books and articles about how the market for military science and technology drains such skills away from the civilian economy. For example, he pointed out that the United States is no longer competitive in some industries for lack of innovation and inferior production engineering. Nearly a decade ago, when New York City requested bids for new subway cars, not one came from a U.S. manufacturer. Other industrialized countries are not burdened by spending half of their operating national budgets on military expenditures the way the United States does year after year. No country, however, can match our nuclear submarines, missiles, and drones for their destructive accuracy.

The 1970s saw the birth of the rallying cry "science for the people"—a call for science to meet the many needs of society. These were the years when the Pentagon's expensive mobile MX missile program was satirically referred to as the nation's leading public transit project.

The "science for the people" movement was about priorities. But it was also about who controls or inhibits the scientific establishment. It raised the basic question of what role we as citizens play in determining the direction of the R&D initiatives we fund with our tax dollars. Such money often resulted in such dubious contributions to our communities as nuclear power plants, fracking, and avoidable waste storage sites, not to mention free-floating pollution. This question—whether science and technology are driven by the concentrated power of the corporate government or shaped by democratic participation—has drastic implications for our society and world.

One telling example comes out of the Vietnam War, when the second cause of hospitalization for U.S. soldiers was malaria. The Department of Defense could not interest the drug companies in doing research to develop more effective pharmaceuticals against this debilitating disease; there simply wasn't much profit in such an effort. So the Pentagon started what in effect was its own drug company at Walter Reed Army Medical Center and Bethesda Naval Hospital. With minuscule budgets, officers with PhDs and MDs went to work on the problem. Their productivity was remarkable, their results published in peer-reviewed scientific journals. By 2000, three of the four most widely used antimalarial drugs used in the world had come out of this Pentagon unit along with other important, clinically tested medicines.

Almost no one in Washington's media circles knew about this work. The Office of the Secretary of Defense (OSD) and even many Pentagon managers I spoke with neither favored publicity for these scientists nor encouraged them to connect with Congress. At a meeting in the late 1990s with the brigadier general in charge of the program, and the colonels and captains who were developing the drugs, I learned that each of these drugs cost roughly $5 million to $10 million each, plus payroll, to get to market. This was less than 5 percent of what Big Pharma said their new drugs cost to develop. At the meeting, the brigadier general told me they were working on a new malaria drug, but they needed a few million dollars more for clinical trials. I facetiously asked how much of a B-2 bomber's cost would be enough. "A wheel," he said with a smile.

The motivations of corporate science, almost by definition, run contrary to the public interest. In the 1960s, for instance, General Motors (GM) boasted that it employed twenty-one thousand scientists and engineers. But they were not assigned to do research on crashworthiness; in fact, they were behind European automakers in tire and brake improvements (including radial tires, developed by Michelin, a French company) and were behind the curve when it came to handling and safety. Even when they did pursue safety features—such as air bags, which they were testing way back in the 1950s—they kept the whole thing secret. Only when the government stepped in to regulate safety features in 1967 did the GM brass recognize the need to support their scientists and engineers. In the meantime, decades' worth of motorists had been denied the life-saving efforts of these capable researchers. The toll in human life and limb was clear.

Corporate sponsorship creates problems when it comes to science, because the corporate context is so different from academia. In a university setting, science is conducted in the open, subject to peer review, and not for profit. Research conducted in a corporate setting, by contrast, is generally kept secret (in order to protect the corporation's proprietary interest), not peer-reviewed, and yoked to the company's scheduled profit-seeking strategies. And it's all controlled by the unseen hand of the corporate political, economic, and promotional power that underwrites it. Corporate science is also backed by the corporate, political, economic, and promotional authority that hires and controls it.

This misbehavior was brought home to millions of Americans, through such outlets as *The Phil Donahue Show*, after the publication of the Public Citizen Health Research Group's book *Pills that Don't Work*, led by Dr. Sidney M. Wolfe. This compendium listed 607 drugs on the market that were deemed ineffective by government and university scientists for the purposes for which they were advertised. Sold by major drug companies like Wyeth (now owned by Pfizer), Squibb (now Bristol-Myers Squibb), UpJohn (now Pharmacia, a subsidiary of Monsanto), Eli Lilly, and Merck, these drugs were widely prescribed by doctors who trusted these formulas to combat pain, asthma, inflammation, coughs and colds, allergies, various infections, bleeding and digestive disorders, heart pain, skin diseases, high blood pressure, depression, arthritis and gout, vitamin deficiency, and other ailments. All of them were ineffective. They represented one of every eight prescriptions filled—169 million of them in 1979 in the United States alone. As the authors wrote, "Since all drugs involve risks, this lack of effectiveness means you are exposing yourself to dangers without gaining compensating benefits." Plus the dollar cost. By the mid-1980s, the Food and Drug Administration (FDA) had banned most of these drugs. Were it not for the pressure of the Health Research Group, who knows how many more years would have passed before these costly frauds of junk corporate science were abolished?

Today, the side effects of drugs and the use of drugs for unapproved ailments still claim around one hundred thousand American lives per year. Drug company salespersons are trained to put the hard sell on physicians, often with tempting them with gifts and junkets. Where are the corporate scientists on staff who know better? They are kept silent. Suppression goes with secrecy. By the time the public learned that Merck's Vioxx actually led to heart attacks and other dangers, it was too late for tens of thousands of patients.

In recent decades, corporate science has been very aggressive in exerting its power over academic science, regulatory agencies, and the tort civil justice system. Monsanto and its allies have kept the federal government from requiring labeling of genetically modified food—a disclosure desired by more than 90 percent of consumers. Other companies are swarming over leading universities like Harvard, Stanford, and University of California, Berkeley, offering them joint ventures that will inevitably tie the hands of academic scientists. These joint contracts require that the fruits of all such university research be owned by the companies. Research findings are passed on by corporate monitors before publication; in some cases, the companies actually appoint professors to the faculty for these projects.

This growing corporate-university complex inevitably affects a university's research priorities, including what graduate students choose to study. And that corporate influence is locked in through the use of patents, a commercial tool that stifles free exchange among scientists. After the U.S. Supreme Court, in a 5–4 decision, approved the patenting of life forms (*Diamond v. Chakrabarty*, 1980), the planet's entire genetic inheritance became a hunting ground for monopoly corporate patents. Today, corporations such as Monsanto and Novartis own hundreds of human gene sequences as well as countless genetically engineered seeds—which can migrate undetected from controlled farms to unwilling nearby farms and even to indigenous seed cultures in developing countries, compromising the survival of natural crops.

Profit-driven science can also crowd out important research within corporations. With abundant capital resources—bolstered by tax credits—such companies make free use of taxpayer-funded science and technology developed by government departments (USDA, DOD), institutes (NIH), agencies (NASA), and laboratories (Oak Ridge, Los Alamos) to support commercial product development, displacing research in their own companies on life-saving programs such as vaccines in favor of major moneymaking daily medicines, such as high blood pressure medication or lifestyle drugs like Viagra. Nonprofit foundations are belatedly trying to fill that gap.

This kind of crowding out is a serious consequence of excessively powerful corporate science. As Indian physicist Vandana Shiva has written, "Once priorities shift from social need to potential return on investment, which is the main criterion for commercially guided research, entire streams of knowledge and learning will be forgotten. While these diverse fields might not be commercially profitable, they are socially necessary. As a society facing ecological problems, we need epidemiology, ecology, and evolutionary and developmental biology. We need experts on particular taxonomic groups, such as microbes, insects, and plants, to respond to the crisis of biodiversity erosion."[1]

When large corporations become such centers of power that they can suck scientists and engineers into their commercial maw, massively subsidized by free government R&D, they undermine the objectivity and interests of university-based science—while jeopardizing the freedom of the scientific community to pursue society's most urgent needs.

One example of how the distracted, co-opted science community is failing us is the troubling growth in human resistance to antibiotics.

The more antibiotics are used, especially when they're not needed, the more bacteria mutate and become resistant to specific antibiotics. The term "super bugs" has emerged to refer to resistant microbes that are immune to all but one antibiotic or sometimes immune to all. The spread of deadly drug-resistant tuberculosis in Eastern Europe and some third-world countries illustrates this trend.

Dr. Stuart B. Levy, author of *The Antibiotic Paradox: How the Misuse of Antibiotics Destroys Their Curative Powers*, describes the potential epidemic that could result from this diminished resistance: "The resistance genes, harbored in one group of bacteria, can spread to vastly different types of bacteria and to areas far away. Resistant bacteria . . . do not need passports in order to cross country borders. They can quickly circumnavigate the globe, carried along as stowaways in human, animal, and food products."[2]

Levy cites experts who estimate that "at least half of the human use of antibiotics in the United States, whether in the community at large or in hospitals, is unnecessary or inappropriate." The World Health Organization has named antibiotic resistance as one of the three major health problems of the new century. But you'd never know it, given the drug companies' lack of investment in the problem, or the inadequacy of public budgets to address not only increased mortality and prolonged hospital stays but also more costly treatments and medical complications. Although antibiotic resistance has been documented for more than thirty years as a silent killer, public alarm over the phenomenon has sadly been answered by widespread neglect in the scientific community.

Corporate science-technology, often funded by heavy government contracts for military weapons research at places like the Massachusetts Institute of Technology (MIT) and California Institute of Technology (CalTech), has led to a major "brain drain" on campus. During the 1960s, for example, the Pentagon secretly enlisted university researchers to discover a more virulent form of dengue fever for use in biological warfare—funding the secret project with tax dollars that could have gone to public health research to save lives.

More recently, the Pentagon has lavished massive resources on what many physicists consider the dubious prospect of a long-range missile defense system. Ted Postol, professor of engineering at MIT, has been a lonely public voice in challenging the feasibility of such a system. Budgeted by the Congress at $9–$10 billion yearly, the program has been damaged by dubious congressional testimony, in which Postol charges that several witnesses have engaged in fraudulent misrepresentation of test methods and results. Thus far, few have listened to his charges. When a prime missile defense contractor—in this case Raytheon—speaks, Congress and MIT listen.

The corporatization of universities has created a hostile climate for the few professors who volunteer to be expert witnesses on product liability cases against corporations. Academic science is dedicated to free-minded faculty exercising their intellectual integrity for public causes. But the growth of corporate influence on campuses has long since corrupted this ideal, as fewer and fewer technical specialists are willing and able to challenge the industry's own well-compensated "experts."

Through the decades, when controversies have emerged regarding auto safety, tobacco, nutrition, lead, underground mining and other workplace toxics, pipeline safety, highway pavement design, pollution's effect on children, and more, it has proven difficult or impossible to enlist more than a handful of scientists or engineers to break ranks and testify against their large corporate donors. The fates of innocent victims hang in the balance.

And yet, when a courageous medical professor persists, real change can happen. Over the course of thirty-five years, Dr. Herbert Needleman became a pioneering advocate exposing the damaging effects of chronic lead exposure on the vulnerable bodies of children, especially poor children. He then converted his research into calls for public action to remove the sources of lead contamination from paint and gasoline. Sheldon Krimsky, an environmental policy professor at Tufts University, has called Needleman's work "one of the most successful campaigns in disease prevention of the past century."

Hounded all the way by the Lead Industries Association—comprising companies like DuPont, Royal Dutch Shell, and Ethyl Corporation—Needleman was undeterred in his work at Harvard Medical School for the Environmental Protection Agency (EPA). Then, when he moved to the University of Pittsburgh, the lead industry went after him for alleged scientific misconduct; only after an extended ordeal was he exonerated by the university. A short time later, Needleman received the Heinz Family Foundation Environment Award for his "extraordinary contributions to understanding and preventing of childhood lead poisoning." The award noted that he "worked tirelessly and at great personal cost to force governments and industry to confront the implications of his findings. While this has made him the target of frequent attacks, he has fought off his critics with courage, tenacity and dignity."

Only a university setting that supported his academic freedom, insulating him from industry threats and political

pressures, allowed Needleman to do his scientific and public interest work. Other professors, hamstrung by their universities'
conflicts of interest, have been less fortunate.

Fifty years ago, in his much-heralded farewell address, President Dwight D. Eisenhower added this prescient warning to his
oft-quoted passage on the "military-industrial complex": "The
free university, historically the fountainhead of free ideas and
scientific discovery, has experienced a revolution in the conduct
of research. Partly because of the huge costs involved, a government contract becomes virtually a substitute for intellectual curiosity. . . . The prospect of domination of the nation's scholars by
Federal employment, project allocations, and the power of money
is ever present—and is gravely to be regarded. Yet, in holding scientific research and discovery in respect, as we should, we must
also be alert to the equal and opposite danger that public policy
could itself become the captive of a scientific-technological elite."

Eisenhower was shining a light on the vast expansion of
government-funded R&D, which amounts to a transfer of taxpayer assets—the commons—to universities and then in turn to
corporations through patent licenses or through outright giveaways resulting from their close day-to-day partnerships with
industry. Some of these grants represent the NIH's large investment in health research, mostly in new drug development and
diagnosis and treatment methods. But a far greater portion are
military and space contracts, which have turned some of our
larger universities into technical and promotional arms of the
Pentagon. In an interview with the president of the University of California, I asked whether he was satisfied with having weapons of mass destruction research at its Los Alamos and
Livermore labs as part of the university system's mission. While
he granted that there were arguments on both sides, he came
down on continuing this relationship with the government on
the grounds that "no one can do it any better."

In 1980, as one of his last acts in office, President Jimmy

Carter signed into law the Bayh-Dole Act, which enabled universities to patent federally funded research (instead of having the government hold the patent) and license these patents to private industry. The process of giving away federal R&D via universities opened the door to the wholesale commercialization of university research and to tighter ties between universities and private companies, which were sometimes invited to set up facilities on the not-for-profit educational campuses. One gets the sense that very few university presidents these days are thinking about President Eisenhower's observation that the "scientific-technological elite" should be focused on "the supreme goals of our free society."

Years after Bayh-Dole was passed, in 1988, the respected Office of Technology Assessment (OTA) noted some of the problems of this merging of corporate and university interests. Besides "inhibiting free exchange of scientific information, undermining interdepartmental cooperation, creating conflict among peers, or delaying or completely impeding publication of research results," OTA added this blockbuster: "decreasing university scientists' interests in basic studies with no potential commercial payoff."[3]

The most aggressive co-opters of university talent and facilities are the biotechnology, drug, computer, and chemical industries, and lately the nanotech business. As the corporate-university partnerships have matured, the industry powers have quickly neutralized university specialists as a potential force for regulation. It is a disturbing sign of the times when the two most transformative science technologies affecting the globe—biotechnology and nanotechnology—are governed by no external ethical or legal frameworks to protect public safety and other public interests, despite the fact that both industries have benefited from heavy taxpayer-funded government support.

Genetic engineering and nanotechnology have joined the old standby challenges—waste disposal, pollution, extractive energy, and the like—as clear and present threats to the human biosphere. Yet it is doubtful whether anyone is investing even the cost of a one-minute Super Bowl ad in monitoring these immensely perturbing technologies. With the (often unproven) benefits touted by their public relations machines, the purveyors of these "bios and nanos" spend very little time mentioning the risks.

Genetically modified seeds are growing today on tens of millions of acres, and signs of super-weed mutations are becoming widespread. Likewise, human biotechnology—biologics, stem cell research, cloning, synthetic biology, and more—has not received even minimal public debate or attention from authorities that could regulate these activities. And nanotechnology—the development of "products" at microscopic, near-atomic scale—has been subject to even less study, never mind public legislative hearings or mandatory inspection or safety standards. Nanotechnological products are already included in more than a thousand products—clothing, packaging, computers, cell phones, paints, filters, cosmetics, coatings, and drugs—despite the fact that nanotechnology research was generated by the government with no assent from the governed. We were never informed about the development of this technology, nor were we asked for our consent. In 2010, taxpayers funded nanotechnology research in the amount of nearly $2 billion—with less than 5 percent slated for environmental health and safety research.

Swiss Re, a large reinsurer, observed in 2004, "Never before have the risks and opportunities of a new technology been as closely linked as they are in nanotechnology. It is precisely those characteristics which make nanoparticles so valuable that give rise to concern regarding hazards to human beings and the environment alike." Yet not one citizen group has yet emerged in the United States to challenge governmental and industrial efforts in this area from the standpoints of health, safety, ethics, and law.

Only three citizen organizations monitor biotechnology. One is the Council for Responsible Genetics (CRG), founded by Harvard and MIT scientists searching for a wider framework of public understanding. CRG has come out against the issuing of patents on life forms, and has called attention with some success to the importance of protecting genetic privacy from discriminating employers and insurance companies, and the need to create and protect natural seed banks for posterity. Yet CRG has not yet had great success gaining attention for many of its findings in the mainstream media, which seizes every opportunity to announce questionable new research "breakthroughs."

In a time when the big corporations have such an overbearing presence at the universities, it is difficult to expect public protests from either faculty or administrators. The National Academy of Sciences has declared that "serious and considered whistle-blowing is an act of courage that should be supported by the entire research community." When professors are hog-tied by self-censorship, however, whistle-blowing and public protest can seem like professional suicide.

Over the years, I have asked a number of university presidents whether they have a comprehensive written policy regarding the boundaries between their institutions' interests and those of corporate commercialism. Their replies suggested that their policies were largely ad hoc—a movable set of expediencies, influenced far more by competition for funding among universities than by a well-conceived public philosophy on academic freedom, public service, and intellectual independence.

Corporations have gone into business with universities in order to tap into the schools' intellectual power and to receive valuable rights to taxpayer-funded research conducted there. More crassly, they are also looking for validation of their corporate behavior from highly regarded faculty at prestigious institutions of higher learning. Many corporations have bankrolled articles in medical journals, often without proper disclosure for the readers. They have hired expert witnesses to testify in court and before legislative and regulatory bodies, or retained professors as consultants. Such moonlighting can double a professor's salary at institutions such as Stanford or Harvard.

One egregious example of commercial incursion on academic integrity was the longtime effort by the tobacco companies to sow doubt about the dangers of smoking, long after the issuance of the historic surgeon general's report of 1964. The companies paid academic scientists many thousands of dollars apiece just to write articles or letters to academic journals and other lay media downplaying the risks of smoking. The *Dallas Morning News* reported in 1997 that the University of Texas had agreed to let a professor do secret research for tobacco company attorneys for eleven years in return for nearly $1.7 million.

A more recent example is that of the notorious, now-defunct Enron Corporation, one of the greatest corporate criminals of recent years, which got the Harvard Business School and the Harvard Electricity Policy Group (through donations and close relationships) to produce many reports and articles praising the "Enron model" of electricity deregulation—articles that continued throughout its years of price and supply manipulation and the market collapse in California that followed. In her well-documented book *University Inc.: The Corporate Corruption of Higher Education*, Jennifer Washburn traced the contours of this disgraceful collaboration and quoted Harvard Watch, a student and alumni group that uncovered these seedy ties: "Harvard University should apologize to the people of California for having sold its research institutes and faculty members to corporations."

Our society contains three major sponsors of research and knowledge: government, academia, and business. When academia's nonprofit status and independence are corroded, society loses exactly what President Eisenhower considered the crucial role of a free university: to be a "fountainhead of free ideas and scientific discovery," of "intellectual curiosity," of "the principles of our democratic system—ever aiming toward the supreme goals of our free society."

But how are we to turn the tide?

Liberating science from corporate influence, freeing scientists to conduct their work for the betterment of society at large—for the health and well-being of present and future generations—will require a civic movement. Fortunately, there are some environmental and consumer groups that have spent decades leading the way. Over the past forty years, the Center for Science in the Public Interest (CSPI) has been challenging misuses of food-science technology that enhance corporate profits but undermine healthy eating by maximizing the use of fat, sugar, and salt in most foods. The big food companies have enlisted thousands of food scientists and technologists to find new ways to make their products sensually appealing to consumers, especially children. Their goal was "turning the tongue against the brain," as my mother used to say: to enhance taste and texture, regardless of how the resulting foods promoted obesity, hypertension, and other ills. As former FDA commissioner Dr. David Kessler notes in his confessional book *The End of Overeating: Taking Control of the Insatiable American Appetite*, these foods are more than simply appealing: they trigger responses in the brain that amount to addictive desire.

CSPI, through its popular monthly newsletter *Nutrition Action*, is bringing nutritional science to the people, promoting foods that are both nutritious and delicious. Its staff and colleagues are greatly outnumbered by the food processing giants, with their decades of experience manipulating the taste buds of billions of consumers. Yet CSPI, cofounded by Dr. Michael Jacobson, shows what a few public interest scientists can do for the people. As an organization, it has helped change the food habits of millions of people, altered the terms of the debate to throw the food processors and fast-food industry on the defensive, and pressured the FDA to pay more attention to its duties.

Groups like CSPI are also doing the important work of demystifying science for consumers. The corporate infiltration of the scientific community has blurred the distinction between good science and fraudulent corporate-funded "findings" masquerading as science. The efforts of groups like CSPI reveal how science is used as an instrument of unjust corporate and governmental power. They have demanded that ordinary people be granted access to public laboratories to determine what toxics may be in their air, water, soil, and food. And they have done important work calling attention to the many volunteer "citizen scientists" among us, who engage in rigorous observation of the natural world on behalf of formal institutions.

If scientists and engineers are to consider themselves a respectable profession, then they need to think independently of those who employ or retain their services. Otherwise they are a trade. The National Academy of Sciences says, "The community of scientists is bound by a set of values, traditions, and standards that embody honesty, integrity, objectivity, and collegiality." If that is so, then scientists should recognize the importance of this kind of demystification. They should heed the advice of their distinguished colleague Jane Lubchenco, former president of the American Association for the Advancement of Science, who has called for a new social contract between scientists and the public about "how the sciences can and should advance and also return benefit to society." Lubchenco said nothing about checking with their employers for permission before pursuing their work. The vacuum needs to be filled by some of these scientists organizing themselves into a nationwide advocacy organization.

Faulty and fraudulent science, whether warped by commercial interests or through simple incompetence, must be exposed to the public, not just the priesthood of fellow scientists. In August 2011, the *Wall Street Journal* published a lengthy feature on the surge of research articles that have been retracted because of "mistakes"—often a euphemism for falsification or fabrication of data or other misconduct. "Just 22 retraction notices appeared in 2001, but 139 in 2006 and 339 last year," the *Journal* reported. "Through seven months of this year, there have been 210. . . ."[4]

Mistakes in medical journals can have serious consequences for patients around the world. The newspaper pointed to a study published in the influential medical journal *Lancet*, allegedly proving that well-known high blood pressure drugs were more effective taken in combination than on their own. In the six and a half years before the study was retracted, "the damage was done," the *Journal* reported. "Doctors by then had given the drug combination to well over 100,000 patients [in the United States]. Instead of protecting them from kidney problems, as the study said the drug combo could do, it left them more vulnerable to potentially life-threatening side effects, later studies showed. Today, 'tens of thousands' of patients are still on the dual therapy, according to the research firm SDI." This error was apparently the result of both fraud and incompetence, and the consequences were lethal.

Fraudulent business science has been invoked to protect tobacco sales, to entrench the installation of asbestos, to keep lead in gasoline, and to ignore the vehicle emissions that cause photochemical smog—until, in each case, a combination of public pressure and conscientious scientists came together to place sound science behind effective public health policies.

When Big Science comes under the influence of corporate or governmental power, the scientific community becomes a servant of abusive masters. It can no longer fulfill its role as a public trust that keeps, in the words of mathematician and philosopher Alfred North Whitehead, "options open for revision."

We must democratize science, redirecting the academy's priorities away from corporate and military imperatives and toward the public good. In doing so, we can take inspiration from Mahatma Gandhi, who envisioned the people of Indian villages serving as scientists and their villages as places of practical scientific learning. Anthropologist Shiv Visvanathan makes this point in a piece in *Science* magazine on Gandhi's *Hind Swaraj* (1908), which he described as one of the great critiques of science and technology. "His ashrams," Visvanathan wrote, ". . . were locations for scientific experiments, especially on waste management. His theory of khadi (homespun cloth) was a theory of technological innovation, of communities fighting obsolescence."[5] In his piece, Visvanathan called attention to four tragedies brought about by corrupted science, including the Bhopal chemical disaster of 1984 and the struggle against the environmentally costly Narmada Dam in the 1990s, which taught people that "the resolution of scientific controversies could not be left to experts, but was part of citizenship." He concluded that "the great debates on science and technology came not from the scientific academies but from political movements. It was local struggles against trawlers, missiles, pollution, monoculture, and industrial accidents that re-created the dialogue between science and democracy. These became the dissenting academies of Indian democracy."

The same is true in our country. From the beginning, the environmental and worker safety movements have had to challenge "servile science" in their pursuit of health, safety, and justice for the people. Corporations have trotted out scientists and engineers to contend that coal dust was not the cause of miners' lung ailments; that benzene was not carcinogenic; that GM's air pollution did not cause sickness; that vinyl chloride did not cause liver damage. Professional foresters at the U.S. Forest Service rebelled when they were ordered to approve timber companies' clear-cutting in areas the foresters believed would be seriously harmed by the cutting. In 1996, they formed Public Employees for Environmental Responsibility (PEER) to protect their professional judgment and affirmatively oppose commercial and bureaucratic interests that would override what they believed was best for our national forests.

Western science is also subject to certain ethnocentric beliefs that may hamper its ability to resist corporate influence. The book *Naked Science: Anthropological Inquiry into Boundaries, Power, and Knowledge,* edited by my sister Laura Nader, offers an eye-opening exploration of the relative autonomy of indigenous science—including local knowledge such as Mayan medical practices and a Micronesian navigation system. The contributors showed that in the West, as Stacia E. Zabusky pointed out in a review, knowledge systems are "embedded in social and cultural contexts." In case studies including molecular genetics, nuclear weapons testing, physics, and science policy, the book's contributors probed the connections between power and knowledge, social structures and cultural beliefs.

In the concluding chapter, Professor Nader draws on her longtime participation in a national energy research advisory committee, in which the prospect of self-censorship was a frequent subject of open conversation. Everything about these scientists' dialogue—the way they judged risks, argued for specific alternatives, evaluated costs, valued openness, and respected democratic participation—reflected how unfree these scientists were from the allegiances, pressures, and economic self-interests that often color such proceedings.

The more science and technology policy is democratized through a process of civic demand, the more decisions will be openly arrived at and the more they will serve the public good. As inspiration, we should look to advocates like Kiyoko Okoshi, a farmer in Iwaki, Japan. After the disastrous Fukushima Daiichi nuclear power disaster in March 2011, which affected four out of the thirteen plants in the area, it was revealed that both company officials and their patsy government regulators had wrongly reassured the public about the safety of the remaining nine plants that had been affected by the earthquake and tsunami. Skeptical about statements by local officials that her community was safe, Okoshi, who lived twenty miles from the plant, bought a $625 dosimeter to test the air. The meter beeped wildly, with the screen reading as high as 67 microsieverts per hour, a sign of radiation danger. Thus alerted, a local councilman enlisted a former Health Ministry expert to conduct extensive testing—ultimately confirming Okoshi's findings.

Citizen science can be a hobby, but it can also be a catalyst for change, offering unbiased support to nonprofit and government research programs. *Canadian Geographic* magazine recently devoted a cover story to "the rise and call of citizen science." Canada is a huge country with nearly 9.1 million square kilometers of terrain and 7.1 million square kilometers of ocean territory. "There's no way," writes the magazine, "governments, universities and private companies could deploy the armies of researchers needed to monitor, say, the number of belugas returning to the Gulf of St. Lawrence *and* how many salamanders awaken from their winter hibernation in northern British Columbia *and* the amount of rainfall in the Yukon. . . . So volunteers step up to fill the gaps. . . ."[6] As *Canadian Geographic* points out, scientific "experts" have been wrong or misled us over the years far more than they have been willing to admit. Instead, the magazine gave its Environmental Scientist of the Year Award for 2010 to these citizen scientists "throughout Canada who gauge rainfall, band birds, tag butterflies and take air samples, relying on the same notebooks, binoculars, hip waders, microscopes and keen eyes used by paid professionals."

Professional scientists in large institutions are always calling for people to have more "science literacy." But their calls often seem to go no further than a wish that more people would appreciate the contents of *Scientific American* or *Science* magazine. Or that high school and college students would take more science courses and learn the scientific method in their physics, chemistry, and biology labs. This is all well and good, but this kind of learning is a far cry from harnessing science to serve the civic aspirations of the people. What if high schools and colleges were to give students projects like testing local drinking water for heavy metals, assessing ambient air pollution, or dissecting soil samples? Their public reports on such community conditions would give this kind of curricular citizen science a constructive function, a way to use their skills to improve their surroundings.

Science is about knowing what to ask. The unfettered imagination thinks of questions that professional scientists either don't wish to ask or cannot imagine asking. On September 3, 2011, the *Washington Post* published a page one feature on a question asked by a fifteen-year-old high school student from Arlington, Virginia. Alexa Dantzler wanted to know how much toxic chemical residue remains in wool, cotton, and polyester clothing after being dry-cleaned. "Nobody, I mean nobody, has previously done this simple thing—gone out there to several different dry cleaners and tested different types of cloth [to see how much of the chemical persists]," said Georgetown University chemistry professor Paul Roepe, who allowed Alexa to use his lab and supervised the study. Now, at sixteen, Alexa has published her report in a peer-reviewed environmental journal after winning first place in chemistry at last year's Northern Virginia Regional Science and Engineering Fair. Her findings—that certain chemicals linked with cancer tend to linger in some fabrics, including wool, long after cleaning—have been registered by both the dry-cleaning and chemical industries and government job safety and environmental staff. The *Post* gave its story just the right headline: "From Curiosity to Eureka."

Before the twentieth century, many of the great scientists were amateurs. Antony van Leeuwenhoek, Charles Darwin, and Gregor Mendel all started as amateurs. It has been little more than a century since it took university credentials to earn the status of a "real" professional scientist. This tide may be turning. At least this is the belief of retired nuclear physicist Shawn Carlson, founder of the Society for Amateur Scientists.

Citizen science is more than "popular science." It is a crucial pillar of popular democracy in an age when the internet, and other widely available communications tools, can place unprecedented power in the hands of the people. A citizen science movement will spawn much-needed interest in local management of natural resources, including the environmental impact of cell towers, polluting factories and power plants, and new technologies like fracking. Without such citizen engagement, we will remain complacent, obedient consumers—a prospect that is hazardous to both our health and our pocketbooks.

"The real beauty of citizen science may be that it gets us back to our roots—science as the outcome of a natural, unquenchable curiosity," *Canadian Geographic* observes. "Young or old, educated or illiterate, anyone can pay attention. Coming from all walks of life, citizen scientists bring unprecedented diversity to the pursuit of knowledge."

If we are to persist as a democratic society, we must take action to ensure the honest and unfettered conduct of science, especially as it gets applied in the form of technology. If we fail to do so, it will be to our indefinite detriment. A society with no such oversight would have no protection for its exposed populations or for the health and safety of its workers; no environmental protection against the release of biotech or nano materials; no mandatory labeling of hazardous materials; no public participation in scientific decisions with public health implications; no consideration of potential effects on third parties, such as farmers; and no manufacturer liability for damage. After all, when even the genetic engineering of food is described as "changing the nature of nature"—and nanotechnology advocates promise that it will result in "unprecedented control over the material world"—we'd better pay attention.

A good start would be for our society to spend at least as much time on science as we now devote to science fiction. Indeed, a host of multinational corporations, and their supporting governments, are currently sponsoring a real-life version of science fiction in the form of "synthetic biology." These scientists are building life forms from scratch using synthetic DNA and other human-made parts; if unleashed, these biological products could pose a catastrophic threat to our environment. As of today, no legal or regulatory framework exists to police this activity. Such burgeoning areas of discovery are rapidly incorporated in this commercial laissez-faire world. The same is true for genetically engineered food, which has outrun the science discipline that first gave rise to it. The accelerating release of genetically engineered products is tantamount to flying blind. And there are equal dangers when it comes to nanotechnology.

The long-term protection of the fossil fuel and nuclear power industries is a devastating illustration of the corporate state's power over science and technology. For decades, Washington has lavished subsidies, free government research, promotional attention, and the appearance of legitimacy on these industries, despite vast and obvious environmental concerns and only sluggish efforts to enforce health and safety standards on these dangerous energy systems. Corporations like ExxonMobil, Peabody Energy, and a handful of other titans have succeeded in entrenching oil, gas, coal, and nuclear power as our nation's preferred sources of power, suppressing and crowding out vastly superior energy-efficient technologies and renewable solar and wind power. They have also managed to perpetuate the absurd theory that the growth of the economy is inextricably linked to the growth of energy production—an argument in which they've been supported by complicit scientists.

The conflict of interests between the sellers of energy and its consumers could not be clearer. For consumers, energy efficiency means being able to do more with less energy (in the form of fuel for our cars, oil to heat our homes, or electricity to run our appliances)—more bang for our energy buck. The gallons of gasoline or the kilowatts of electricity you don't waste are gallons and kilowatts you don't have to pay to produce. But wasteful engines, lightbulbs, refrigerators, and other household products are no problem for energy companies, for they only ensure higher sales for them. Waste, in other words, is a perverse incentive for the energy industry. So who wins this struggle? Right now, the forces with the power to control the uses and prices of energy, and dominate the government in their favor, are in the lead.

So what's the conflict with renewable energy? There is none.

Assume, for a moment, that the sun is speaking to Earth— its rambunctious progeny. "From the moment you were born," says the sun, "I've provided you with all the energy you need. Photosynthesis to help you generate plant life; heat to keep you from freezing. When the two-legged ones invented fire and began to dominate you, they went looking for more convenient and efficient ways to harness energy. They found simple ways to extract the energy contained in the solids on your surface and in your crust—first wood, then coal, then oil and gas. Yet, even after their ingenuity led them to develop more efficient and less damaging ways to tap the daily energy I shine down upon your surface, Earth—in the form of sunshine, of wind— they kept digging into the bowels of the planet to dredge up those combustibles, even though the processes they invented destroy lives, so much so that living conditions all over the planet are threatened. Now your whole climate is disrupted, and I cannot help you."

The sun is accessible to everyone, everywhere. No one owns it. No one can subject it to a cartel. No one can make it scarce. No one can contrive a solar eclipse—not even ExxonMobil. And, for the energy companies, that's the problem. Our energy companies derive their worth from those damaging processes—mining, combustion, nuclear fission—that human beings have contrived to create energy from the earth's raw materials. These raw materials are hard to get at, and these processes require much more capital than ordinary people could ever dream of controlling on their own—enough capital that only a big, centralized corporation could be expected to control. Ordinary people just don't have the wherewithal to find coal, gas, oil, or uranium, or to mine them, or to refine them and transport them to market.

Solar energy has been a part of history going back more than two thousand years, when passive solar energy was used in the buildings of the ancient Persians and Greeks and East Africans. An active form of solar energy, wind power, has been in use for centuries. And yet solar energy is a threat to the world's biggest and most powerful energy companies. Why? Because its omnipresent supply lends itself to wide decentralization, small business participation, and homeowner application.

Solar power holds the promise of making our communities self-sufficient, reducing pollution and climate disruption, cutting our dependency on foreign resources, lowering our trade deficits, decreasing our risk of nuclear sabotage and proliferation, eliminating wars over oil, making our economy more efficient, all while demonstrating respect for both our planet and future generations. Until recently, however, it was the fossil fuel and nuclear power industries that received massive federal and state subsidies, free technology giveaways, and favorable tax treatment. The big energy companies took Washington, D.C., as their own occupied territory. Big business and the government alike looked upon solar with derision, as if it were no more than science fiction. Corporate-sponsored scientists and engineers, who should have known better, dismissed solar as too diffuse, too intermittent, too difficult to store, and too expensive to meet the nation's needs. I was once told by a team of engineers at the Hanford Nuclear Reservation in Washington,

D.C., that solar energy didn't even represent an intellectual challenge, like the atom did. It was, they sneered, just "sophisticated plumbing."

For decades, the energy companies found solar energy incompatible with their real goals: maximizing sales, profits, and control over resources. Until, that is, the price of conventional energy skyrocketed, wars over oil proliferated, smaller entrepreneurs swung into action, inventors started expanding solar efficiency, and the government finally started to help, freeing up tax credits and research grants for solar development. Several varieties of solar energy—solar thermal, photovoltaic energy, wind power, and other renewables—are slowly expanding. Pressure is growing for public investment in wind turbine energy systems, capable of sending energy over further distances from many directions. Other renewables, such as hydropower, wood, and biomass, are still major resources. (Although corn ethanol, which requires huge subsidies and reduces food production acreage—leading to higher food prices—has proved a dead end.) The infrastructure is being established, and today's pioneers are learning from the predictable bumps and setbacks along the way: some U.S. solar manufacturing companies, unable to keep up with Chinese competitors, which receive superior largesse from Beijing, have filed for bankruptcy and moved to China. Overall, however, solar energy and wind power are here to stay—and grow. How fast they grow and come to replace fossil fuels and nuclear energy may be a function of how loudly we, as citizens and responsible consumers, demand the long-overdue transition to the solar age.

This transition won't happen until we all get better informed about the potential benefits of the transition to solar energy and start calling on our neighbors to join the movement. There will be resistance: every local community has businesses—gas stations, trucking companies, and countless others—that are deeply enmeshed in the oil economy and will be unwilling or unable to change. But that was true for the horse and buggy business when automobiles came onto the scene. As the solar energy business expands, and with homeowner support, the tide will turn. Some fossil fuel companies may not survive the change, but many will move into the solar business. This change will not be sudden, but it must not be too gradual. We need a national strategy to convert to major conservation and renewable ways to power our economy as fast as the pressures—serious climate change, oil spills, nuclear meltdowns—demand.

As a nation, we have fallen behind Western Europe and fast-moving China in adopting solar energy. Their advances have been driven largely by government mandate, political pressure, and their short supplies of oil and gas. Our federal government, meanwhile, has been paralyzed by the chronic gridlock between presidents and Congress and by the omnipresent grip of the fossil and nuclear lobbies. For the past eighty years, the best interests of the American people have been blocked.

The conflict dates at least as far back as the 1920s, when the synthetic chemical industry—DuPont, Dow Chemical, and the like—stymied a remarkable recommendation by Thomas Edison, Henry Ford, and the heads of MIT and Harvard to build a carbohydrate-based economy rather than a hydrocarbon-based economy. After World War II, President Truman's Materials Policy Commission urged that the nation go solar. But no strong constituency for the transition emerged, and the country went nuclear under President Eisenhower's "atoms for peace" program.

To say these were missed opportunities is to massively understate the millions of lives that would have been spared, wars and illnesses avoided, trillions of dollars saved, and damage to our planet that would have been averted if we had listened to Edison, Ford, and their colleagues. But the big money was with a centralized, petro-based hydrocarbon economy, which co-opted the power of Washington and used its force against the people.

Hopes for solar energy rose again during the Carter administration. In 1979, President Carter announced that 20 percent of U.S. energy needs would be served by renewable energy by the year 2000. The Solar Energy Research Institute (SERI) in Golden, Colorado, was to lead this effort. But his successor, President Reagan, had other ideas. He cut SERI's budget by 80 percent, fired half of its employees, and tore the solar water heaters off the White House roof for good measure. In early 2009, SERI's first director, Denis Hayes, wrote, "The successive administrations of George H. W. Bush and Bill Clinton, bobbing along on a sea of cheap oil, did little to promote energy efficiency or to shift America's economy to renewable energy. And for the past eight years, the United States was led by a president whose energy policy began and ended with Arctic drilling."[7] Since 1981, he observes, the energy situation in the United States has grown much worse, with oil imports more than doubled and greenhouse gas emissions far higher.

I first met Hayes when he was the lead implementer of the first Earth Day in 1970. In the years since, he has always struck me as a philosophical pessimist but a practical optimist. But he had great hopes for Barack Obama to turn our country around, reestablishing leadership in solar and conservation through a variety of job-creating public works programs.

So what did President Obama do? He saved the domestic auto industry—but allowed it to get away with a loophole-adjusted 40 mpg average fuel efficiency standard by 2025! He answered the BP Gulf of Mexico disaster by granting permission to open 20 million more acres to drilling. And, before and after Fukushima, he supported the development of more taxpayer-funded nuclear power plants.

True, with some assistance from Washington, D.C., both the solar and the conservation industries are growing. Sharp rises in fossil fuel prices assure that upward curve. And our economy is more energy efficient, measured against our GDP, than it was in 1975. But the United States and Canada are still the most energy wasteful countries in the world. That is why Amory Lovins, the leading architect of energy conversions—both efficiency and renewables—says that our main energy source right now is in Detroit: that is, in the huge potential for energy-efficient vehicles.

"We understand too little the wise use of power," Lovins says. He later writes, "[If] we can't keep the bathtub filled because the hot water keeps running out, do we really (as Malcolm MacEwen asks) need a bigger water heater, or could we do better with a cheap, low technology plug?"[8]

Lovins is the most powerful advocate for the "soft path" of renewable energy, arguing in the mid-1980s that it can help to "inhibit nuclear proliferation, abate acid rain and marine oil spills, save wild rivers, secure troubled utilities, cut electric rates, forestall the CO_2 threat to the global climate, make farms and industries more profitable, rebuild distressed local economies, and save enough money to pay off the National Debt [while lowering] oil imports." Lovins has cited example after example of the economic, environmental, and geopolitical superiority of soft paths over traditional "hard path" fossils and nuclear. In the first quarter of 2011, according to the U.S. Energy Information Administration (EIA), renewable energy sources (biomass/biofuels, geothermal, solar, water, wind) already provide 11.73 percent of U.S. energy production—5.65 percent more than that from nuclear power.

But small-scale successes, here and there, will not give the movement enough political power to overcome the entrenched powerful oil, coal, and nuclear lobbies. Denis Hayes says that we need "the moral equivalent of war," citing the astounding conversion of our peacetime economy to the world's largest war machine on land, air, and sea in the months after December 1941. He cites America's "unparalleled scientific and engineering excellence, formidable financial muscle, bountiful natural resources, a democratic political system and an entrepreneurial culture well-suited to helping lead the world into a prosperous, carbon-neutral era. For a fraction of the taxpayer money being spent to bail out an overpaid, under-regulated collection of investment banks, brokerage firms, mortgage companies and insurance companies, we can usher in a solar-powered era."[9]

What Hayes leaves out is that we also have the least organized citizenry against the most organized corporate state in our history. If our past teaches us one thing, it's that citizens will not mobilize for change without full-time organizers at the community level. The first step in sparking that change is for foundations and private fortunes to enlist such organizers in every congressional district in the country, to press Congress to unlock this mother of all logjams when it comes to energy conversion policy. Everything else is in place for this great change—a movement to seize absolute control over science and technology away from big business and return it to the people.

4

Protect the Family Unit

This chapter is dedicated to parents and grandparents. The family is the most effective unit of human development in history. That is why it has lasted so long, despite any number of conflicts and challenges. Powered by love, biology, protectiveness, generational nurturing, and the desire to procreate, the family is also marked by internal relations among its various members—parents, siblings, and extended family—that are driven strongly by selflessness and generosity, not by any desire for material gain. Anyone who doubts the sheer value of family should consider how much it would cost society if the responsibility for supplying these daily functions were shifted to the marketplace. Indeed, as more of the feeding, training, clothing, entertaining, counseling, child and elder care, and other functions of family life are being commodified, they are taking up ever larger percentages of the GDP.

The family shapes the character and personality of our children from birth and protects them against danger both physical and moral. The family possesses a remarkable resilience, a tendency to land on its feet when provoked or perturbed. In recent decades, as divorces have increased, the growth of single-parent families has only further demonstrated this familial resilience—often in the person of the "single mom."

No one studies the family—its vulnerable strains and its

stresses, its desires and its gratifications—more closely than corporate retailers, who see the family as a market of endless opportunities. Today, almost invisibly, a struggle is intensifying between corporations and parents and their children. It is a struggle over the time and place, bodies and minds, self-image and values of tens of millions of children and the world in which they are growing up. There is a strange and seductive tension between these retailers and our families: the corporations know what they want and how to enlarge their profits by nonstop selling, while the parents generally know what they do not like. But every year the parents are losing control over their own children to what marketing seminars call the "corporate parent" planning the "corporate week." For modern retailers are increasingly focusing their efforts on selling directly to children, motivating them to nag their parents (which the marketers privately refer to as the "nag factor") to buy the attractive new products they want—thus undermining the parents' authority to choose how to raise their children. Additionally, children have more and more money of their own, at younger and younger ages, to purchase what they want—even when it upsets their parents.

Companies have not always been so bold. Back in my childhood, they did try to sell us bubble gum and comic books directly, but they were wary of going much further. But breaking down our resistance is what modern marketers do. Year after year, corporations have used direct marketing to broaden their reach into the child's sensory temptations—especially with taste, but also with sound, color, dynamic cartoon characters, cartoonish violence, and (for slightly older children) sexual appeal. The more trouble there is inside the family, and the more parents want their offspring to remain safe by staying home, the more the big corporate retailers try to commercially induce or seduce these children into buying their way into such bliss. The pattern is only enhanced when parents allow TV, video games, and the internet to serve as electronic babysitters, further delivering their children to marketers.

These corporations are very adept at inducing dependency. One of their greatest victories was deceiving vulnerable mothers—right in the hospital delivery room—to accept gifts of infant formula instead of breastfeeding newborns mother's milk. From their earliest years, children today are growing up corporate, seeing the world through thousands of ads and logos. The long-lasting power of brand loyalties is demonstrated by "the cradle-to-grave marketing at McDonald's, and how well it works," says James U. McNeal, a path-breaking marketer to children. "We start taking children in for their first and second birthdays, and on and on, and eventually they have a great deal of preference for that brand. Children can carry that with them through a lifetime." Corporate marketers are targeting kids "younger and younger all the time," says Dan Acuff, a former marketing consultant to Mars, PepsiCo, Coca-Cola, and Frito-Lay. "Babies don't distinguish between reality and fantasy, so they think, 'Let's get them while they're susceptible.'" Coke provides their drinks, McDonald's their food, Time Warner their entertainment, PlayStation their video games, Gap their clothing, the drug companies' pediatric divisions their overmedication; then, as they approach their teen years, the addictive industries grasp them with cigarettes, alcohol, and other temptations. Today's information technology increasingly allows the corporations to track purchases, where they're stored in meticulously micro-mined databases the companies can use to target consumers for further offers. The corporations even call upon the services of so-called influentials, studying their buying habits, providing them with free samples, and even hiring them to pitch certain products to their friends.

What all this means is that children are spending far more time in the "virtual reality" of corporate vendors and their screens—mobile phones, video games, computer monitors, TV sets, and other platforms—than with their parents, who often spend much of the week away from home. Polls show that youngsters trust their computers more than they trust their parents. Clearly, lines of family influence that were once considered inviolable are now being crossed with impunity by corporations. This aggressive corporate culture is indiscriminately handicapping American children, reducing their attention spans, their vocabularies, and their social time with family, friends, and neighbors. Children are more and more remote from real events, history, nature, knowledge of, and interaction with their own communities unfiltered by images on screens and gossip spread on social media.

But families do not have to succumb to this corporate mandate. Corporations do not have to ruin their children's lives. There is a whole other children's world available and accessible to parents—a world that can strengthen the family, leading children to use their minds, enrich their imaginations, learn self-discipline, enlarge their range of experience in their communities, develop household skills, make more friends, enjoy themselves as participants rather than spectators, and unleash their ideals for the common good through shared interests and activities. Of course, many parents already do encourage their children to partake in organized sports, crafts, the arts, and music. But how many parents have managed to avoid the rancor, the arguments and whining that come with their kids' demands to go to some mall, stop at some fast-food drive-through window, or click on some easy online retail site and make a purchase, all to keep up with their friends' purchases because they just saw it advertised in some medium or other? How often do parents hear another kind of demand from their children —to go to a town meeting, a protest rally, the local historical society, the local courtroom, the drinking water purification facility, or the senior citizen center? Of course, many children do participate in charitable activities, go to church, and join the Girl and Boy

Scouts or 4-H associations. Yet most live lives focused on commercial products tailored for their consumption, drowning out any potential impulse toward civic life.

This trend is also confirmed in the kinds of information children and young adults consume in their daily lives. No one doubts that children have more access to information than ever before. Yet the percentage of children reading newspapers on an average day has plummeted from 42 percent in 1999 to 23 percent in 2009. In the 1990s, in the Prospectus for the Cultural Environment Movement, communications expert George Gerbner expressed concerns over this drift, in words that ring even more true today:

> For the first time in human history, most children are born into homes where most of the stories do not come from their parents, schools, churches, communities, and in many places even from their native countries, but from a handful of conglomerates who have something to sell.

The corporations' campaign to dominate childhood is relentless. It comes at parents from every direction, respecting no limits or boundaries, no traditional or worthy family values.

These intrusions have caused no little fear and anxiety among parents. The more children see themselves as independent consumers, the more they tend to flaunt disrespect for their parents, teachers, and other authority figures. And the purchases they're encouraged to make harbor all kinds of threats to their safety and health. Corporate processed foods, full of addicting fat, sugar, and salt, are endangering millions of children by predisposing them to diseases such as type 2 diabetes, cardiovascular disease, stroke, and some forms of cancer. More than one out of three American children and teenagers is now overweight or obese, which is more than a threefold increase in thirty years. Tobacco companies, internal documents have shown, have deliberately passed out free cigarettes and other enticements near schools to hook them early: the earlier children are hooked, the more likely they'll smoke until they die. Over promotion of medicine, leading to overmedication or unnecessary medication, has produced serious complications and worse for the children of unwary parents. And, perhaps most viscerally troubling, youngsters imitating the sadistic mayhem they see on television, online, or in video games have committed serious acts of violence.

These companies, in countless ways, are electronic child predators. They should be recognized as such—and their work should be countered through conscientious parenting at every age.

It is no secret that many corporations pollute our air and water and manufacture and sell hazardous or unhealthy products to unsuspecting consumers, which include children whose bodies are more vulnerable to toxins than adults. Less well-known, but potentially even more destructive, are the many ways that corporate commercialization destroys the essence of childhood. Enlisting child psychologists, marketing experts, advertising agencies, communications specialists, and government lobbyists, companies have created a system that allows them to bypass parents and market directly to children, wrapping youngsters in a cocoon that warps their lives. Children under twelve years old spend far more time with corporate products than with their parents and other adults. And the economy is a silent conspirator in this tragedy, driving undercompensated workers to take second jobs, when they can, to pay the rent—further reducing the time they have to spend with their families. Under such conditions, it's no surprise that parents are losing the war with amoral marketers over the minds, bodies, time, and space of their children.

This corporate takeover of childhood was never announced or decreed. It just happened. At the turn of the twentieth century, reformers argued that a shorter, five-day workweek would allow parents to spend more time with their children. We got the shorter workweek but not the wholesome family life the reformers envisioned. Today's children are raised by products and brands and social media as surely as they are by their own families. They are the Facebook generation, the PlayStation generation, the YouTube and iPhone generation.

As these corporations grew throughout the twentieth century, they exploited a change in the American household. Unlike in poorer times, in modern times parents no longer expect their children to contribute to the household economically. Where once they worked in the fields or performed chores around the house, today's children are primarily consumers rather than producers. As disposable income has increased, more and more household functions have been assigned to the marketplace: food, clothing, repairs, entertainment, day care, and counseling. Today, most teenagers who work do so to increase their personal spending income rather than to support their families.

This evolution within the family occurred in stages. After World War II, when children were seen as less economically necessary, the family assumed a different shape. Children spent their after-school time playing in the den or the backyard, overseen by Mom; Dad returned from work in time for the entire (often extended) family to sit down together for dinner. But this new culture of the American family did not last. Over the next few decades, the growth of the two-earner household, the increased prevalence of long commutes, and the decline of the extended family residence caused the post–World War II household to dissolve. This dissolution coincided with the emergence of television and direct selling to children. The less time adults spent with their children, the more the children went seeking gratification elsewhere. And the corporations were ready to fill the vacuum, offering children a commercial culture that touched everything from their sweet tooth to their self-esteem. Home alone and trusting any huckster with a smile and something to sell, children became increasingly prone to the sweet profit-pickings of corporate marketers stripping them of their innocence.

In exchange for peddling junk food and drink, violence, addiction, and varieties of tawdry sensuality, today the companies reap billions annually. To "earn" these profits, they employ thousands of experts to analyze, test, and interview children to learn how best to stimulate and exploit their drives, anxieties, and fears at various ages. These legalized child molesters are tireless in the pursuit of profit. A few years ago MTV boasted that it targets young people "24 hours a day, 365 days a year, while network television only targets them 22 percent of the time."

This commercial onslaught shows little restraint or respect for boundaries. Whatever the companies can sell is fair game, and thus their products keep becoming more coarse, more violent, and more "interactive"—a word that's increasingly becoming a euphemism for products that seduce youngsters into addictive, mayhem-driven behavior. Under the rubric of interactivity, the television-video game-music-cable moguls have transformed children from observers of video carnage to active participants—right down to do-it-yourself massacres and dismemberments. Thousands of studies over the decades demonstrate that daily exposure to violence desensitizes children. Anyone who claims that such desensitization has no effect either lives in a cocoon or profits from the phenomenon. For example, former West Point psychology professor Lieutenant Colonel Dave Grossman argues in his book *Stop Teaching Our Kids to Kill: A Call to Action Against TV, Movie and Video Game Violence* that first-person shooter video games (in which the player holds a toy gun or gunlike controller) are teaching kids to "act out violently without remorse."[1] Grossman argues that corporations that manufacture such toys should be held partially responsible for some school shootings and other violent tragedies perpetrated by children and teenagers. "Our children are learning to kill and learning to like it," he writes.

Privately, some business executives have acknowledged misgivings about what they transmit to their little customers. They offer a weak rationalization: if they don't do it, someone else will do worse. They recognize the squalor of their products, which they would not want for their own children or grandchildren, but pretend they have no choice. Even a universally admired filmmaker like Steven Spielberg has admitted that he wouldn't let his own eight-year-old watch *Jurassic Park*, but he didn't complain that many children that age and younger were seeing the hit movie. Instead of competing for market share in the childhood-destroying industry, these corporate power brokers should show courage and speak out as citizens.

A new coalition of parents and friends called the Center for a New American Dream (www.newdream.org) is organizing public opinion and resistance. According to a poll commissioned by the Center, 70 percent of parents with children ages two to seventeen believe that marketing negatively affects kids' values and worldview, making them too materialistic and putting pressure on them to purchase things that are harmful to them. More telling, over half of the parents polled admitted to buying things for their children that they disapproved of because their children expressed that they needed the products in order to fit in with the crowd.

Why are parents losing the war over their children? In large part, it's because the corporations have overwhelming resources at their disposal and because the perverse logic of the marketplace dictates that they put those resources to the most exploitative possible uses. The food and beverage industry alone spends nearly $2 billion each year on advertising and marketing to our youth. Driven by billions of dollars in sales, profits, bonuses, and stock options, the men who lead these giant companies are in a race to the bottom with their competitors, constantly expanding the spectrum of unhealthy products they peddle to our children through ever more manipulative delivery systems. Parents cannot match the vast sums of capital, technology, and influence these highly focused predators have at their fingertips—especially not when the average parent is working hard elsewhere to make ends meet.

Short of throwing out their TVs and computers, iPods and iPads, mobile phones and video game consoles, and homeschooling their children away from their peer group (a strategy that has other potential downsides), no parents can completely insulate their kids from these marketers' multilevel commercial assault. Single parents, often overworked and overstressed, are hard-pressed even to spend time with their children, and the situation is not much better in homes where both parents work full-time and can't adequately monitor their children's activities or exposure to aggressive corporate culture. Parents learn about such exposure only after the fact, when they notice their children imitating behavior and language they've picked up from television, movies, and the internet. With parents absent or too busy to inculcate values, children absorb and adopt values from the commercial entertainment industry.

Today, many children experience the "corporate week," spending more than forty hours weekly (seven hours each day) in the world of corporate products. To make matters worse, the entrepreneurial gurus shrewdly exploit parents' misgivings about how little time they spend with their children, enticing parents to salve their guilt by buying them video games, toys, sugary foods, and other dangerous products. The combination of guilt, weariness, and nagging by their children drives parents into dependence on corporate entertainment. The result is the delegation of child raising to electronic babysitters whose owners view children as sensory profit centers.

The corporate selling machine offers a seductive landscape—full of colorful imagery and reassuring slogans, a pace and excitement that can't help but fill children's senses and arouse their interest and appetites. This swirl of activity has given rise to an annual children's market that's valued at well over $200 billion. But the loud and addictive world that engulfs children exacts a corrosive and enduring price. Spending endless hours sitting and watching, listening to, or interacting with idle entertainment creates youngsters who are fatter and less fit than at any time in recorded history. The obesity epidemic and its associated illnesses, especially diabetes, are now viewed by public health officials and First Lady Michelle Obama as a national emergency. The Centers for Disease Control and Prevention (CDC) notes that "approximately 17% (or 12.5 million) of children and adolescents aged 2–19 years are obese. Since 1980, obesity prevalence among children and adolescents has almost tripled."

Children spend less and less time reading; writing; studying; talking; playing actively with their family, neighbors, and friends; or thinking at a level more sophisticated than the simplest Pavlovian response. When children do spend time with friends, they often share violent or sexualized toys and entertainment or scarf down junk food, not to mention smoking, drinking, and using drugs (both illegal drugs and their parents' own prescriptions). As a result, they get less out of school—which, in turn, limits their futures.

Television and other sources of electronic entertainment lie at the heart of the distortion of childhood. Polls show that Americans have a starkly negative view of commercial culture and blame television more than any other single factor for teenage sex and violence. Many Americans see a direct connection between the fictional world young people are exposed to and their behavior in real life, recognizing that portrayals of sex and violence on television, in movies, and in music lyrics contribute substantially to inappropriate teenage behavior. Former North Dakota Democratic senator Byron Dorgan once asked people to imagine an executive from New York City coming to their front door accompanied by a troupe of actors and high-tech props. The executive offers to bring these actors into our living room and entertain our kids with graphic scenes of violence and gore. The actors, he promises, will shoot and stab and maim one another. The blood will flow. They will return and repeat these displays day after day, as long as we let them in. Needless to say, most parents would slam the door in his face and call the police. Yet this activity takes place every day across America—on television.

Hundreds of studies confirm the connection between violent TV and aggressive behavior in real life. For example, a landmark University of Michigan study found that children who viewed higher levels of violent television "displayed a higher frequency of very serious antisocial and violent behaviors"[2] in adulthood. The study even found that such men were convicted of crimes at more than three times the rate of other men. "Exposure to violent electronic media has a larger effect than all but one other well-known threat to public health," says L. Rowell Huesmann, one of the authors of the media violence study. "The only effect slightly larger than the effect of media violence on aggression is that of cigarette smoking on lung cancer." The Congressional Public Health Summit and American Academy of Pediatrics found that more than one thousand studies and thirty years of research point to a "causal connection between media violence and aggressive behavior in some children." They also found that young children who were exposed to violence were more likely to consider it an effective way to settle a conflict; to be emotionally desensitized toward violence in real life; to perceive the world as a violent and mean place; and ultimately to engage in violent and aggressive behavior themselves later in life.

The eight or ten hours a week earlier generations of kids spent reading books are superseded by the thirty hours modern kids spend at the television. (Many inner-city youth have been blocked watching TV eleven hours a day, with thankful parents saying it at least keeps them off the dangerous streets.)

The corporate week offers children entertainment shorn of any historical or social context. Its world is heavily populated by cartoon characters on violent or repulsive missions, from *The Simpsons* to *South Park* to *Family Guy*, depicted through animation and dizzying scene changes, leaving no room for reflection. These celluloid-saturated children must negotiate life with sharply reduced attention spans and shriveled vocabularies.

And yet we forget that We the People own the public airwaves that are contaminating our children. We are the landlords of the broadcast spectrum; the television industry is the tenant. But the tenants pay us no rent for their FCC licenses and decide what is shown on their stations. Those who disapprove of their programming are told to switch channels or turn their sets off. That is the extent of our power as owner-landlords—even as the broadcast industries are preying on our vulnerable children, who can be counted on to switch prohibited shows back on as soon as we've left the room.

Shouldn't We the People demand something meaningful in return for handing these monopoly licenses to very profitable cable companies? Of the thousands of cable/satellite channels, why shouldn't we demand that several be devoted to education and the development of children's critical faculties? Might not a few stations be dedicated to evaluating the quality of the other hundreds? Shouldn't a few channels be programmed by organized viewers using the companies' amply funded studios, programmers, and reporters? Shouldn't there be a national audience television network, chartered as a nonprofit by Congress, giving the public owner-landlords of the airwaves the chance to take back even one prime-time or drive-time hour a day on all licensed television and radio stations, and devote it to healthier fare?

We need a systemic response from caring adults to challenge the electronic violence and other addictive debris polluting our children's environment.

By entering our living rooms and children's bedrooms and speaking directly with our children, television, mobile phones, and the internet have become the nation's major education system. They glamorize violence, presenting it to children as the way adults solve problems. This has been an issue almost since the beginning of the television age, but in the last two decades the problem has escalated to unimaginable levels. Yes, crime has many roots, but is it pure coincidence that the generations of kids who absorbed a deluge of bloodshed on the tube during the 1990s and 2000s are now mimicking it on our city streets? And the problem isn't limited to the cities. Pediatricians around the country describe a new cause of injury they frequently encounter: injuries children inflict on one another as they copy television characters.

The fallout from all this is almost too horrible to imagine. Writing in the *Los Angeles Times*, Richard Rodriguez observes that "we are entering a Stephen King novel: We are entering an America where adults are afraid of children. Where children rule the streets. Where adults cower at the approaching tiny figure on the sidewalk ahead. . . . Was there ever a generation of adults so ill-prepared to assume the central responsibility of adulthood—that of raising children?"[3]

Advertisers are constantly striving to deepen their penetration into the inner worlds of our children. In recent years, they have enjoyed particular success at influencing youth through new technologies, such as video and computer games, mobile phones, instant messaging (IM), viral videos, social media, and branded "entertainment" websites. Mobile phone use among children and teenagers is skyrocketing. According to a Kaiser Family Foundation report in 2010, "Over the past five years, there has been a huge increase in [mobile phone] ownership among 8- to 18-year olds: from 39% to 66%." Marketers are using mobile phones to advertise to children with great power and precision, using micro-targeted messages based on age, location, shopping history, and other personal information. Google's manager of mobile products, Sumit Agarwal, boasts that the mobile phone is the "ultimate ad vehicle" because it's "the first one ever in the history of the planet that people go to bed with."[4] In September 2011, the advertising industry publication *Adweek* featured an article, by Brian Braiker, titled "The Next Great American Consumer: Infants to 3-year-olds: They're a new demographic marketers are hell-bent on reaching." The article noted that mothers are increasingly allowing their children to use mobile phones. "In 2010, the average age they said children could have their own mobile phone was 13-years-old. In 2011, however, 1 in 4 mothers allowed their children to interact with a mobile phone by age 2."

Children are also spending more of their time online, and advertisers are following them. *Adweek* recently trumpeted the finding that "80 percent of kids under the age of 5 use the internet weekly, and 60 percent of kids 3 and younger are now watching videos online." Social media like Facebook have made it their business model to immerse teens and other users in a sophisticated framework of advertising. Companies can now use Facebook's new "sponsored stories" to advertise directly in a person's "news feed." Market research shows these ads are unusually potent: according to *Adweek*, these ads "have a 68 percent recall, with users twice as likely to remember a brand and four times as likely to take action."[5] This is just one small part of Facebook's new effort to cram ads into nearly every part of the Facebook experience. One Facebook vice president recently explained that Facebook advertising is only "1 percent of where we need to be."

Nearly every new technology is subject to such commercialization. American youth are increasingly using IM as a way to communicate with each other, for instance—and marketers now use a variety of techniques to embed their ads into instant messages. Many children and teenagers regularly spend hours each week playing computer and video games—so market researchers have found ways to implant ads within these games and even to create games whose purpose is solely to promote a product, both of them powerful and cost-effective ways of influencing youth to buy products. Advertisers are also creating branded games and websites filled with a great variety of engaging content, but also full of advertising, such as EA Sports FIFA International Soccer games, featuring Adidas billboards, or online games featuring Subway restaurant blimps floating in the background. Mobile apps allow you to download them for free in exchange for filling the game with advertising breaks. Apps such as Words with Friends and Draw Something are examples of free mobile games filled with advertising. You can opt out and pay for the app, but most people don't buy the app and instead are inundated with ads. General Mills features many games on its website, as does Kellogg's. There are games where you have to shoot at Cheerios to reach the next level. There are games in which kids have to follow what Tony the Tiger (Frosted Flakes) tells them to do.

Ads are especially influential when it's less obvious that they are ads—hence the rise of product placement as a marketing technique. "There are a lot of corporations that realize being integrated [into a TV program] from a product placement standpoint has a greater value than a 30-second spot," says Steve Rasnick, vice president of UPP Entertainment Marketing. "Irrespective of what ad agencies tell you, there's a falloff in [viewership during] a commercial. People get up, they change the channel and TiVo gets around commercials altogether, so by being integrated into the program, you have a large, captive audience—and an interested one." Some programs are so saturated with product placements that they have essentially become program-length ads. For example, *American Idol*—one of the most popular shows in the history of television—has served as a de facto infomercial for Coca-Cola. Between January 15 and March 31, 2008, for instance, Nielsen Media Research measured 2,337 product placements for Coke on *American Idol*.

Similarly, images of stars smoking in movies exert a deadly influence in luring youthful new smokers. In such movies, smoking is often used to dramatize relaxation, glamour, independence, and socializing. When a child or teenager identifies with a movie character who smokes, this especially promotes tobacco use. According to an aggregation of all available studies of smoking in movies, about 44 percent of all new smokers are recruited by images of tobacco in movies. Each year, about 390,000 American kids start smoking because of movie imagery of tobacco; roughly one-third of them will eventually die of smoking-related illnesses.

Today, the corporate assault on childhood occurs through the internet as well, with advertisers and marketers pursuing the spending dollars of children—"lucrative cybertots"—online. These corporations solicit personal information and exploit young computer users through deceptive advertising. Advertising and content have been interwoven in online "infomercials" that lure children into interacting with product-characters like Frosted Flakes' Tony the Tiger; Fruit Loops' Toucan Sam; Rice Krispies' Snap, Crackle, and Pop; Lucky Charms' Lucky the Leprechaun; and Cocoa and Fruity Pebbles' Flintstones.

The advertisers use data gathered about the children's online use to personalize each interaction so effectively that the children are transported into a "flow state" of total absorption. Erica Gruen, former senior vice president of strategic media resources at Saatchi & Saatchi Advertising, has exulted about the potential "for advertisers to build relationships with kids" through such schemes.

The "one-to-one marketing" of children via virtual reality, cyberspace, and interactivity is particularly difficult for parents to control. In a report titled *Web of Deception: Threats to Children from Online Marketing*, the Center for Media Education notes how hard it is for parents to monitor their children's use of online services. Unlike television, which many families watch together, most children use computers alone. Many children have greater computer skills than their parents, which further complicates monitoring. In addition, because computers do have important educational uses, many parents prefer that their children be online rather than watching television, often unaware that the websites their children are viewing can be more intrusive and manipulative than the worst children's television. In such ways, these online marketers are taking children away from their parents and into a commercial world that knows no time restraints, shows no concern for the child's development, and is under little or no regulation.

The big businesses that market to children use consulting firms that psycho-research the "youth market." One such firm, Boston-based FIND/SVP, noticed the potential for corporate takeover of childhood as early as the 1990s. In a report titled *Heroic Kids: The Emerging Family in the 21st Century*, FIND/ SVP looked at various statistical trends (family income, age, marriage and divorce rates) and concluded that modern children have uncommon emotional stresses due to greater family instability. The report observed that family tragedies can become the hook of sales strategies. Companies can "help kids build their own islands of happiness, independent of parental interaction" by creating a separate children's world to give the child power, peer acceptance, and a sense of identity separate from the family world.

These companies are succeeding beyond their wildest dreams. Pediatricians William Dietz and Victor Strasburger have estimated that 2- to 5-year-olds average more than 27 hours a week watching television. And a 2010 Kaiser Family Foundation study found that children aged 8 to 18 spent an average 7 hours and 38 minutes per day using media such as television, music, video games, and movies (totaling more than 53 hours per week). By contrast, these youngsters spend just 30 hours a week in school, 9 months a year. The study showed that these children spent an average of only 8 minutes a weekday in "meaningful conversation" with their father and 11 minutes with their mother.

Parents are the only real defense children have against the kind of product-centered separate world these marketers envision, but there's one catch: parents also provide the dollars. Accordingly, companies have worked out a three-step strategy to overcome or circumvent parents' control over their children's spending. First, they entice children to nag their parents. Second, they take advantage of the absence of parents who travel or work long hours outside the home. Third, they undermine the authority, dignity, and judgment of parents in the eyes of their children, thereby inducing kids to purchase or demand items regardless of their parents' opinions.

Most parents still don't realize how crafty the hucksters are at defeating their efforts to shield their children by sending subtle and oblique messages encouraging children's liberation. It's no accident that the Marlboro Man—which *Advertising Age* called the most powerful brand image in the twentieth century—evokes teenagers' yearning for independence and freedom. Over time, the message against parental authority becomes more blatant and, in the face of "liberated" children, parental resistance weakens. Consider McDonald's McWorld campaign, which includes both advertisements and a virtual world online that carries the tagline "It's a kid's world where kids rule!" Every McWorld ad has a different theme, but they share one common element: the portrayal of adults as lame, stupid pains-in-the-butt (with the exception of the McDonald's workers, of course). Other corporate commercials, most egregiously by video game firms like PlayStation and Xbox, explicitly degrade and devalue parents, as do programs like *South Park* and *The Simpsons*. As social scientist Laura Sessions Stepp writes, "For children and adolescents, the advertisers' message is clear: We understand you better than your parents (something teens are only too willing to believe). Parents often are incompetent and tyrannized by their children."

Selling to kids also means displacing parents as role models. This isn't a difficult task, given the number of single-parent households and families where both parents work and lack time to spend with the kids. In the past, the children in such families have turned to MTV, the movies, or the sports world for adult role models. Parents who did try to teach their children found their lessons undermined by television and other media in a campaign that knows almost no limits in terms of time, space, or taste.

The time, talent, image making, and resources that companies use to create a "kids only" world seem obscene when we consider the poverty of millions of America's children. Millions more are deprived of necessities by a malfunctioning political economy. Yet instead of seeking innovative ways to meet these crucial needs, corporate America uses its ingenuity to inspire desire for sordid, addictive entertainment and other unwholesome habits that harm children's bodies and minds.

Take the fantasy world for kids created by Kool-Aid's advertising in the 1990s. Each packet of Kool-Aid came with a number of points on the back, which could be exchanged for toys and prizes. To promote its point system, Kool-Aid created an imaginary Wacky Warehouse. One ad campaign showed children visiting the warehouse while their parents were put into a huge playpen. Frenzied kids ran around collecting toys while drinking Kool-Aid. In the words of Bob Skollar, the executive vice president of advertising who developed this campaign, "All kids like to drink Coke, but they have to have their own drink. Kool-Aid is going to be a kid's own world; it belongs to the kids. A world that only kids can understand, and that adults just were not allowed into. . . . We showed the commercials to adults and they did not get it. Then we showed it to a group of kids, and we showed it to them just one time, and they played back almost every element of the campaign. They got it. They knew that it was something different [for children] and they loved it."

Companies come after children in every way they can, penetrating not only the media and cyberspace, but also malls, magazines, movie theaters, day care centers, fast-food restaurants, theme parks, and schools. Every part of a child's life can be touched and shaped by corporate products. Everything in their lives has a corporate logo, theme, or message. This represents a complete integrated marketing system—a world where children are reared to bolster the corporate bottom line. University of California, San Diego, professor Herbert Schiller explains the nonstop nature of these marketing pitches: "The reason that commercials are particularly insidious is because there is a cumulative, a sedimentary buildup. There is a growing base of these kinds of images, impressions, and ways of looking at that world. . . . This base will not help kids when they become teens, and adults, to grow up healthy."

When children are a bit older, addictive industries like tobacco and alcohol lure children with "integrated imaging" and ersatz "role models," building on the Pavlovian purchase response they've been conditioned to feel from near infancy. Older children often go out of their way to see and sample things their parents disapprove of, absorbing the messages they've learned from the sales machine and parroting them back contemptuously under the rubric of "adults just don't get it." What the children don't get is how the corporations got them.

Of course, the commercialization of childhood is a subset of the larger commercialization of America. Over time, corporations have entered virtually every aspect of our lives. In countless areas that were once off-limits to commerce, the mercantile juggernaut has moved in—into our schools and colleges, public media, amateur sports, arts, holidays and rituals, religious institutions, environment, and politics. Historically treasured cultural values are either viewed as marketing impediments or are commandeered, co-opted, or outright commodified in the service of corporate profits. For example, national holidays have become sales days, overwhelming their original inspirations—from celebrating religious or patriotic milestones to honoring our veterans.

Some might assume that such aggressive sales techniques are as old as the country itself. Didn't President Calvin Coolidge say back in the 1920s that "the chief business of the American people is business"? Haven't the command of commerce, the lure of profits, the focus on markets been around since the days of the thirteen colonies?

In truth, nothing in the past remotely compares to what we're experiencing today: the corporate intrusion into formerly noncommercial space with a pervasive sales pitch that sweeps away all prior restraints and decorum. Megachurch preachers talk more about marketing themselves than about Mammon. Ad agencies use revered former presidents such as George Washington, Thomas Jefferson, and Abraham Lincoln as pitchmen for car dealerships, furniture stores, and banks. In one Maryland elementary school, a teacher held up a picture of Ben Franklin and the children identified him as a car salesman they saw on television. There are virtually no limits or boundaries to commercialism. What's next: Ads on postage stamps and school buses? Billboards on the Grand Canyon or below the faces on Mount Rushmore?

Advertisements like these would hardly come as a surprise

today, as we've routinely come to accept what would once have been considered unthinkable. Public schools now allow into the classroom commercial television replete with product advertising (claiming they couldn't otherwise afford the donated television equipment). Channel One News is a twelve-minute commercial TV program shown to captive audiences of "nearly six million" students in about eight thousand middle and high schools across the nation. Since its inception, it has promoted to schoolchildren an unsavory stew of junk food, soda pop, prescription drugs, violent and sexualized entertainment, and movies that encourage schoolchildren to smoke. In 1994, Joel Babbit, the channel's then president, explained why advertisers like the programming: "The biggest selling point to advertisers [is that] we are forcing kids to watch two minutes of commercials." As Babbit explained, school is a perfect backdrop for sales pitches: "The advertiser gets a group of kids who cannot go to the bathroom, who cannot change the station, who cannot listen to their mother yell in the background, who cannot be playing Nintendo, who cannot have their headsets on." Channel One has drawn opposition from across the political spectrum, from the American Family Association and Phyllis Schlafly's Eagle Forum, to Global Exchange and the Organic Consumers Association, and including education groups like the National PTA. The company was so desperate for political protection that it even hired the legendarily corrupt Jack Abramoff as its lobbyist.

Scholastic is another company that helps marketers bypass parents to promote directly to children products and values that parents may not approve of. Under the guise of its "book club," Scholastic has marketed toys, makeup, jewelry, and video games such as M&M Kart Racing and the Dairy Queen "DQ Tycoon" game to elementary and middle school students.

But isn't the glass half full? Hasn't the wholesale commercialization of American culture also produced unprecedented material comforts for the general population? In fact, rampant commercialism has failed to deliver for ordinary Americans. The rich are getting richer, but the gap between the rich and other Americans is only growing. Nevertheless, the obsessive commercialization of America in the past fifty years goes unchallenged, in part because it shapes our minds—starting at a young age.

In the face of such an all-encompassing assault, it's easy for parents to feel helpless. But it's worth remembering that things haven't always been this way. There are lessons to be learned from previous civilizations, even when it comes to such modern problems as the commercialization of society.

In ancient times—from biblical lands to dynastic China— commerce was forced to respect boundaries, lest it contaminate noncommercial practices, traditions, and customs. In old China, merchants were near the bottom of the social status ladder. A similar strain of anticommercialism has always marked American culture—or, at least, a traditional concern that other values not be trampled. At the time of our founding, Ben Franklin preached thrift and moderation. He and his fellow founders feared that greed and financial overreaching posed a serious threat to the virtuous republic they envisioned, a civilization that aspired to higher purposes in life.

Of course, the founders' concerns have been borne out—at times shockingly so. During the Civil War, profit-maximizing munitions manufacturers produced defective equipment that took the lives of soldiers, angering senators and President Lincoln to no end. But there have also been uplifting counterreactions. The populist-progressive movements were designed to decentralize power, reclaiming it from the mighty railroads and banks and shifting it to the common people. They sought to build a power base for values beyond commerce—the values of self-reliance, family, and a just democracy—as part of their efforts to create a people that lead decent lives shielded from absentee corporate predators. To judge by America today, their reforms have been overwhelmed.

Any culture that surrenders its self-sustaining human values to the narrow dictates of commerce will be neither free nor just. Commercialism damages the substance of democracy, if not its forms. It leads to self-censorship in the media, the indentured servitude of politicians, and an overall coarseness that deprecates the people's humanitarian impulses and civically creative drives.

This is our challenge today. But there are solutions—strategies we can seize together, in an effort to drive our nation's priorities in a new direction.

To start with: parents need to gain a larger perspective on what the big corporations are doing to their children and what they have in mind for years to come. More than twenty years ago, a Minnesota mother exclaimed: "I try to teach my children something, and then when I turn my back for a moment, the TV is undermining what I said." Those words are still more resonant today—but not every parent even recognizes the ever-present threat of these commercial enticements or feels empowered to do anything to counter their influence.

Which is why caring American parents need to join forces at the neighborhood level, to compare notes, share stories, and start a movement to fight back the encroaching public influence over their children's private lives. Every major movement starts small.

In particular, we need a systemic campaign to challenge the electronic violence and other addictive debris that are polluting our children's environment. While it's too late to turn back the clock completely on the commercialization of our children's lives, there are concrete measures we can take to restore the essential blessings of childhood. We can begin by demanding that, if nothing else, corporate America respect our children's privacy.

In recent times, commercial brokers have actually sold lists of the names and personal information of middle school students. One list sold by the Student Marketing Group included middle schoolers' ages, gender, e-mail addresses, and phone numbers. American Student List boasted at one point that it sold a list of "over 20 million students ranging in age from 2–13."

In 2004, U.S. senators Ron Wyden (D-OR) and Ted Stevens (R-AK) introduced legislation to stop this despicable practice. Their proposed bill would have prohibited corporations from selling the personal information of children under sixteen for commercial marketing purposes without parental consent. Such legislation warranted congressional passage and the president's signature, yet it was sent to the Senate Committee on Commerce, Science, and Transportation and never became law.

A citizen's organization I helped found, Commercial Alert (www.commercialalert.org), backs various measures to restore balance to our ultracommercialized society. In 2004, the organization launched a campaign for a worldwide ban on marketing of junk food to children twelve and under. This sensible proposal would combat the rising global epidemic of childhood obesity— and thus help save or enhance millions of young lives. Numerous health professionals and organizations have called on the World Health Organization to incorporate such a ban into its global anti-obesity initiative or to enact the ban through international health regulations.

Commercial Alert also backs a package of measures it calls a Parents' Bill of Rights to help combat the destructive commercial influences on children, promote wholesome values and products, and resist the epidemic of marketing-related diseases (including obesity, alcoholism, addictive gambling, and deadly smoking-related illnesses). This Parents' Bill of Rights includes nine proposed pieces of legislation, a few of which have been introduced in Congress:

- The Leave Children Alone Act, banning television advertising aimed at children under age twelve.
- The Child Privacy Act, giving parents the right to control any commercial use of their children's personal information and to know precisely how such information is used.
- The Advertising to Children Accountability Act, requiring corporations to disclose who created and conducted market research for each ad directed at children under age twelve.
- The Commercial-Free Schools Act, prohibiting corporations from using schools and compulsory school laws to bypass parents and pitch products to impressionable kids.
- The Fairness Doctrine for Parents Act, applying the Fairness Doctrine to all advertising to kids under age twelve by granting parents and community equal time in response to such ads.
- The Product Placement Disclosure Act, requiring corporations to disclose any and all product placement in television shows, movies, video games, and books, preventing advertisers from sneaking ads into media that parents assume to be ad-free.
- The Child Harm Disclosure Act, requiring corporations to disclose all information suggesting that their products could substantially harm the health of children.
- The Children's Advertising Subsidy Revocation Act, eliminating federal subsidies, deductions, and preferences for advertising aimed at children under age twelve.

Of course, we as individuals still shape our culture from within. We are still responsible for actively teaching children positive values and promoting wholesome activities and learning experiences with family, neighbors, and teachers. Parents today must focus their energies on warding off the daily commercial saturation of childhood. Still, the measures listed above and others—such as shareholders' challenges at corporate annual meetings—can contribute toward seizing control over childhood from the corporations and returning it to the family unit. The existence of groups like Commercial Alert and the Center for a New American Dream suggests that parents are no longer willing to roll over and allow corporate America to wrest their children away from them, sacrificing healthy childhood at the altar of megaprofits.

It won't be easy. One thing is for sure: corporations fight tenaciously for their bottom line. We can't expect to combat the pernicious effects of their marketeering if we aren't prepared to fight back. But we have the means—through such organizations, through internet-based national campaigns, and through our votes—to organize pressure on these corporate hucksters to change their practices and on our legislators to enact proposals such as those presented by Commercial Alert. And we can do it—if we are really serious about defending our children from these marketers.

In communities all over the country—at all income levels—there are already parents who have opted out of corporate childhoods. They put the TV in the closet, the cell phones in the drawer, and eat their family meals together. They organize their time around family conversations, family outings, family work around the house, family recreation, family readings and discussion, and family community service. The common thread of such engagements is that the family is connected and each of its members is involved as an active participant. And it sure beats Junior waking up and texting Mom down in the kitchen to tell her what he doesn't want to eat.

And there are community organizations in place that can help to set a different rhythm for family life. The local papers are full of listings for family activities—so much that you might have a problem choosing what to do. Interested in community storytelling? Nature walks? Running a 5K? Presentations on your community's history or geography or animal life? Local libraries are another source of information on community events and groups, including book clubs, poetry readings and contests, amateur sports teams, and art circles. There are museums, theaters—sometimes with special children's sections and even roles to fill—children's film festivals, arts and crafts programs, family oral history projects, and more. And many communities offer the chance for youngsters to spend time with elderly residents, learning from their experience and skills—from kite flying, to knot tying, to playing a musical instrument—while absorbing their stories. All these interesting groups rarely complain that they are overbooked; many are free and the volunteers who administer them are eager for you to visit.

Participating in community economics is another way for parents to change their children's views of the world. Families can participate in credit union and food cooperatives, health clinic boards, community energy production, and local markets. They can also get involved in important civic matters at the local level. Take them to town or city council meetings and have them observe the participants. Most children grow up to adulthood having never seen their communities' public works departments, which keep highways, bridges, dams, schools, and sewage systems in working order, or having never sat in the courts watching the way justice is (or is not) dispensed. My mother once wrote an article titled "Touring Your Own Home Town." At that time, our hometown of ten thousand people had numerous factories, artisan shops, dairy farms, and firehouses, along with a hospital, a daily newspaper, a county court, and other facilities—sites that even then were rarely visited by local families. Common experiences create common bonds.

More Americans need to give serious thought to the family's untapped potential as the essential building block of our democracy. The kinds of constructive people our society desperately needs—both leaders and "participators," to use one of

Thomas Jefferson's favorite words—are raised not by corporations but by caring, thoughtful, engaged families. The Greek philosopher Heraclitus observed that "character is destiny." I would add also that "personality is decisive." Boys and girls who are raised within healthy, mutually supportive families are most likely to possess those two attributes—character and personality—and to reach maturity with both of them intact and ready to take flight.

5

Get Corporations Off Welfare

When President Bill Clinton proudly joined with House Speaker Newt Gingrich in 1996 to enact their reforms of welfare for the poor—you know, those pesky single moms receiving three hundred dollars a month—I wrote a letter to Clinton, urging him to follow the move with a much more important encore: ending the hundreds of billions of undeserved dollars regularly doled out by Uncle Sam in direct and indirect corporate welfare to just about every large company in America. Clinton never responded. No surprise: unlike single moms, corporations that feed off the taxpayers are important contributors to political campaigns, including his own.

For decades, I've been calling on Americans to recognize the phenomenon of corporate welfare as the poster boy for both the exploitation of taxpayers and the hypocrisy of free-market anti–big government ideologues. As early as 1971, I denounced giveaways like the Surface Transportation Act, which handed an open-ended $5 billion in financial assistance to the railroads and trucking companies, and a $250 million loan guarantee to the Lockheed Corporation, which narrowly passed Congress despite extensive public hearings and an uproar of opposition. And yet today, consider how quaintly modest this Lockheed sum was compared with the humongous taxpayer subsidies and trillion-dollar guarantees during the speculative Wall Street crash of

2008–9. But corporate entitlements have been trending sharply upward that way for decades.

A specific comparison illustrates both the gigantic escalation of corporate welfare and its descent into secrecy. One weekend in October 2008, Robert Rubin, former secretary of the Treasury and deregulation advocate for Bill Clinton, went to Washington in his capacity as chairman of the giant but teetering Citigroup for a supersecret meeting with Treasury secretary and former Goldman Sachs chair Henry Paulson and Federal Reserve chair Ben Bernanke. By Monday morning, American taxpayers awoke to the news that their government—without congressional approval—was purchasing $45 billion in Citigroup preferred stock and guaranteeing $365 billion of Citigroup's shaky paper. Just like that. Could a dictatorship have taken such unilateral action more swiftly and unaccountably? It was the corporate state in action.

Corporate welfare is the business of Washington, D.C., these days. The government has devised literally hundreds of programs giving out taxpayer money to corporations—in the form of credits and exemptions, grants, subsidies, and loan guarantees. The government offers free access to taxpayer-funded R&D assets, natural resources on our public lands, and our public airwaves to corporations; these companies offer no return on their profits to Uncle Sam, whether in royalties or by fulfilling the promises on jobs they made to get the giveaways. There are many ways to deliver corporate welfare: the energy, timber, mineral, and agribusiness industries benefit from complex, backdoor, over-time transfers through the Treasury Department through the Departments of Interior or Agriculture, for instance, while technology companies profit from inflated contracts through NASA and the Pentagon, and the medical industry receives almost clinic-ready medicine and hardware from the NIH. Uncle Sam's sugar daddy largesse is so rampant that no one has managed to compile a comprehensive survey of even a single department's or agency's giveaways.

In public, at least, no one approves of corporate welfare. Politicians from right and left fall over themselves to say how much they dislike it and the sleaze that goes with it. Yet when it comes to bringing the bacon back to their own district or state—or enlarging their campaign coffers—they're all for it, especially when the corporate giveaways can be readily camouflaged as job-creating measures. Dependent on corporate donations to fund their reelection campaigns, these politicians support these giveaways even when they lend corporations an unfair competitive advantage over other companies in the same region. This imbalance tends to hurt small businesses, which pay their property taxes even as new competitors, such as Walmart megastores, are given lengthy abatements.

This kind of government favoritism has been going on for years. After Ronald Reagan lost his bid for the Republican presidential nomination in 1976, I participated in a public discussion on the government-business relationship with Reagan and Senator Hubert Humphrey. At one point, I challenged Reagan, the self-proclaimed champion of business and foe of government spending, to make good on his rhetoric. "If you make that your campaign theme next year," I told him, "you'll be making a major contribution to the American dialogue." I urged Reagan to "speak out against corporate socialism, government subsidies of big business, corporations that are so big they can't be allowed to fail so only small business can go bankrupt. A company that is big, like Lockheed Martin and those other giants, can go to Washington instead of going out of business. And you are absolutely right that in that situation there is massive outflow of the taxpayers' revenue into the coffers of the giant corporations. It certainly doesn't make them more efficient."

Reagan insisted he agreed with me. "Mr. Nader, I've been

speaking out against this for a long time," he said. "I often tell my business friends not to put their hand in the Washington trough. . . . I've been addressing business groups and asking them if they believe in free enterprise—because I believe that we should return as much as possible to the marketplace." Yet, sure enough, once Reagan became president in 1981, he never lifted a hand to stop the accelerating corporate welfare train; indeed, he supported it. Critique in theory, surrender in practice: that's how the money keeps flowing from Washington to hypocritical corporate capitalists, thanks to their ideological apologists. Only the lonely libertarians have been brave enough to address the contradiction.

Of course it's not just Washington that sends these rivers of taxpayer funds into corporate coffers. In 2000, in one of the most foolish and cruelly ironic urban policy moves ever, New York governor George Pataki and New York City mayor Rudy Giuliani collaborated to provide a clutch of state and local subsidies, amounting to more than $1 billion, to construct a new building for the growing New York Stock Exchange (NYSE). In December of that year, Giuliani signed a letter of intent to acquire land for the new exchange building and to join the state to construct a new trading floor for the NYSE. The plan also involved exempting the NYSE from the facility tax and providing it with subsidized energy benefits—while charging it only a nominal annual rent, for appearances' sake.

Can you imagine a more potent symbol of free-market global capitalism than the NYSE? And there it was, shamelessly putting its hand in the taxpayers' trough. The sole purported rationale for this bonanza was to keep the stock exchange in New York City and out of New Jersey. This is a time-tested strategy, one whose flames are often fanned by specialized consulting firms: pit state against state, city against city, forcing them to submit their most profligate bids to keep important businesses from migrating or to attract new businesses to their area. Such standoffs create no new jobs for the country as a whole—yet they inflict a huge cost per job for the taxpayers.

There was never a chance that the stock exchange would leave New York City for Hoboken. Around that time, I visited the NYSE trading floor and asked veteran traders about the possibility of the exchange moving across the Hudson River to Jersey. They laughed, dismissing it out of hand. The very reputation and identity of the NYSE—not to mention the personal connections between its members and the Wall Street banks and brokerage firms—were too wound up in its New York location to make the threat credible. And the Pataki/Giuliani offer was mooted in any event, a short time later, by a combination of space-saving automation and the 9/11 disaster in lower Manhattan. The deal dissolved from its own overreaching greed and recklessness.

Still, this spectacle has not stopped one large financial firm after another from trying to cut its taxes and gain other advantages by floating unwritten threats to move their operations to New Jersey or Connecticut. The mayors of New York have all played along with the ruse; it has become routine for the big guys to get these breaks, with no public hearings, while the thousands of brick-and-mortar small businesses that line New York's streets pay full fare.

The corporate welfare state exists because we allow it to exist.

In November 1998, *Time* magazine unleashed its star reporters Donald L. Barlett and James B. Steele on the corporate welfare kings—including the magazine's own parent company, Time Warner Inc., which has received millions of dollars in tax exemptions and free public services from federal, state, and local governments. Barlett and Steele had a knack for exposing the complex system of corporate favoritism by comparing it with the budgets of working families: "How would you like to pay only a quarter of the real estate taxes you owe on your home?

And buy everything for the next 10 years without spending a single penny in sales tax? Keep a chunk of your paycheck free of income taxes? Have the city in which you live lend you money at rates cheaper than any bank charges. Then have the same city install free water and sewer lines to your office, offer you a perpetual discount on utility bills—and top it all off by landscaping your front yard at no charge?"[1]

They could have gone further with their questions: How would you like the taxes corporations pay to your state be rerouted to your bank account? Such was the outlandish agreement the state of New Jersey struck in 1996, when the new cable network MSNBC pitted New York against New Jersey to bid for the location of the cable network with jobs. New Jersey won the contest with a bevy of goodies, including this astonishing giveaway: the state government agreed that all state taxes paid by MSNBC employees would be reimbursed to the coffers of the network's two parent companies: the superprofitable Microsoft and General Electric. Corporate attorneys and the consulting firms that specialize in getting states or localities to engage in this kind of bidding frenzy are always thinking of creative new ways to game the system. As *Time* reported: "It's a game in which governments large and small subsidize corporations large and small, usually at the expense of another state or town and almost always at the expense of individual and other corporate taxpayers. . . . It has turned politicians into bribery specialists, and smart businesspeople into con artists. And most surprising of all, it has rarely created any new jobs"—because the jobs in question were being created anyway. Only the location, and the jobs' surprising cost to taxpayers, was up for grabs.

Barlett and Steele came up with a simple definition of corporate welfare: "any action by local, state or federal government that gives a corporation or an entire industry a benefit not offered to others. It can be an outright subsidy, a grant, real estate, a low-interest loan or a government service. It can also be a tax break—a credit, exemption, deferral or deduction, or a tax rate lower than the one others pay." But there are even more forms of corporate welfare. Governments have exercised eminent domain—as in Detroit's Poletown area, where it condemned four hundred homes, dozens of businesses, twelve churches, a hospital, and schools in the early 1980s to clear four hundred acres for a GM plant promising six thousand jobs. GM also demanded and received $350 million in national, state, and local subsidies. Among the casualties of the move was a beautiful Polish-American Catholic church, lovingly built by Polish immigrants earlier in the century, torn down to provide space for shrubbery in the corner of a parking lot. The priest, Father Joseph Karasiewicz, said this would never have happened in Communist Poland. He died a short time later, his heart broken. GM needed less than two hundred acres for the plant and staging areas. But with the city fathers falling all over themselves to keep the plant from being built over the city border in Hamtramck, they were happy to grab twice the space, forcing the expulsion of four thousand residents. The new GM plant employed only three thousand workers, and the auto giant failed to give back a proportionate share of the subsidies.

For years, the practice of eminent domain has been used in similar fashion: to seize a small factory to allow the expansion of a larger one in Pittsburgh, to seize land for a casino parking lot in Atlantic City, New Jersey; and to seize other private holdings around the country. In the 2005 case *Kelo v. City of New London*, the Supreme Court ruled 5–4 that such seizures could not be challenged by the dispossessed. This verdict was so outrageous that it did lead to a rare setback for corporate welfare kings, after public indignation at *Kelo* sparked new laws in numerous states banning the local government taking from private property for purposes of private business.

It is difficult to overstate how many tactics the government uses to support corporate activity here and abroad—from subsidizing sellers to paying buyers; from setting agricultural market quotas to absorbing nuclear power insurance risks; from offering taxpayer support for overseas marketing campaigns for corporate giants (such as McDonald's) to giving corporations free access to immensely valuable inventions and assets that were developed with taxpayer dollars. You may not be aware of these tactics—no one involved is eager to call attention to them, and they are often cloaked in contracts that are difficult to retrieve for public examination—but the government has used them to send your tax dollars to Hollywood filmmakers, corporate prisons, profitable computer chip factories, and biotech facilities.

In their *Time* investigation, Barlett and Steele touched on a wide array of profitable corporations that engaged in such windfalls—including Intel, General Motors, Mercedes-Benz, UPS, PepsiCo's Frito-Lay subsidiary, Caterpillar, Union Carbide, Chrysler, R.J. Reynolds, and Georgia-Pacific. Also on the dole were AlliedSignal, Microsoft, Bechtel, Boeing, Hughes Aircraft (now owned by Raytheon), AT&T, General Electric, Archer Daniels Midland, Monsanto's Searle subsidiary, and Exxon. Polluting companies are paid to try not to pollute. Large sugar producers, even assorted foreign corporations, are given welfare. The list went on and on, often with the color photograph of each CEO: the corporate welfare boss at the top.

The *Time* investigation was responding to a growing momentum for change. Conservative think tanks like the Cato Institute and the Heritage Foundation were issuing reports denouncing corporate welfare, as were liberal/progressive groups such as Good Jobs First, Common Cause, and Public Citizen. Public opinion was rising in that same direction, provoked by billionaire sports owners who were demanding more and more money from city taxpayers to build their stadiums and ballparks, lest they move their beloved franchises away. John McCain and other senators were pressing for an independent federal commission to eliminate "unnecessary and inequitable federal subsidies" to private companies. The national TV networks reported on case after case on such shows as the ABC News segment "It's Your Money" and CBS News's *60 Minutes*.

Seven months after the *Time* report, the first congressional hearing entirely on "Unnecessary Business Subsidies" was called by the House Budget Committee, chaired by Republican John Kasich, now governor of Ohio. In a long opening statement, Kasich expressed the view, shared by millions of small-business owners, that corporate welfare went mostly to the big companies and thus constituted an unfair form of competition. He referred to "millions of small businesses that pay taxes that do not participate in these special programs" and called the hearing "a matter of fairness."[2]

Witnesses from opposite poles of the political spectrum—from conservative economist Grover Norquist to myself, from the Cato Institute's Stephen Moore to the Citizens for Tax Justice's Robert McIntyre—were largely unanimous in condemning corporate welfare. The entire text of the *Time* series was read into the record, as was an impassioned statement by T. J. Rodgers, CEO of Cypress Semiconductor Corporation. His tough-worded "Declaration of Independence: End Corporate Welfare" was signed by the CEOs of leading technology companies including Applied Materials, Xilinx, Seagate Technology, and Sun Microsystems, who signed on to the document's principles "even if it meant funding cuts to my own company." Indeed, many of the signatories presided over companies that had received forms of corporate welfare, such as R&D tax credits.

So all in all, for a moment, it looked like the tide was turning against the corporate welfare state. But it wasn't. The forces, both economic and political, were too organized, too powerful, and often too cleverly hidden to be brought down by a few investigations and a governmental hearing. The courts remained inhospitable to reform—often to the extent of throwing out citizens who challenged these handouts, deferring to their respective legislatures or asserting that the petitioners had no standing to sue. Worse yet, beyond a handful of smaller groups and political parties—including the Green Party and Libertarians—existing institutions like the Republican and Democratic Parties were silent on the issue.

The same is true today. The major-party candidates, their campaigns, and their parties' platforms all refuse to recognize the problem—and it's a rare candidate indeed who challenges any opponent on the issue. Foundations rarely provide grants to the kinds of civic groups that might lead such reform movements— even if the group is trying to fight, say, a move to take important funds intended for recreational facilities in urban neighborhoods and use them instead to fund a professional sports stadium. John McCain's commission proposal went nowhere in Congress, and he hasn't reintroduced it since. Governor Kasich himself has failed to follow up on the many ways Ohio puts companies on the dole at the local and state levels; these days, he spends his time pushing deep cuts in social services.

And yet there are individual stories of citizen groups and public movements turning the tide by focusing public opinion on the issue of corporate welfare. In 1998, Robert Kraft, the owner of the New England Patriots, sparked a public outcry when he drove from Boston to Hartford, Connecticut, to present his "request" for $500 million from Connecticut's taxpayers as an incentive to move his team to a new stadium on the banks of the Connecticut River. He met with state legislators, the governor, and the fawning media. The local TV network affiliates interrupted their afternoon shows to report on the story. After allowing protesting citizens *just one minute each* to express their disapproval, the legislature met until midnight and finally passed the bill. Polls in the Nutmeg State showed a 3–1 margin of approval for the deal. That was in December. The state was gripped with euphoria at the prospect of getting its first big-league team. Never mind that a team that plays less than a dozen days per year doesn't generate many jobs—even those selling hot dogs and soda. Never mind that sports economists repeatedly point out that taxpayer-funded pro sports facilities cannot be justified as creating jobs, much less decent-paying jobs, other than the already-employed players.

In their rush to ink the Patriots deal, the lawmakers failed to inform the public about the costs of the deal—or its lack of benefits for the state. Within days after the signing ceremony, civic groups from left and right began a statewide drive to spread the truth about what the deal entailed. Connecticut is a small state; between radio and TV appearances and town meetings, it took about three months to turn public opinion around and convince state residents that they were being taken for a ride. In addition to the stadium, taxpayers would be forced to spend $50 million on a practice field. The site chosen for their new stadium was soaked with toxic chemicals, potentially endangering construction workers. The promises about jobs were revealed to be baseless. Before long, an embarrassed Robert Kraft drove back to Hartford for a press conference, this time announcing he was pulling out of Connecticut and housing his Patriots in a privately funded stadium near a Boston suburb. This gigantic potential freeloading came to an end because of organized and effective civic opposition, which turned public sentiment around just in time.

The insidious thing about most corporate welfare is that, once enacted, it does not have to go through any annual review and approval process the way normal budget appropriations do. Once granted, a tax abatement remains in effect indefinitely. When a huge agribusiness purchases a public water license for a pittance, it remains in possession of that license without having to be reviewed by Congress or even the licensing agency. And countless new giveaways occur every year. In the Telecommunications Act of 1996, our digital television spectrum—worth an estimated $70 billion—was authorized to be handed over to existing broadcasters. The deed was enacted by the Federal Communications Commission on April 7, 1997—but not before Bob Dole, the Senate majority leader, objected, saying that there was no conceivable reason that the incumbent broadcasters should be given exclusive rights to our public airwaves year after year. "The airwaves are the Nation's most valuable natural resource and are worth billions and billions of dollars," Dole said. "They do not belong to the broadcasters. They do not belong to the phone companies. They do not belong to the newspapers. Each and every wave belongs to the American people, the American taxpayers. Our airwaves are just as much a national resource as our national parks." Despite a move from competing businesses eager to participate in a public auction for the rights, the National Association of Broadcasters prevailed.

When the government fails to collect certain taxes because of what are known as "tax expenditures"—that is, tax credits and exemptions—it is basically spending our money. And when the government fails to collect taxes because of legal preferences it extends to certain corporations, it is subsidizing those firms as surely as if it were making direct payments to them. When drug companies like Eli Lilly or Bristol-Myers Squibb, or tech companies like Microsoft, Cisco, or Intel, receive billions in tax credits to support their R&D programs—work they should be doing anyway for their own business interests—that's exactly like the U.S. Treasury writing them checks for those billions of dollars. Except, that is, for one prohibited deduction: for lobbying expenses and campaign contributions, which ensure that the privileges of power are not disrupted.

Another area not often publicized is the underpayment of federal income tax by foreign corporations. A Government Accountability Office (GAO) report concluded that foreign-controlled companies doing business in the United States pay roughly half as much in taxes, as a percentage of their sales, as U.S. companies pay. Former senator Byron Dorgan (D-ND) pointed to this as evidence of manipulative "transfer pricing" by foreign multinationals. Transfer pricing refers to a conscious practice of paying too little, or charging too much, in paper transactions between the United States and foreign affiliates in order to artificially lower the income of the U.S. affiliate. In short, these foreign corporations game the governmental tax systems more than their U.S. counterparts do on their U.S. sales—and they get away with it.

This kind of multinational tax avoidance takes many forms. One reform group, the Citizens for Tax Justice, has decried a kind of shell game that occurs when companies pay interest to nontaxable offshore subsidiaries, deduct the interest payments against their worldwide taxable income—and yet claim an exemption from U.S. antitax haven laws by asserting that, for U.S. tax purposes, the interest earned by the offshore subsidiaries does not exist. The Treasury Department has nowhere near enough auditors to police such schemes, assuming they would even be allowed to by Congress.

More than forty years ago, I founded the Public Citizen Tax Reform Research Group to help call attention to how politicians conspire with corporations to game the federal tax system. At the end of each year, before Congress adjourned, our public interest attorneys would spot an array of obscure special "Christmas tree" tax breaks for specific companies and industries. Each amendment usually could be traced to the lawmakers who were pushing to get it through in the frantic last days or hours before Congress went home for the holidays. Our legal eagles would search and spot millions of dollars' worth of these escape hatches, connect them to campaign contributions to their congressional sponsors, and then release them to the media. Many a gross loophole was plucked out and defeated by the glare of public opinion, especially when reporters like the *New York Times*'s Eileen Shanahan picked up on our leads. This kind of activism worked then—and it could work now, if the press were to uphold its former sense of newsworthiness.

The large multinationals have also taken extraordinary measures to limit the liability of their companies, not just of their shareholders, in the case of catastrophe. As the saying goes, they privatize their profits and socialize their risks. The nuclear power industry, entirely born out of U.S. government R&D after World War II, has managed to lay the risks of nuclear meltdown almost entirely at the feet of the government under the Price-Anderson Nuclear Industries Indemnity Act, which holds that the federal government—in other words, we the taxpayers—assume the vast proportion of liability for any meltdown or disaster at a nuclear reactor.

This is no abstract theoretical threat, as recent history tells us. In March 2011, when the Fukushima Daiichi complex of six reactors in northeast Japan was overwhelmed by the earthquake-tsunami, the disaster caused three reactors to melt down and the rest to collapse in various stages of dysfunction. More than a year later, the costs of the Fukushima disaster continue to accumulate as contaminated soil, food, water, and air spreads far and wide, upsetting lives within a growing circumference. The disaster wreaked havoc with Japan's supply chains, disrupting exports to the rest of the world. Apart from the human tragedies as the only society struck so severely by both the wartime atom and the peacetime atom, the immediate economic cost of the disaster is already estimated to top $257 billion (U.S.).

Among the more than one hundred reactors currently operating in the United States, several are similar in design to the Fukushima Daiichi plant. These aging facilities are vulnerable not just to earthquake risks but to sabotage, to erosion, and to human error. Although the Price-Anderson Act requires a two-tier pool of insurance coverage totaling $375 million (private insurance) and $12.6 billion (self-insurance) for catastrophic claims resulting from a large nuclear accident, just think: How large could the affected area be? As early as 1957, the U.S. Atomic Energy Commission was estimating that such an accident could affect an area the size of Pennsylvania. Who would bear the cost—economic, social, and human—of dealing with the deaths, injuries, horrific illnesses, relocations, dispossession, and physical and emotional trauma that would result from such an accident? We the People.

If an industry, whose profitability is guaranteed by virtue of a legal monopoly it has enjoyed for forty-five years, is too risky to qualify for private insurance, what are we to conclude? That the industry should be closed, that's what. This is one case where corporate welfare is endangering not only our pocketbooks but also the very habitability of our land.

That's what corporate welfare often does: by protecting corporations from accountability, it tempts them to assume more and more risk in exchange for greater and greater rewards for the top executives and their rubber-stamp boards of directors.

Fannie Mae and Freddie Mac, the mortgage agencies created by the federal government (and later privatized) to buy mortgages from banks, were initially conceived to free the banks up to offer mortgages for more homeowners. This is known as the secondary mortgage market. Fannie and Freddie made their stockholders rich as their soaring profiles—helped by the U.S. government's implicit guarantee, exemption from state and local taxation, and other advantages over their competitors—kept rising. In just ten years, their stock appreciated more than 1,000 percent. Then, in the first decade of the twenty-first century, greed overtook caution. The companies inflated their accounting records to boost executive stock options, leading to scandals in 2004 and the departure of several top officers of Fannie and Freddie. But untamed greed tends to endure from one executive team to the next. In the few years before 2008, the banks and mortgage brokers sold Fannie and Freddie securitized packages of subprime mortgages that carried distinctly greater risk than the companies were used to guaranteeing. Even as the inevitable collapse loomed overhead, from April to July 2008 government officials offered a chorus of sickening reassurances about their viability. While their stocks were gradually falling, Freddie and Fannie were "adequately capitalized," said their regulator, James Lockhart. Federal Reserve chairman Ben Bernanke and Treasury secretary Henry Paulson assured the investment community—small and large institutional shareholders alike—that their companies were "adequately capitalized." Within weeks, Fannie and Freddie had collapsed, along with their share values. The companies were placed in a federal conservatorship, where they received regular doses of bailout money.

Obviously, the existing protections were inadequate to prevent the Fannie and Freddie disasters. Their government overseers engaged in knowingly deceptive assurances. Innocent shareholders, assured by their advisers that Fannie and Freddie shares were the safest investments after Treasury bonds, lost everything. Congress, garnished with large campaign contributions and lobbied by many of their former staff, turned a deaf ear to the few warnings from their unconvinced colleagues. As the sweet music played on, the essential question was ignored: namely, what was the real motive guiding Fannie's and Freddie's directors in these years? Helping middle- and lower-income people become homeowners, or playing the market in outlandish and unneeded arbitrage games? How much of their government subsidy was used to benefit consumers, and how much was siphoned into shareholder assets and staggeringly bloated executive compensation arrangements? Such questions would have been unnecessary if the firms had been held to rigorous standards of transparency and trust.

Even when the government appears to be investing responsibly in our future, the real beneficiaries may be lurking behind the scenes. Such was the case with the government's "Supercar" initiative, a plan to devise "an environmentally friendly car with up to triple the fuel efficiency" of contemporary cars "without sacrificing affordability, performance, or safety" announced in September 1993 by President Bill Clinton, Vice President Al Gore, and the CEOs of GM, Ford, and Chrysler. The program was called the Partnership for a New Generation of Vehicles (PNGV), and if you were paying taxes at that time, you and other taxpayers paid for it.

The partnership included seven federal agencies, twenty federal laboratories (such as the Oak Ridge National Laboratory), and the Big Three automakers. According to the Department of Commerce, the PNGV aimed "to strengthen America's competitiveness by developing technologies for a new generation of vehicles"—drawing on taxpayer funds to do so at a time when these well-capitalized auto companies were making record profits year after year.

So what did you get out of this ten-year effort? Worse than nothing. You funded a decade holiday for GM, Ford, and Chrysler from competing with one another. The main accomplishment of this partnership with the government was to exempt the Big Three from both the antitrust laws and regulatory fuel efficiency upgrades, allowing them to pool their resources in the interest of automotive progress.

Instead they colluded to do nothing.

This giveaway—this license for stagnation—broke new ground in pillaging taxpayer-funded R&D. Under the PNGV contract, all taxpayer-funded intellectual property developed by government scientists and engineers was transferred to Ford, Chrysler, GM, and some other large private firms. These agreements were arrived at with Clinton and Gore in secrecy, with no public comment.

The initiative also served as a smoke screen behind which the automakers protected themselves from higher air quality standards. The PNGV agreement did not require the Big Three to mass-produce the technologies it purportedly sought to develop. In the years since, the leading innovators in fuel efficiency have been Toyota and Honda—companies that did not participate in PNGV.

Alerted to the forthcoming Clinton-Gore announcement in 1993, I wrote a letter objecting to the deal and predicted that its structure was made to provide the domestic industry with the mechanisms for doing nothing and getting away with it. Before PNGV collapsed in 2001, the taxpayers had been billed $1.5 billion and gotten nothing in return but continued low gas mileage and increased air pollution. A lost decade! Corporate welfare at its destructively innovative best. Sixteen years later, Chrysler and a smug GM, relying on SUVs and more powerful gas-guzzling engines, transformed their stagnant mismanagement into a bailout bankruptcy and welfare rebirth—compliments of more than $60 billion in taxpayer dollars. Corporate welfare is a national and local problem. Corporate freeloaders make brazen threats to move away and object to paying taxes to fund schools and other essential local services.

What can be done about such unfairness, such profiteering, such reckless behavior—all of it carried on the backs of taxpayers?

The first step in ending this kind of rapacious corporate welfare is to advocate for a better alternative: a more equitable partnership between government and corporations, one that is open, publicly deliberated, nonexclusive to its recipients, and requires the corporations to pay back the government's investment wherever possible. There is a place in our society for taxpayer-funded projects that fulfill urgent public goals not being met by the market, to the benefit of consumers and workers and always subject to periodic review and renewal. For example, life-saving drugs, worker safety inventions, and energy-saving technologies developed by the NIH, National Institute for Occupational Safety and Health (NIOSH), and NASA could be made available under nonexclusive licenses to promote competition, paying royalties back to the U.S. Treasury or, better yet, directly back to the programs that developed them, to help underwrite expansion of their life-saving missions. Obviously, corporations vying for such licenses would be doing so to make a profit, but along the way they would be serving the public, not pillaging its coffers. The key is reciprocity: any such agreement must pave a two-way street between the company and the taxpayers.

Any program that fails this test—any program in which the government gives more to private companies than it gets back—should be challenged as undesirable corporate welfare.

Of course, to the average citizen, corporate welfare must look like one of the most intransigent social scourges. As American taxpayers, though, we must remember that what's at stake are *our own taxpayer dollars*—the money we earn each year with our hard work, money that for years has been siphoned out of our pockets, "laundered" through the arcana of government programs, and deposited in the coffers of the biggest, most megaprofitable corporations. It's time for us to liberate these resources, which belong to We the People for our own use and that of our descendants. How revealing that unlike health and safety regulations to save lives, corporate welfare has been under no obligation to register a public cost-benefit justification that is challengeable in court.

The American people have never been shy about fighting for their rights when their own interests—and their own savings—are at stake. The successful public opposition to the Patriots stadium in Connecticut demonstrates that we can still mobilize to defeat an undesirable plan. But the current governmental system tends to discourage us from thinking we can make real changes to policy through personal activism.

The practice of corporate welfare is so insidious that it points to how badly we need to correct this shared sense of disempowerment. We need new strategies, new processes, through which everyday Americans can air their grievances and call for change.

For a lesson in effective citizen empowerment, we can look to Sweden. When the Swedish people are confronted by a major decision that requires more than the participation of its Parliament, the government announces national town meetings to address the issue. The government provides ample budgets to maximize citizen engagement across the country to help ensure that a national consensus can be reached.

In the 1980s, this process was engaged as the Swedish people weighed whether to continue building nuclear power plants. The people's consensus? No.

The American people should start pushing for a similar process to help insert our voices back into the political process. Such meetings could be funded by our government—but they could also be funded by foundations or individual wealthy philanthropists, and could reach tens of millions of viewers through the internet.

Knowing is the first step to doing. The feedback from these meetings would stimulate congressional hearings to review any program that smacks of corporate welfare and make it prove itself anew—sector by sector—under public scrutiny. Those programs that cannot pass the test would be ended; those that do would be subject to rigorous annual review in the normal congressional appropriations process, ending the practice of extending unlimited subsidy to such giveaways as tax expenditures or corn ethanol subsidies. Many of these programs thrive in the dark and cannot survive the illumination of sunlight.

It's impossible to imagine our politicians passing a comprehensive bill to end corporate welfare outright. But the next best thing—and a more realistic goal—would be a bill to make any existing corporate subsidy subject to congressional review and renewal, modification, or rejection after three years. Congress should support this by calling for annual agency corporate welfare reports, listing every program under its purview that confers below-cost or below-market-rate goods, services, or other benefits on corporations. The Securities and Exchange Commission (SEC) could require publicly traded corporations to disclose the subsidies they receive, by both type and amount received, by publishing the information in their annual reports and on their websites.

Pending these major changes, there are intermediate ways to police the conduct of corporate bosses who want to continue to receive these windfalls. Congress should prevent any corporations from receiving subsidies if its chief officers are convicted of criminal wrongdoing. It should call for corporate welfare beneficiaries to agree to return the favor through nonmonetary actions. When the government saved GM and Chrysler through its 2009 bailout, for instance, it should have required the corporations to adhere to higher fuel efficiency and safety standards—and extend fairer contracts to the consumers whose tax dollars saved them. Instead, GM and Chrysler lobbied *against* energy and safety proposals from the Obama administration, while using the bailout to shrug off a raft of pending liability suits from injured motorists. Government subsidies should be seen as a tool to *promote* competition—by requiring competitive bidding, nonexclusive licensing, and market-based prices for any government assets being sold, leased, or rented to the corporations. Such measures would establish, once and for all, that the free lunches are over for the nation's corporate welfare kings. The taxpayers are coming to town.

There is one final tool taxpayers need in order to set these changes in motion, without having to beg for their congressional representatives to act. That tool is called "standing to sue."

At the federal level, the courts routinely reject taxpayer suits not on the merits but on the procedural premise that the plaintiffs have no standing to bring the suit. The courts have decided, in essence, that no individual taxpayer—not one of the 150 million taxpayers in the United States—has a specific enough interest to allow such a suit. It's a notion held over from the common law of medieval England, but one that's desperately outdated today.

We need new legislation that can give a taxpayer standing by awarding a $10,000 "bounty" (plus reasonable attorneys' fees) to anyone who successfully challenges unlawful agency action in doling out corporate welfare. We should also reward plaintiffs in such successful suits by giving them a percentage of the money recovered and saved through such suits. This has worked since the 1986 passage of the False Claims Act, which allows whistle-blowers to report corporate fraud ripping off government programs like Medicare and defense contracting and operations. If the Justice Department agrees and pursues the culpable company to a resolution, the whistle-blower gets a percentage of the recovery. In the ensuing twenty-five years, more than $30 billion in taxpayer money has been recovered this way—and probably much more saved as a result of the deterrent effect on corporate contractors.

Finally, beyond what we can all do as individual advocates, we should be working to create a national coalition of taxpayers, workers, and small-business owners as a countervailing force against the corporate state, which has devoted such massive effort to seizing taxpayer dollars and assets for private profit. For too long corporate welfare has been undercutting our political process, using the financial power of the corporations—through campaign contributions, ultimatums, and the like—to influence public policy far more directly than we possibly can as individuals. This effect of corporate welfare only heightens the disparities of wealth, influence, and power in American society—making it increasingly difficult to realize our ideals of self-governance and national sovereignty. The sentinels of our democracy—our lawmakers, regulators, and judges—have all failed to stem this continual raid on the Treasury. When the sentinels fail, the people themselves must make them act.

6

Crack Down on Corporate Crime

On the evening of February 27, 2011, Charles Ferguson, winner of the Academy Award for Best Documentary for the banking industry exposé *Inside Job*, strode to the stage to accept his award. Before a worldwide television audience of more than one billion people, he declared: "Three years after a horrific financial crisis caused by massive fraud, not a single financial executive has gone to jail, and that's wrong." In the 2008–9 Wall Street crash, trillions of dollars in savings and pension funds were looted or drained by finance bosses, enriching themselves as they pushed through their gigantic Washington bailout.

The story was quite different in December 2007, when Roy Brown, a fifty-four-year-old homeless man, walked into a Capitol One bank in Shreveport, Louisiana, without a visible weapon, and told the teller to give him money. The teller handed him three stacks of bills, but Brown took only a single hundred-dollar bill. He said he was homeless and hungry. The next day he surrendered to the police voluntarily, telling them that his mother hadn't raised him that way. He pleaded guilty. The judge sentenced him to fifteen years in jail. Brown is currently serving that sentence, which in its entirety will cost taxpayers at least half a million dollars to keep him there.

Crime in the suites has always been punished much more lightly than crime in the streets. Yet corporate crime exacts a far greater toll. While politicians cry out about cracking down on street crime, they collect campaign money from politically powerful corporate crooks who are eager to see that enforcement budgets, prosecutorial will, and even data collection about their fraud, violence, and systemic abuse are kept to a minimum. These corporate supremacists have achieved such control over the system that they're able to ensure that criminal laws are drafted to exclude their kind of crimes or to divert responsibility away from corporate bosses toward underlings or hollow company subsidiaries. They have managed to drive federal and state cops off the corporate crime beat to protect business as usual.

Consider the size of this corporate crime wave. In just the medical sector alone, patients and taxpayers pay at least $250 billion a year due to computerized billing fraud and abuse. The nation's expert on this heist, Harvard's Malcolm Sparrow, says it might be even a larger chunk of the $2.7 trillion health bill. Preying on Medicare is so lucrative that drug lords in southern Florida are finding it easier and more lucrative than the drug trade.

Twenty years ago, the savings and loan banksters cost savers and taxpayers, who had to bail out the remnants of this financial debacle, $300 to $500 billion. Former Republican U.S. Attorney General and now corporate lawyer Richard Thornburgh called it "the biggest white collar swindle in history."

We think of street crime as more dangerous than corporate crime—because street crime involves immediate physical danger, often takes place at nighttime, and is viscerally upsetting. But each year far more people die, become injured or sick, and lose their money, homes, and other property because of corporate crime than they do because of street crime. The scale of devastation isn't even close. Year in and year out, roughly 60,000 Americans die from workplace-related diseases and trauma,[1] 70,000 from air pollution,[2] 100,000 from hospital negligence,[3] and another 100,000 from hospital-induced infections.

At least 45,000 die because they cannot afford health insurance to get diagnosed or treated.[4] And the list of preventable, silent violence goes on. If one of your kin or close friends was a victim of such corporate violence, would it be any consolation to hear that at least the loss of your loved one didn't occur at the hands of terrorists or a crazed killer on the street?

The point is that these fatalities, and many more injuries and illnesses, are preventable. It's in our hands to prevent them. We surely wish to do so, don't we?

But the only way to stop them is to arrest the march of corporate crime.

It's important to understand the reason high corporate crimes go undetected. First, the law enforcement community posts no database on corporate crime. This is not an oversight; it's a concession to corporate power. For forty years my associates and I have tried to convince the Justice Department to create such a public, widely publicized information system, just as it produces each year for street crimes. We have met with U.S. attorneys general from both major parties, written, testified, spoken, and campaigned to get this adopted—all to no avail. Some authorities assured us that such a timely source of information would be useful, but when they sought direction and funding from Congress, neither the Republicans nor the Democrats took up the cudgels. Attorney General Eric Holder has repeatedly refused to discuss this proposal with us. Better to keep people in the dark and light up the corporate campaign cash register.

Second, corporate crime persists because there's no public outcry against it. With no federal database tracking corporate crime from year to year, the justice system gets little real pressure to prosecute and even less of a budget to enforce the law. The issue is off the evening news or the front page of newspapers. Politicians don't talk about it. Reporters don't ask about it. Pollsters don't poll it. And even the best-intentioned prosecutors often quit earlier than they would in a more encouraging environment—and end up going to work for the corporations.

Third, the legal community has devoted little scholarship or law school instruction to corporate crime. This kind of indifference does not exactly prepare thousands of lawyers to take corporate crime cases, to become prosecutors, or just to take a stand against this recurring insult to equal justice under the law. Worse, this tolerant atmosphere has opened the door to a craven type of pseudo-scholarship from the University of Chicago Institute for Law and Economics. Federal judge Frank Easterbrook and coauthor Daniel R. Fischel once argued in a *Michigan Law Review* article that corporations might find it in their best interests to violate the law, so long as they pay the fine, if such violations benefit the corporation more than obeying the regulation.[5] Imagine telling people who've been fleeced of their life savings, or who are recuperating in the intensive care unit of a hospital, that their suffering was inevitable, sanctioned by legal scholars like Easterbrook and Fischel. This kind of thinking can only come from a dehumanized, monetized mind.

Fourth, corporate crimes come in silent, often invisible fashion. Violations of standards for air and water pollution, asbestos, lead, PCBs, and coal dust; illegal dumping of toxics in rural areas; and more—these are examples of the silent violence we too charitably call pollution. These crimes have taken millions of lives over the years—and the fact that they don't inflict immediate pain, or offend the senses, means that the illnesses they cause are harder to trace and punish. In the same vein, drug companies cause untold danger by promoting off-label or unapproved uses for their medicines through their salespeople and physicians. In 2009, Eli Lilly and Pfizer were criminally fined $515 million and $1.2 billion, respectively, for such unlawful and willful marketing. The overpromotion of antibiotics, which can lead to bacterial resistance, costs around one hundred thousand lives a year in our country—roughly three times the number of people who die on the highways in America. Unnecessary operations have long been a scourge in hospitals, sometimes driven by profit, sometimes by ignorance or negligence. Medical "errors" or "mistakes," as official announcements call them, cause another estimated one hundred thousand deaths a year—most of which could be prevented by stronger, more enforceable standards for hospitals and stronger regulation of medical prescribers.

Fifth, these business outrages hammer taxpayers or consumers *indirectly*. When, for example, military contractors in Iraq were caught cheating the army, it's not as though the bills for such massive multibillion-dollar frauds on government procurement were sent to you directly. But you end up paying for them all the same—through higher taxes in years to come. The same is true for widespread billing fraud. Try to read the inscrutable computerized bills you or your health insurance company pays. Even when you don't opt to buy, you can be defrauded: a July 2011 Senate committee report estimated that the phone industry crams charges for *unrequested* services or products onto our phone bills to the tune of $2 billion yearly.

Sixth, even when corporations do knowingly and willfully violate existing safety laws, endangering their customers or workers, business lobbyists make sure there are no criminal penalties in the statutes to enforce. I saw this firsthand as far back as 1966, when auto industry lawyers persuaded members of Congress to delete the *criminal penalty* in the motor vehicle safety law, even for companies who knowingly sold defective cars or parts—and willfully declined to recall the cars even after their use resulted in injuries and deaths.

Seventh, unlike street criminals, corporate criminals are in business with the very entities that are supposed to keep tabs on them. Corporations spend billions in advertising dollars each year, after all, and the media can't help but remember that investigating corporate rackets could mean biting the hands that feed them. Auto dealers have been especially successful in silencing local radio and television stations that are looking into fraud and deception, cutting their advertising when such segments make it onto the air. This happened to the *Washington Post* and to *The Phil Donahue Show* years ago in Dayton, Ohio, and sent a message to the other media to look for their journalistic prizes elsewhere. Moreover, corporate cash is abundant in the campaign coffers of the elected officials in Congress and the executive branch. In 2008, as a presidential candidate, Barack Obama raised more money from Wall Street and corporate lawyers than any candidate in American history—far exceeding John McCain, his Republican opponent. Worse, as the *Corporate Crime Reporter* has documented, the Democratic and Republican parties received $9.3 million from thirty-one major convicted corporations in the 2002 election cycle. Their crimes include antitrust violations (Archer Daniels Midland), price-fixing (Pfizer), environmental crimes (Chevron), and so on. These companies' corporate objective is to dismantle the regulatory institutions of government and make it difficult for victims to pursue remedies against corporations in our courts of law—a phenomenon grotesquely called "tort reform" by the corporate wrongdoers' lobby.

Eighth, some corporate crimes take decades to wreak their long-term damage on millions of people. Every day, for instance, millions of people in motor vehicles creep along congested highways wasting time, burning polluting gasoline, and getting into collisions. The massive scale of our highway system can be traced all the way back to 1949, when GM, Phillips Petroleum, Standard Oil of California, and Firestone Tire were convicted in federal district court in Chicago of criminal violation of the antitrust laws. Their crime—which lasted for about two decades—was a deliberate conspiracy to buy up and dismantle one hundred electric trolley systems in cities across America and replace them with automobiles and buses. Instead of expanding in-city rail systems, these public transit systems—including the largest one in the world, in the Los Angeles area—were destroyed. People had to rely on cars and roads, whether they wanted to or not. The result was bumper-to-bumper traffic, then, now, and in the foreseeable future. What commuters ever swear at GM, Standard Oil, or Firestone when they get into traffic jams or highway pileups? As the documentary *Taken for a Ride* pointed out, "These companies . . . eliminated systems that in order to reconstitute today would require maybe $300 billion."[6] In punishment for this massive antitrust violation—one that scholars like Brad Snell have called one of the twentieth century's greatest crimes—GM paid a whopping $5,000 fine.

The abstract, anonymous nature of corporate-produced deaths and illnesses can make them seem like crimes without perpetrators—ensuring that they get little public attention. Unlike in street crime, where the results of bad acts are usually immediate, the crimes of corporate America often appear to be the result of impersonal forces over a long period of time. Decisions made by American corporate leaders have infected our environment with toxic chemicals, particles, gases, radiation, and the like; poor quality standards have led to defects in construction sites and machinery. But such crimes are rarely traced back to individuals. Moreover, some consumers are prone to excuse such mishaps as inadvertent, as inevitable mistakes occurring within companies that are beyond reproach because of their importance to the economy. Most do not understand that gross carelessness, safety violations, or willful suppression of criminal evidence—as with the tobacco bosses—can be considered criminal negligence or involuntary manslaughter under existing laws.

Penalties for such crimes are weak. For example, federal law calls for a maximum six-month prison term for a company official responsible for willful violation of workplace safety rules leading to the death of workers. (Meanwhile, under federal law you can spend up to a year in jail if you harass a wild burro on federal lands.) In one of his finest television investigations, *Trade Secrets* (2001), Bill Moyers used internal corporate documents and other studies to show "how the chemical companies, through their silence and inertia, subjected at least two generations of workers to excessive levels of a potent carcinogen—vinyl chloride—that targets the liver, brain, lungs, and blood-forming organs."

For many decades, workplace-connected diseases and traumatic deaths were viewed as the price of having a job: regrettable but inevitable. This kind of resignation to industrial forms of violence still persists in some families—until a family member falls victim, as in the corner-cutting coal mine disasters of recent years.

The level of public outrage can remain low, even after the government catches business crooks, when the cases are settled confidentially, without publicity. Public corporate crime trials— with the resulting disclosure—are rare as hens' teeth, in large part because of the imbalance between prosecutors' limited budgets and the ample coffers of defendant companies. About ten years ago, Sara Lee pled guilty to two misdemeanor counts for the deaths of at least twenty consumers and a hundred people seriously sickened from a listeriosis outbreak in the company's frankfurters and other processed meat. The company's Chicago power lawyers overwhelmed the few federal prosecutors into accepting the plea in exchange for a $200,000 fine, a $3 million grant to Michigan State University for food safety research, and $1.2 million to the government in a separate settlement over meat sold to the government. The Justice Department and Sara Lee actually issued a joint press release announcing the weak settlement!

When business theorists insist that corporations exist to make profits, and that so-called social responsibility is not their business, they tend to ignore the fact that obeying the law— and not corrupting its enforcers—should also be corporate business. The media (which itself is another big business, of course) has adopted a laissez-faire attitude toward the problem, as if somehow the corporate world is not part of the moral community. Mainstream business magazines run feature stories that are great on the facts but forlorn in their conclusions—from *Fortune* magazine articles such as "Enough Is Enough: White-Collar Criminals: They Lie, They Cheat, They Steal, and They've Been Getting Away with It for Too Long" and "Why Chief Executives' Pay Keeps Rising" to *Newsweek*'s famous cover story "Corporate Killers." And the problem is only getting worse. For the most part, corporations are immune to *60 Minutes*–style exposés because few are ever followed up by law enforcement or official investigations. And tight enforcement budgets are increasingly leading the justice system to grant corporations immunity from prosecution, in what are called "deferred prosecution agreements"—a measure corporate attorneys love because it allows their clients to avoid pleading guilty.

John Braithwaite, a corporate crime scholar and author of several books on the subject, maintains that "if we are serious about controlling corporate crime, the first priority should be to create a culture in which corporate crime is not tolerated."[7] He believes that "the moral educative functions of corporate criminal law" are enhanced with regular adverse publicity "as a social control mechanism."[8] It appears that the most effective corporate crime attorneys for corporate defendants agree, which explains why they want these deals with law enforcement. You don't see your local evening news regularly covering any crimes beyond the street or household variety. Where is the public outrage toward the enormity of these corporate crimes, which deceive, defraud, steal, pollute, bribe, injure, destroy lives, and rip off consumers and taxpayer funds and natural resources?

Even though the citizenry, preoccupied with its own pressures, is quiescent, professor of criminology Gilbert Geis points out that despite its quiescence, the public does share an underlying revulsion for such corporate crime. As far back as 1969—long before the growing and diverse corporate crime wave—Geis observed that a "Louis Harris Poll reported that a manufacturer of an unsafe automobile was regarded by respondents as worse than a mugger (68 percent to 22 percent), and a businessman who illegally fixed prices was considered worse than a burglar (54 percent to 28 percent)."[9] So the American people do recognize that more people are hurt by corporate crime than by street crime. Yet most people feel that the vast majority of the business crooks and their companies get away with it, that it's just the way the system operates. They're not mistaken about the way things have been—but that doesn't mean we can accept the same going forward, not if we want a country where we can expect justice to be done as a normal condition rather than as an exception.

There are plenty of realistic tools to deter, punish, and reverse the incidence of corporate crime, fraud, and abuse. But tools require someone to hold them and put them into play. The arena where we must enforce this turnaround is the very arena where the corporatists currently hold sway: the U.S. Congress. Consider this anomaly: corporations, unlike citizens, have no vote in Congress—but they do have money. Each year, thousands of corporations regularly get their way with a majority of the 535 members of Congress.[10,11] We the People, back home in the congressional districts, are the only ones who have the vote—and without our votes the members of Congress are soon unemployed. But there may not be 1,500 people out of tens of millions of voters who spend a week's worth a year demanding that Congress, or even just their own representative and senators, get tough on corporate crime.

If you went to a county fair to watch the tug-of-war, would you stay very long if only one side was tugging on the rope? When it comes to congressional influence, corporations and their trade associations are tugging on a rope with no opponent tugging the other way. Before we start worrying about how to enforce prosecution and punishment for corporate crime, we need to start by getting Congress to put the power of enforcement in the executive branch under regular congressional watchdogs. The good news is that "public sentiment," to use Abraham Lincoln's words, will be overwhelmingly on your side.

All reform movements start small. They grow slowly as the people catch on, until the early pioneers find themselves driving a bandwagon. So here's how to start small, so that we can all make this anticorporate crime movement bigger.

Every congressional district has at least 630,000 people. Roughly 450,000 in each district are old enough to vote. And in every district there are especially motivated people—people who have been harmed directly, or who have felt the anguish of having a loved one injured, sickened, or fleeced, by corporate rampages. Among them are a few lawyers and law professors who know the score. Among them are some progressive local officials who won their elections because they wanted to serve the people, not their careers. Among them may be some members of the clergy who know that runaway commercialism has been condemned by every major religion and who are appalled at what Mammon is doing to our country's moral fiber. Among them are existing organizations whose leaders and staff have long been fighting the effects of corporate rip-offs on poor people in urban areas; the toxic air, water, and soil getting into people's bodies; the pugnacious commercial greed that holds workers down in penury and deprivation; the politicians who are bought and sold by developers or other big corporations. Among them are social studies teachers, from middle school to colleges and universities, who see their students being raised in a commercial marketplace, trained in a Pavlovian market of conditioned responses.

Don't think you can find twenty-five like-minded people in your district to get the bring-them-to-justice ball rolling? Don't worry. Start with a half dozen determined allies. The connections you have in your own community, and the information available on the internet and your libraries, can provide you all the evidence you need to find people whose moral sensitivity has been punctured by corporate misdeeds. Before you know it you'll have the makings of a movement with substantial popular support, buoyed by the irrefutable evidence of your allies' own experience.

What reforms should your movement call for? As the ancient Romans used to say, "Out of the facts come the laws." There are plenty of facts available to show these corporations and their officials that their crimes will no longer pay. What we need to get through Congress are a series of reforms designed to ensure that these corporations, with all their clever lawyers, will never be able to escape—will never be able to make their complex, under-the-radar crimes pay big dividends for their own enrichment.

The first priority must be a complete overhaul of the weak, outdated, underfunded, insufficient federal criminal laws. This overhaul must start with a series of highly visible Senate and House congressional hearings to get the vast array of grievances from around the country onto the public stage.

We need a comprehensive, modern federal corporate criminal law, one that starts by making both corporate institutions and their governing executives accountable. When both the group and its individual members are potentially responsible for criminal wrongdoing, each will police the other—long before they give in to the temptation to break the law.

We need laws that require corporations to hire compliance officers to monitor key sectors of their operations horizontally and vertically, up to the CEO and board of directors. These compliance officers would be responsible for making sure their corporations maintain proper records, fulfill all public disclosure requirements, and in many other ways save their companies from serious travails. Ethical whistle-blowers inside corporations must be protected, given due process when their jobs are in peril, and rewarded when their allegations are proven correct by their own company or by law enforcement. As previously noted, the 1986 False Claims Act—conceived by a single California public interest lawyer, John Phillips, who lobbied his idea through Congress—has already returned more than $30 billion back to the U.S. Treasury as of 2011, with around $21 billion being recovered by whistle-blowers. (Note: in 2012 alone the number is expected to surpass $11 billion, with $11 billion already being recovered by June 2012.)[12] The law protects whistle-blowers who take evidence of fraud against the government—such as fraud on Pentagon contracts or Medicare—to the Justice Department and guarantees them up to 25 percent of the total recovery if they are successful. This idea needs to be expanded. Few people have the courage and the stamina to endure the arduous road from their protest to its conclusion. But such protection certainly allows those who have such courage to take their conscience to work.

As owners of their companies, investors need to be given more authority over the hired hands at the top of the business. A pyramid company that gets caught engaging in unlawful activity eventually devalues that company stock to all shareholders. At present, the only incentives shareholders and reluctant institutional investors have, if they don't like what the company executives are doing, is to sell out. Selling out, though, doesn't solve the problem; it leaves the top rascals in charge. Only by voicing their protest in public do the owner-shareholders have a chance of recovering the value of their stock—by evicting the reprobates who have been poisoning the company. But not without changing the present proxy system, which is rigged to allow top management to perpetuate both themselves and their corrosive policies.

To force the large institutional investors—such as Fidelity and Vanguard, who after all are investing the pooled savings of millions of Americans—to respect the importance of honest corporate governance, we should fight for a law that explicitly establishes a fiduciary relationship between the manager-brokers and their customers.

The law should recognize that the investors are the ones who bear the losses, and for that reason, they should be given full rights and remedies in courts of law to hold reckless and criminal corporate officers—and their aiders and abettors (law firms and accounting firms)—accountable for the loss of shareholder value. The mere prospect of empowering investors in this way would deter executives from cooking the books to increase their own pay. Shareholders should also employ full-time watchdogs—which in many cases could be funded by some shareholders contributing one penny per share annually—to protect their interests.

CEOs, board members, and other high officials of global corporations will find that their impulse to take the high road tends to intensify when they know they'll be held accountable for their actions. When they know they'll pay a personal price for reckless speculation, looting, and indifference to the safety and security of their employees and shareholders, they're much more likely to straighten up and fly right.

The key is to have an arsenal of sanctions that can be tailored to each particular violation. One such punishment would be forcing companies to forfeit illegal profits and/or the criminally inflated holdings of top officials. Another could be banning convicted violators from employment in the industry for a specified period of time, as labor laws do for guilty trade union officials.

Many corporate bosses have told me that the most effective penalty would be a likely prospect of imprisonment for individuals who have committed serious violations. One said that even the six-week jail term doled out to the culpable executives in the giant heavy electrical equipment price-fixing conspiracy back in 1961 sent tremors through the big boys in executive suites. William Ginn, former General Electric vice president, told a Senate

committee that the "taint of a jail sentence" made people "start looking at the moral values a little bit." Another GE executive, who did jail time, testified that, "They would never get me to do it again . . . I would starve before I would do it again."[13] It is more difficult to create comparable punishments for a corporate entity itself, because corporations are not human beings capable of imprisonment. But corporations causing violent crimes could have their charters revoked—the states revoked corporate charters in the nineteenth century—or be forced into bankruptcy for creating widespread dangerous conditions for their workers or their customers. Corporations can be placed on probation, as Consolidated Edison was in New York after being convicted of an environmental crime. After a probation official was assigned to the company to collect employee evidence of wrongdoing, which he would relay in reports to the judge, the company changed its wayward ways.

The United Kingdom and Canada now have laws designed to strengthen criminal liability standards for corporations as well as executives and directors. The UK's Corporate Manslaughter Statute, enacted in 2008, makes companies criminally responsible for gross negligence that leads to death. According to the Center for Corporate Policy, penalties "include unlimited fines, as well as a 'publicity order' (requiring the company to publicize its crime). In addition, the courts can order the organization to take remedial steps to correct the source of the law-breaking activity."

In March 2005, the Federal Trade Commission closed down three consumer debt companies charged with violating the Do-Not-Call Registry and defrauding low-income people of $100 million by promising debt relief that actually expanded their personal debts. While running for attorney general of New York in 1998, Eliot Spitzer declared, "When a corporation is convicted of repeated felonies that harm or endanger the lives of human beings or destroy our environment, the corporation

should be put to death, its corporate existence ended, and its assets taken and sold at public auction."

Strong but appropriate corporate sanctions, demanded by an angry public, may be one of many reasons wily corporate attorneys have devised ways to avoid having their corporate clients plead guilty, using such devices as the deferred prosecution plea, which the budget-strapped Justice Department is accepting more and more frequently.

Of course, it's unlikely that anything like a fair corporate "death penalty" statute for large companies could be enacted, due to the damage it would cause to innocent pensioners, shareholders, and workers. As an alternative, the Justice Department decades ago proposed enforcement measures that would secure significant structural changes in recidivist corporations without damaging innocent parties. These included reincorporation—with new directors and officers—under public ownership, federal chartering, and/or the "deconcentration and divestiture" of designated assets or specific divisions or subsidiaries involved in the violations.

Existing federal law allows corporate violators to be barred from bidding for government contracts for a period of time. Given the huge amount of government outsourcing the Pentagon, the Department of Health and Human Services, and many other departments engage in every year, this could be an effective deterrent if it were ever applied forcefully—which, sadly, seldom happens. Since corporate lawyers are very adept at shifting risks and costs from the corporation itself to innocent individuals, the justice system must find other effective deterrents—such as a ban on tax deductions for fines and penalties, as some banks have taken after reaching a settlement with Uncle Sam. Then there is the "equity fine," an elegant sanction devised by Columbia University law professor John Coffee. In an article aptly titled "Making the Punishment Fit the Corporation," Coffee noted that when shareholders benefit from criminal activity,

one way to make them more alert earlier would be to force their guilty company to issue stock that would reduce the value of existing shares along with the values of executive stock options.

Some members of Congress have suggested additional measures. Congressman George Miller (D-CA) has a bill that makes it a federal crime, after thirty days upon discovery, for an appropriate manager to knowingly fail to inform the appropriate federal agency and warn affected employees in writing of a serious danger associated with one of the company's products or business practices. Congressman John Conyers Jr. (D-MI) has introduced H.R. 322, the Dangerous Products Warning Act, which toughens Miller's legislation. These are the kinds of bills and legislators we must rally around.

What is the economic cost of corporate crime to our nation each year? W. Steve Albrecht, a professor of accountancy at Brigham Young University, once estimated that white-collar fraud alone costs the country $200 billion a year—and that was in 1995! Two major corporate crime waves later, plus inflation, and the figure is likely closer to $1 trillion in financial fraud alone—putting aside violent crimes, product defects, and toxic exposures perpetrated by corporations.

The most important change we must push for is to make corporate crime a law enforcement priority, with a permanent corporate crime division in the Department of Justice (DOJ), a continually updated corporate crime database, and much larger enforcement budgets in that department and in the several regulatory agencies, from the SEC, to the Occupational Safety and Health Administration (OSHA), to the EPA, to the National Highway Traffic Safety Administration (NHTSA), to the FDA. Law enforcement against corporations more than pays for itself: even the anemic SEC brought in fines twice its budget in 2010. The payback is far greater for the antitrust enforcement agencies. Professor Malcolm Sparrow of Harvard University, an applied mathematician and the nation's leading expert on computerized billing fraud in the health care industry, estimates that law enforcement budgets should be at least 1 percent of the estimated corporate crime volume. Instead it is routinely under 0.1 percent. Recall Sparrow's estimate that health care billing fraud amounts to anywhere from $250–$400 *billion* or more a year—and then measure that against the law enforcement maxim that, for every $1 spent, at least $17 comes back. The stakes are even higher for prosecuting corporate tax evasion. Yet enforcement budgets are not popular in Congress, where the prevailing calculation on the corporate crime lobby is: *Why bite the hand that feeds you?*

At the 2007 Taming the Giant Corporation conference, presented by myself and the Center for Study of Responsive Law, *Corporate Crime Reporter* editor Russell Mokhiber told the packed auditorium that "corporate criminals are the only criminal class in the United States that have the power to define the laws under which they live."[14] In his estimation, corporate crime is underprosecuted by a factor of, say, a hundred. Corporate fugitives from justice, Mokhiber noted, are at large everywhere:

> For every company convicted of health care fraud, there are hundreds of others who get away with ripping off Medicare and Medicaid, or face only mild slap-on-the-wrist fines and civil penalties when caught.
>
> For every company convicted of polluting the nation's waterways, there are many others who are not prosecuted because their corporate defense lawyers are able to offer up a low-level employee to go to jail in exchange for a promise from prosecutors not to touch the company or high-level executives.
>
> For every corporation convicted of bribery or of giving money directly to a public official in violation of federal law, there are thousands who give money legally through

political action committees to candidates and political parties. They profit from a system that effectively has become legalized bribery.

For every corporation convicted of selling illegal pesticides, there are hundreds more who are not prosecuted because their lobbyists have worked their way in Washington to ensure that dangerous pesticides remain legal.

For every corporation convicted of reckless homicide in the death of a worker, there are hundreds of others that don't even get investigated for reckless homicide when a worker is killed on the job. Only a few district attorneys across the country have historically investigated workplace deaths as homicides.

Mokhiber has interviewed more important people engaged on all sides of corporate crime enforcement than anyone in the country. He told the conference: "White collar crime defense attorneys regularly admit that if more prosecutors had more resources, the number of corporate crime prosecutions would increase dramatically. A large number of serious corporate and white collar crime cases are now left on the table for lack of resources."

One way to understand the extent of the corporate crime problem in America is to imagine it as a raging street crime epidemic in New York City—with only one hundred police on duty to enforce the law and with all the police superiors taking contributions from the gangs. Roughly sixty thousand Americans die each year due to workplace-related toxics and trauma. OSHA has an annual budget of some $550 million to diminish the occupational disease, death, and injury epidemic, but only a portion of that budget is used for actual inspections and enforcement. Violations that pose a substantial probability of death or serious injury incur an average penalty of only $910.

Compare that to the 2010 contractor budget that whizzed

through Congress to guard the U.S. embassy and its personnel in Baghdad: $675 million!

Finally, any attempt to curb corporate crime must include safeguards against prosecutorial abuse. Every agency that prosecutes corporate crime and civil offenses should be required to issue annual compliance reports, reviewing what they have done and could do better in the coming years. The guards must be as accountable as the criminals.

So those of you who share the view that corporate crime is a cancer that is spreading through our society and must be stopped, you've got plenty to work with. The experts are on our side; the tools are within reach; public opinion is firmly behind us. We're facing a formidable challenge. But our representatives cannot resist our demands for justice forever—not if we join together to shine a light on corporate greed and abuse. Remember, the corporations have the money—but we have the voice and the vote. When the latter collides with the former, we win.

7

Create National Charters
for Large Corporations

Ask most people who creates a corporation, and they'll reply "investors." They will be disappointed to know that they're mistaken. Corporations are created by state governments issuing charters of incorporation. They are *financed* by investors. No U.S. corporation exists without its investors or officers-to-be applying for a birth certificate that stipulates the company's rights and the powers and duties shared between its board of directors, officers, and shareholders. The charter acts as the company's granting constitution; it is a compact that state governments make on behalf of the society at large.

The best-known privileges granted to a publicly traded corporation are the ability to provide its owner-shareholders with limited liability—extending only to the amount invested—and the privilege of perpetual life in the form of an unlimited term. Beyond that, state incorporation laws generally allow a company's management to rule with an iron fist over its largely powerless owner-shareholders. These owners are told in many ways that, if they don't like their company's management policies, their one recourse is to sell their stock. That is, they have the freedom to *exit* and leave the rascals in charge, rather than the freedom to voice their concerns and otherwise take action to redirect the officers and board or replace them altogether.

Things were not always this way. When the first public-stockholder corporations emerged in the early 1800s, at the height of our industrial revolution, corporate charters were granted one by one as "special charters" by the state legislatures. (Today one can get a charter in a matter of days by submitting pro forma paperwork to the state secretary of state.) These early charters—say, for textile manufacturers in New England—were limited to a certain amount of time, subject to renewal for good behavior. They were chartered for a specific purpose—manufacturing clocks, for instance—and could not stray from that mission or engage in cross-corporate stock manipulations. The corporations were granted their privileges in return for meeting a worthy public purpose, and their charters were contingent on acceptable fulfillment of that purpose.

In the mid-nineteenth century, states like Ohio, Michigan, New York, and Nebraska weren't shy about revoking the charters of oil, sugar, bank, and whiskey corporations—but those days are long gone. Over the course of the nineteenth century, clever corporate attorneys moved relentlessly, in state after state, to weaken the incorporation laws to enable corporations to own anything, buy anything, issue various kinds of stocks and bonds, and engage—through acquisition, merger, or holding company formation—in whatever business activity they chose. Decade by decade, corporate lobbyists loosened state restraints and standards, using state constitutional amendments and revised statutes to change the rules. There were bumps along the way: during the Civil War, profiteering corporations selling defective weapons and contaminated food outraged President Lincoln, and their public disrepute temporarily slowed the process of granting corporations more privileges and immunities.

After the war, a phenomenon emerged known as "charter-mongering": states competing for corporate charters by racing to the bottom of the well of permissiveness. In 1891, the governor, secretary of state, and other leading politicians in New Jersey accepted bribes in return for passing the most permissive incorporation law in the nation. The state became a corporate chartering paradise, drawing countless corporations across the Hudson River from New York City.

What these companies wanted, and got, from New Jersey was the right to buy and sell the stock or property of other corporations and to issue their own stock as payment. Holding companies came into play, and soon all limits on corporation size and market concentration fell by the wayside. In 1892, New Jersey repealed its antitrust law; four years later, it eviscerated the provision for investor control, allowing corporate directors to amend company bylaws without the consent of the shareholders. Corporations flocked to charter in New Jersey. By 1902, New Jersey was earning enough from corporation filing fees and franchise taxes to abolish all property taxes and pay off its entire state debt. This corporate free-for-all started a race to the bottom that was eventually won by Delaware, New Jersey's southern neighbor, and today that state remains the easiest jurisdiction for incorporation—hosting roughly 60 percent of the Fortune 500 corporations, including GM, Ford, and Citigroup.

Throughout the twentieth century, corporations grew and metastasized—and the states, hungry for tax dollars, abdicated their role as overseers. In 1959, Harvard Law professor Abram Chayes wrote, "The modern business corporation emerged as the first successful institutional claimant of significant unregulated power since the nation-state established its title in the sixteenth and seventeenth centuries."[1] By 1972, Professor Ernest Folk declared that the regulatory role of state corporation law had effectively come to an end: "Statutes have become so broad and sweeping that they let a corporation do just about anything it wants. . . . State law does not and cannot exert any real controls. Corporation statutes and most judicial decisions largely tend to reflect the interests and orientation of management or, to use another popular term, insiders. In short, state law has abdicated its responsibility. As a result, so the argument must run, only federal law can handle the situation."

Of course, business barons of yesterday and today still complain about our modest government regulations as excuses for their business failures—such as the auto companies' fuel-economy fiascos. In reality, however, few regulations are issued without heavy tinkering by corporate attorneys; the results are often obsolete before they are enacted, if they even make it to that point, and attempts at enforcement are subject to further weakening by those same corporate lawyers.

Which is why the solution we need is a system of *federal* chartering for corporations. We need to rewrite the compact between ourselves and the corporations in ways that foresee and prevent the kind of harmful, ruinous misbehavior that currently falls to the beleaguered, underbudgeted regulatory agencies.

The idea of federal chartering has been around since the days of the founding fathers. As early as the Constitutional Convention of 1787, James Madison twice proposed that Congress be given the authority to "grant charters of incorporation in cases where the public good may require them and the authority of a single state may be incompetent." No formal vote was ever taken. In 1864, an act of Congress allowed for nationally chartered banks, but these charters were not much different from their state counterparts, except for which regulatory agency oversees them.

By the time of the robber barons, the days of the giant corporate trusts in oil, timber, steel, and other industrial resources in the late nineteenth century, the idea of corporate chartering as a tool of accountability began to receive attention. William Jennings Bryan supported the idea and enlisted President Theodore Roosevelt in 1901. Between 1903 and 1914, Presidents Roosevelt, Taft, and Wilson all came out for a federal incorporation or licensing system in their annual messages to Congress. President Taft sent a draft bill to Congress in 1910—two years after the *Wall Street Journal,* no less, and the National Association of Manufacturers endorsed "federal incorporation." But support for the idea never reached critical mass, and its momentum was interrupted by the passage of a series of antitrust and regulatory laws viewed by legislators as substitutes. The idea was revived by Wyoming senator Joseph O'Mahoney in the late 1930s in the form of chartering bill S. 3072; the Temporary National Economic Committee on the issue concluded in 1941 with these prophetic words: "The principal instrument of the concentration of economic power and wealth has been the corporate charter with unlimited power."

World War II, which, like other major wars, produced greater concentrations of wealth in its aftermath, broke any momentum generated by O'Mahoney's hearings. The subject of corporate chartering faded from public view, except for a brief hearing in the late 1970s by Senator Vance Hartke of the Senate Commerce Committee. The focus in the postwar years shifted to regulation, litigation, tort law, and antitrust enforcement. But all these approaches dealt with the products of the current system: unfettered power, injustice, and corporate crime. And they were all susceptible to undermining and evasion by the unholy alliance of the corporations, the government, and the media, which together wielded an awesome power of attrition against would-be challengers with far lesser resources. The laws providing for corporate accountability have become largely a myth—and myths are designed to divert our collective attention away from the harsher sides of reality. In this case, the myth of corporate regulation masks our need to constitutionalize the private governments of giant corporations, to ensure that their ultimate masters are We the People. If we are truly to be a nation of "equal justice under the law," there is no way that powerful entities like ExxonMobil, Pfizer, DuPont, Citigroup, or Lockheed

Martin can be equally subject to regulation without some controlling governmental authority.

Our current system, in short, has returned us to a kind of medieval feudal society—one in which citizens are expected to live in obedient resignation under the thumb of the corporate society—in an uneasy détente between the rulers and the ruled.

Thus, for example, we see millions of Americans unwittingly sign fine-print contracts that grant immunity from lawsuits and other overweening economic advantages to vendors from American Express, Apple, Prudential, and MasterCard to smaller firms peddling payday loans and rent-to-own rackets. Corporate contracts with consumers is a form of private legislation that is part of a larger historical trend, one that started with limited liability for investors and escalated to include limited liability for the corporation itself and, finally, outright immunity for the corporation and its indemnified managers. These provisions allow Wall Streeters to use other people's money—pension and mutual fund savings—recklessly, to loot or drain trillions of dollars while enriching their executives, collapsing the economy, firing 8 million workers . . . only to turn around and demand (and receive!) a massive taxpayer bailout.

The consequences of this slippery slope include de minimis punishment for the perpetrators of corporate crime—as the recent economic crisis confirmed. Twenty years ago, a notorious but smaller series of scandals sent 1,600 S&L executives to prison. Those companies that weren't merged outright were saved with taxpayer subsidies and guarantees. In the economic collapse that began in 2008, almost no executive was sent to prison—and $300 billion in bonuses was handed out to the culpable company employees between 2008 and 2011. And executives like JPMorgan Chase CEO Jamie Dimon expect the boom-bust cycle to happen all over again.

This spread of corporate domination has long since overcome the ever-weakening hand of past attempts at reform. Large corporations are placing more of their executives in high government positions. They are sending more and more money to political campaigns and strengthening their agendas with more mass media. They are hiring ever more lobbyists to press their cause—such as the 450 drug industry lobbyists assigned to Congress in 2003 to win a drug benefit law that was structured to be hugely profitable for them. The corporations' tax attorneys have created a tax code of complex provisions, all designed to lower the effective tax rate toward zero. Twelve major corporations—including GE, Verizon, Honeywell, and Boeing—made a total of $171 billion in U.S. profits from 2008 to 2010—and paid zero federal income tax, even while receiving a total of $2.5 billion in benefits from Uncle Sam.

For every federal department and agency, including the Department of Labor, the most powerful outside lobbying force is corporate. The corporate-influenced North American Free Trade Agreement (NAFTA) and World Trade Organization (WTO) trade agreements pull down the United States toward lower levels overseas. They were designed to "pull down" higher-standard-of-living nations by allowing industries to shift activity to countries with communist or fascist regimes, such as China and Mexico—exploiting serf labor with modern capital equipment and shipping back to our country products that were once produced here.

It all amounts to one of the more astounding coups d'état of the modern era: the corporate world has come close to avoiding the rule of law and the authority of their owner-shareholders over their hired managers.

This juggernaut of out-of-control commercialism—so contrary to the precepts of all moral and ethical thinking—has crippled the restraining power of civic and community values. The multinational corporation is a relentless, ubiquitous, power-driven, strategic planning machine of unparalleled reach. It has taken it upon itself to plan out our electoral, governmental, environmental, agrarian, media, educational, worker, pension, and even our water futures—with only its own profit as a goal.

The corporations are ahead of any other entity in planning our genetic futures, as Monsanto is doing. They are determining the futures of our children with their onslaught of heavily advertised junk food, violent programming, and other wares that are harmful to our youngsters' physical and mental health. They are certainly setting the priorities for our public budgets: witness the massive growth of what President Eisenhower dubbed the "military-industrial complex." They are planning our taxpaying future by minimizing their own tax obligations (or eliminating them entirely). The mining, timber, oil, and gas companies have taken over the management of our nation's commons—the great public lands that make up one-third of America—helping themselves to our most precious natural resources at bargain-basement prices. And the media companies, which control the broadcast spectrum twenty-four hours a day, are deciding who says what and when—and who doesn't get to say anything—on the public airwaves, courtesy of licenses that are given without any compensation to We the People who grant it.

Other corporations have depended on the largesse of government for trillions of dollars in taxpayer-funded research and development, which have built most of today's modern industries. By now, most people know that the Pentagon created the internet. But few people know that much of the modern pharmaceutical, aerospace, biotechnology, agronomy, computer, containerization, and detection industries flow from R&D enabled and funded by the taxpayer.

To be sure, the corporations have not won every battle. From time to time they lose. But after a loss they often rebound and prevail. They do an effective job in camouflaging their domination with propaganda, publicizing their charities and inundating citizens with entertainment, including sports, all of which serves as a distraction. And, of course, the corporations all benefit from the free-market fundamentalism currently taught in schools and celebrated by the media.

The ultimate yardstick by which to judge these corporate wealth producers is whether they have delivered for the people—for the families, workers, consumers, savers, and retirees, and for generations to come—and whether they have been good stewards of our planet. By just one measure—worker productivity—these companies have failed to share. Since 1900, worker productivity has increased twentyfold, along with a large growth of the traditional GDP measurements. Raw poverty afflicts 49.1 million Americans while tens of millions more have seriously deprived livelihoods, are ridden with debt, and are languishing in the lowest economic brackets. Yet the concentration of income and wealth in the top 1 percent has never been higher.

What of our democratic processes? What of Thomas Jefferson's observation that the purpose of representative government is to curb "the excesses of the monied interests"? We have fallen far below passing grades on that assignment, and the slide is accelerating. We have failed to heed President Franklin D. Roosevelt's 1938 warning to Congress that "the liberty of a democracy is not safe if the people tolerate the growth of private power to a point where it becomes stronger than their democratic state itself." In FDR's time, he described that threat as fascism. Today, it can be found in the merger of big business and big government, in our fast-maturing corporate state, which is wholly inimical to the precepts of a democratic society.

It is almost quaint to recall a statement by William Gossett,[2] former vice president of Ford Motor Company and president of the American Bar Association, in 1959, that raised some plutocratic eyebrows. He said the modern corporation was the most dominant institution in our society. Eleven years earlier, in 1948, Henry Simons, the founding father of what came to be known as the conservative Chicago School of Economics, wrote: "Few of our gigantic corporations can be defended on the ground that their present size is necessary. . . . Their existence is to be explained in terms of opportunities for promoter profits, personal ambitions of industrial and financial 'Napoleons,' and advantages of monopoly power."[3]

The most important impact of federal chartering would be to plant the seeds of restraint and better behavior within corporate culture. A federal charter would give stakeholders the access and power to nurture this transition, to reshape these immense systems of authoritarian, hierarchical power over labor, capital, and technology and their excessive influence. An equitable system of corporate governance—the kind that could be enforced by a federal chartering system—would oblige corporate bosses to answer to their owner-shareholders and force criminal perpetrators to answer to their victims.

Consider the way Halliburton, the corporation that profited wildly from its relationship with the government during the Bush era, protects its basic goals of sales and profits—not all that unusual for a large company buffeted by both governmental investigations and adverse publicity. CorpWatch, a nonprofit investigative research group, released a report that describes how the usual human deterrents—from shame to sanctions—don't work on large companies:

> In the introduction to Halliburton's 2004 annual report, chief executive officer David Lesar reports to Halliburton's shareholders that despite the extreme adversity of 2004, including asbestos claims, dangerous work in Iraq, and the negative attention that surrounded the company during the U.S. presidential campaign, Halliburton emerged "stronger than ever." Revenue and operating income have increased, and over a third of that revenue, an estimated $7.1 billion, was from U.S. government contracts in Iraq.[4]

"In a photo alongside Lesar's letter to the shareholders," the CorpWatch report continues, "he smiles from a plush chair in what looks like a comfortable office. He ends the letter, 'From my seat, I like what I see.'"

At the time of the CorpWatch report, "sixty of the company's employees had been killed in Iraq so far, and several families [were] suing the company, claiming that Halliburton misrepresented the true nature of its civilian employees' duties, and intentionally placed them in harm's way." The company was grappling with investigations by the FBI, the SEC, and the DOJ, pursuing claims "regarding everything from possible bribery in Nigeria to over-billing and kickbacks in Iraq," the latter of which the company was already under fire for "acknowledged and alleged over-charging in Iraq," and had given $6.3 million back to the military after admitting that its employees had accepted bribes from a Kuwait company. Furthermore, Halliburton was fighting a mutiny within, posed by former accountants charging the company with "'systemic' accounting fraud."

And yet, as the CorpWatch report noted, "Halliburton was awarded two additional contracts [in Iraq] in January 2004," and the company's Iraq revenues that year would almost double those of the previous year.

Now consider how federal incorporation could have prevented such a rapacious company from sailing through such investigations unscathed. A responsible federal chartering system would have required full public disclosure of all of Halliburton's contracts with the government (redacted only for strict national security considerations). It would have required full disclosure of the company's federal, state, and local tax returns, including foreign tax returns. It would have required full disclosure of all official investigation and audits of Halliburton's activities, and similar disclosure of all filings against the company by government workers, subcontractors, suppliers, and customers. Such disclosure is an early alert tool for internal whistle-blowers, conscientious staff, outside law and accounting firms, journalists, congressional committees, and inspector generals. As the great newspaper publisher Joseph Pulitzer once wrote, "There is not a crime, there is not a dodge, there is not a swindle, and there is not a vice which does not live by secrecy." Federal chartering would put an end to the secrecy under which many corporations conduct their shadiest business.

As to mistreatment of workers, Halliburton is not unionized—and, given its antiunion position and the restricted labor laws in this country, that's not likely to change soon. Federal chartering would require corporations to observe union rights, subject only to a majority vote by the employees. In short, if a company's employees want their own union, they would get it—without the customary obstruction and union-busting corporations have perfected. In addition, a federal charter would require corporations to disclose all toxic substances to which workers and nearby residents might be exposed in their air, water, soil, or working conditions.

Federal chartering would also empower shareholders to discipline or replace top management in the wake of wrongdoing or to vote in new board members. At present, these corporate rulers have nothing to fear from their owner-shareholders, who have neither the information nor the practical authority to disapprove executive-enriching mergers, bylaw changes, or executive compensation overreach or withholding of dividends. The officers and board members must be relieved of their present immunities and exposed to standards of liability that invite responsible behavior. Imperious deniability would not be an acceptable alibi.

There are some encouraging precedents for this kind of punishment of corporate malfeasance—though it takes some digging to find them. In the 1975 case *United States v. Park*, for instance, the Supreme Court unanimously held a corporate executive to a standard of strict criminal liability following his firm's violation of the Federal Food, Drug, and Cosmetic Act for failure to implement measures to ensure that violations of that law not occur. John Park, the CEO of Acme Markets Inc., was found guilty after repeatedly failing to keep conditions in his companies' food warehouses sanitary and exposing food to be sold in interstate commerce to rodent infestations in Acme warehouses in Philadelphia and Baltimore.

Other kinds of violations require other corrective measures. Monopoly or monopolistic practices are the responsibility of the Justice Department and the Federal Trade Commission. A combination of global markets, weakened enforcement, and corporatist judges have allowed an epidemic of mergers in numerous industries—big oil, big cable, big airlines, big drug companies, and big health insurers—to go unchallenged. Better antitrust laws are needed to promote efficiency, competition, and innovation, which are sacrificed by complacent corporations that have very large market shares.

After all, economists have long recognized that massive concentration of power in a few corporate hands is not good for our economy. Look at how such concentration, and the resulting bureaucratic stagnation, wrecked our steel and auto industries. A proper federal chartering system could include limits on any one corporation's market share, requiring companies that are nearing a preset share of the market to start shedding assets—in other words, deconcentrating themselves. Decades ago, the Justice Department announced concentration guidelines that promised an increased possibility of enforcement if *four* companies in an industry controlled 75 percent of the relevant market. These guidelines were jettisoned when Ronald Reagan became president; we should revisit them today.

A democratic society cannot long withstand the kinds of massive inequalities in power, privilege, and immunity that exist today between large corporations and individual citizens. Supreme Court Justice Louis Brandeis once observed, "We can have democracy in this country, or we can have great wealth concentrated in the hands of a few, but we can't have both." By reasonably democratizing the giant corporation, and subordinating the rights of corporations to those of the people, we will allow the better people and priorities within the corporations to rise to the top. In this regard, the rules of the street also apply to the boardroom: when there is no law enforcement, bad business will drive out good business every time.

Corporations are different from citizens. Unlike individual human beings, they can be in many places around the world at the same time. They cannot be imprisoned. Under the current system, they are allowed perpetual life. And they have no conscience or accessible sense of shame, regardless of their effect on the world around them. Most corporations are administered with one single-minded mission: to maximize profits. They can reverse course with impunity, as with pensions and fine-print contracts, and can combine with other companies or create their own holding companies and subsidiaries for the purposes of advantage or evasion. Finally, with their massive political power, as Public Citizen president Robert Weissman has observed, "they are able to define, or at very least substantially affect, the civil and criminal regulations that define the boundaries of permissible behavior. Virtually no individual criminal has such abilities." Corporate lobbies have effected changes in the law that reduce or escape fines, cap damages under tort law, hold enforcement budgets down, appoint enforcers from their own executive ranks to head agencies, and pour money into the coffers of political parties and their candidates. They have even turned Chapter 11 bankruptcy into a business strategy to shed creditors, claimants, and shareholders before being reborn.

This list of corporate powers makes it clear what our reforms must accomplish.

Federal chartering must prohibit corporations from lobbying, from contributing in any way to electoral campaigns, from advertising deadly products like tobacco, and from obstructing regulators' inspection rights. Corporate attorney Robert Hinkley has urged that corporate charters abide by twenty-eight words mandating "the duty of directors to make money for shareholders, '. . . but not at the expense of the environment, human rights, the public health or safety, the communities in which the corporation operates or the dignity of its employees.'"[5] Hinkley argues that such a code would relieve corporate officers from slavish adherence to the "doctrine of 'shareholder primacy,'" embedded in corporate law, that arguably could expose them to shareholder suits if they should fall short of certain profit expectations.

Along with balancing out this doctrine of "shareholder primacy," we need to abolish the legal fiction that establishes corporations as "persons" with all the attendant rights enjoyed by individual citizens. A free people must never accept this principle, which can only lead to domination by the artificial entity of the corporation, which is driven by the singular yardstick of profit. There are simply too many other critical values that define the kind of civilization we need to protect. For this reason, a new federal chartering system must strip corporations of this dubious claim to personhood—a reform that will surely be questioned by the present Supreme Court—and frame the matter for a constitutional amendment.

Whatever the Court's position, however, a large majority of the American people are ready to hold big business accountable. In 2000, *BusinessWeek* conducted a poll asking if respondents would agree with the statement: "Business has gained too much power over too many aspects of American life." Seventy-one percent of respondents said yes. After the ensuing decade of corporate crime waves, the results would probably be much higher. That same poll asked Americans which of the following two statements they agreed more strongly with:

U.S. corporations should have only one purpose—to make the most profit for their shareholders—and their pursuit of that goal will be best for America in the long run.

or

U.S. corporations should have more than one purpose. They also owe something to their workers and the communities in which they operate, and they should sometimes sacrifice some profit for the sake of making things better for their workers and communities.

Ninety-five percent of respondents chose the second proposition. Of course, polls are generally suspect; they often reflect ideology or ignorance. In this poll, however, people responded on the basis of their experience and their living in communities as workers, customers, and human beings subsisting in a natural environment that has long been compromised by unaccountable corporations.

Abraham Lincoln believed that "public sentiment" should help a nation's political leaders to accomplish great goals. With public sentiment on our side, we must work to support meaningful, constructive federal charters for the gigantic corporations that are currently dominating our lives and threatening our democracy. If we revise our business standards to reflect our values, we will drive out bad business practices—and make way for the kinds of good business practices that are good for our economy, our lives, and our posterity.

8

Restore Our Civil Liberties

The celebrated psychologist and philosopher Erich Fromm once wrote about what he called the "two freedoms." The first was freedom *from* arbitrary, malicious, and forceful authority—whether wielded by the government or by other sources of power. This freedom was the central motivating concern of our Bill of Rights, which enshrined our freedom *from* dictating authority. The second freedom Fromm described was the individual's freedom *to* shape a community's and country's condition and futures—as a citizen, a voter, or a candidate. The First Amendment to our Constitution ensures this freedom to speak, to assemble, and to petition our government.

Defending and strengthening these two freedoms is crucial to the survival of our democracy. The health of civil liberties and civil rights in a society is directly related to our willingness as citizens to stand up and speak out for our beliefs in the public arena—and if we as citizens lose confidence in the right to speak out about the country's direction, self-censorship—a reluctance and inhibition to go public with dissenting views and proposals—will cripple our nation's future.

After the attacks of September 11, 2001, the reactions of our government, its militaristic supporters, and its jingoistic apologists generated exactly that: a climate of self-censorship, fear of retribution, arbitrary arrests without charges, and outright panic. This kind of atmosphere is poisonous to healthy social discourse; it can destroy any democratic society's capacity to respond wisely and resourcefully.

The dictatorial side of American politics emerges most obviously when the president begins to beat the drums of war. In such circumstances, every check and balance built into our government—the democratic processes, the congressional and judicial restraints, the media challenges, the facts themselves— can fall by the wayside. Dissenting Americans may hold rallies in the streets, but a flag-draped, dictatorial president promoting fear from the bully pulpit to induce obedience from Congress and the people easily drowns their voices out.

In the wake of 9/11, George W. Bush drove the United States into the invasion and occupation of Iraq. The resulting quagmire was Bush's most egregious foreign policy constitutional violation. But Barack Obama has exceeded Bush's lawless example with his unconstitutional presidential war in Libya, launched without any congressional authorization or appropriated funds and even without compliance with the War Powers Resolution of 1973 (which was passed despite President Nixon's veto). These Bush-Obama military actions, however, reflect a broader trend in our nation's relationship with the rest of the world. Remember retired general Wesley Clark's stinging indictment of the administration: "President Bush plays politics with national security. Cowboy talk. The administration is a threat to domestic liberty." The Bush administration, in this regard, was a dress rehearsal for its successor.

As president, Barack Obama signed the National Defense Authorization Act of 2012, which crowns the president with the power to employ the military to detain—for life, without accusation or trial—American citizens who are suspected of substantially aiding a group associated with al-Qaeda to conduct hostilities against a coalition partner of the United States— Poland, for example. Even before this act, Obama authorized the assassination of three American citizens in Yemen, who were never charged with crimes, based on secret evidence and secret law and with no postmortem proof that any had engaged in hostilities against the United States. Several major news outlets reported that the Yemeni imam Anwar al-Awlaki and Samir Khan, the editor for al-Qaeda's online magazine, were killed in a drone strike in late September 2011. Soon after, the Obama administration vaporized al-Awlaki's innocent sixteen-year-old son, Abdulrahman al-Awlaki, also a U.S. citizen, and his younger Yemeni cousin using a Predator drone. With such acts, President Obama has claimed the power to determine unilaterally who lives and who dies—a giant step beyond the Lord High Executioner's little list in Gilbert and Sullivan's *The Mikado.*

Presidents often cloak their jingoism in terms like "freedom," "liberty," and "our way of life." The politics of fear sells: it did during the Cold War, and it has during the war on terrorism. But these sales pitches have come at a great cost to the American people. Even after the dissolution of the Soviet Union in 1991, America's national security budget increased to half the operating federal budget—greater than the collective military spending of all other nations on the globe. Even as America's economy has struggled—as the majority of workers fell behind and our infrastructure crumbled—our politicians have diverted vast resources and specialized skills away from rebuilding our schools, roads, bridges, hospitals, and utility and transit systems, and used them instead to develop and produce redundant and exotic weapons of mass destruction. This is the price of empire, charged to the account of a compliant people. As Edward R. Murrow reminded us, "A nation of sheep will beget a government of wolves."

How do presidents sell America on this diversion of funds and focus?

With the politics of fear. Our twenty-first-century presidents have openly touted the state of permanent war on every square inch of the planet. There are no acknowledged limits to their imperial hubris. The same administration offices that apply rigid and rigged cost-benefit analysis to deny overdue government health, safety, and environmental standards for American consumers and workers annually send astronomical, insupportable budgets to Congress to fund the war on stateless terrorism. The GAO has deemed the Pentagon budget un-auditable. Even before 9/11, then secretary of defense Donald Rumsfeld complained that a stunning $2 trillion to $3 trillion of Pentagon funds could not be traced. But all such runaway spending was easily appropriated in the name of homeland security; the powers that be needed only to scream one word: "terrorism!"

A cost-benefit analysis of the amount of money expended on the war in Afghanistan ($120 billion in 2011 alone) would easily capture the Golden Fleece Award, once granted ruefully by Senator William Proxmire in recognition of outrageous and unnecessary government spending. In exchange for its munificent adventure in Afghanistan, the United States has received a fraudulently elected, corrupt, lawless, and popularly despised government, which has driven countless Afghans to support the enemy. With its bottomless military spending—and causing the deaths of countless innocent civilians in war crimes—the U.S. government has not only created new enemies in a devastated country but also unleashed the massive opium trade conducted by Afghan warlords. And, despite the claims of both presidents, none of this spending has made the American people any safer—because no inhabitant of Afghanistan possessed both the capability and intent to conduct warfare against Americans on American soil.

If you ask administration officials how much a war effort will cost, they recite a fetching mantra: "Whatever it takes to protect the American people." But no government can ever eliminate all risks of terrorism without bankrupting its country and destroying liberty by imprisoning every person capable of evil. Trillions of dollars annually would not suffice to fully secure our ports; border crossings; railways; chemical, petrochemical, and nuclear plants; drinking water systems; shipments of toxic gases; dams; subways; airports and airplanes; and so forth. And so "whatever it takes" is actually a prescription for unlimited spending—and for infringement on our liberties. The war on terrorism has included the employment of countless domestic guards and snoops, all in the service of "freedom"; the mantra "terrorism," endlessly repeated by presidents and their associates, has taken on an Orwellian quality as a mind-closer, a silencer, an invitation to Big Brother and Bigger Government to run roughshod over a free people.

The fact that our country, with its many highly vulnerable targets, cannot be 100 percent secured against determined, suicidal, well-financed attackers obviously doesn't mean we shouldn't take prudent measures to reduce our risks, just as we do to diminish the risk of conventional homicide. But we must allocate funds realistically, not just throw money, at some mischaracterized or exaggerated menace, which could be used for major life-saving programs at home. And our policies and expenditures must address the climate in which terrorism flourishes. The attacks on September 11 would never have happened without the military and financial complicity of the United States in the chronic oppressions and persecutions of entrenched Middle East despots. The idea that 9/11 was provoked by radical Islamic hatred of freedom in America is fatuous. Muslims throughout the world have never demonstrated against freedom of the press, freedom of speech, freedom of religion, free elections, or due process in the United States. In contrast, they violently oppose the killing of Muslim civilians and the overall destruction caused by American Predator drones and armed forces.

Then there's the great unmentionable: the question of how legitimate and extensive the threats against us really were. If you listened to the claims of the national security establishment under Bush, you heard countless assertions that our shores were teeming with well-financed suicidal al-Qaeda cells. If so, why haven't any of them struck since September 11? No politician dares to raise this issue, though it's on the minds of many puzzled Americans. As General Douglas MacArthur advised in 1957, and General Wesley Clark did much more recently, it is legitimate to ask whether our government has exaggerated the risks facing us, especially when such exaggeration serves political and profiteering purposes—stifling dissent, sending government largesse to corporate friends, deflecting attention from pressing domestic needs, and, by concentrating more unaccountable power in the White House to pursue wars, providing a recruitment ground for more stateless terrorists.

Our presidents have willingly moved us toward a garrison state through the politics of fear. The wave of militarism we've experienced in this century has resulted in an invasive campaign of domestic intelligence gathering and a concurrent disinvestment in civilian economies. The tone of our presidents has become increasingly imperial and even un-American. President Bush once told his National Security Council, "I do not need to explain why I say things. That's the interesting thing about being the president. . . . I don't feel like I owe anybody an explanation." Bush had a messianic complex that made him as closedminded as any president in history. Not only was he immune from self-doubt, but he also failed to listen to the citizenry prior to making momentous decisions. In the months leading up to the heralded invasion of Iraq on March 20, 2003, Bush didn't meet with a single major citizens' group opposed to the war. In the weeks leading up to the war, thirteen organizations— including clergy, veterans, peace activists, former intelligence officials, labor union members, business leaders, and students— representing millions of Americans, wrote Bush to request a meeting. He declined to meet with a single delegation of these patriotic Americans, some of whom had returned from Iraq, and

didn't even answer their letters. The media greeted these entreaties with a news blackout. Bush also unilaterally resorted to
an executive agreement, in lieu of a treaty, to conclude a status
of forces agreement with Iraq and evade congressional consultation or input before taking action.

In much the same way, in matters of national security Barack
Obama has acted like an emperor issuing decrees. He alone decided to raise the number of troops in Afghanistan in 2010. He
alone decided which U.S. citizens to place on his assassination
list. He alone decided to perpetrate war crimes by employing
Predator drones without any military objective beyond targeted
killings for their own sake, which result in civilian casualties.
The role of Congress, in all these moves, was as inconsequential
as an extra in a Cecil B. DeMille production.

Bush's authoritarian tendencies preceded the march to
Baghdad—from demanding an unconstitutional grant of authority from Congress in the form of an open-ended war resolution,
to incessantly touting the evils of Saddam Hussein (an ally of the
United States from 1979 to 1990), trumping up false charges
that his alleged weapons of mass destruction and ties to al-
Qaeda posed a mortal threat to America. The administration's
voice was so loud and authoritative, and the media so compliant,
that all other American voices—of challenge, correction, and
dissent—were overwhelmed. And so Bush plunged the nation
into war based on fabrications and deceptions, disregarding not
only large public marches but dissent from inside the army, the
Pentagon, the CIA, and especially the State Department. This
was a costly, bloody war launched by chicken hawks, counter
to the best judgment of battle-tested army officers inside and
outside the government.

In retrospect, it is clear that there were no weapons of mass
destruction except those possessed by the invading countries. It
also seems clear that Saddam Hussein was a tottering dictator
"supported" by a dilapidated army unwilling to fight for him and

surrounded by far more powerful hostile nations (Israel, Iran, and Turkey). The notion that this man posed a mortal threat to the strongest nation in the world fails the laugh test. Bush's dishonest and disastrous maneuvers to initiate war against Iraq met the threshold for a "high crime and misdemeanor" justifying impeachment proceedings under Article II, Section 4, of the Constitution.

Scores of prominent Americans, including retired highly ranked military, national security, and diplomatic officials, did speak out publicly against the war or at least expressed grave reservations. These included former advisers to the first President Bush, Brent Scowcroft and James Baker, as well as retired generals Anthony Zinni and William Odom, who earlier headed the National Security Agency. The media were mostly cheerleaders: uncritical of their leader, dismissive of dissenters, indifferent to their obligation to search for truth and hold officialdom's feet to the fire. And, sadly, even the legal profession—except for a handful of law professors, law school deans, and Michael S. Greco, when past president of the American Bar Association—provided very little organized resistance to the Bush war. The situation was even worse within the Justice Department.

President Obama's lawless record on initiating war is more atrocious than Bush's. In usurping the exclusive constitutional power of Congress to authorize war (Article I, Section 8, Clause 11), Obama's presidential war against Libya rested on the claim that he has the right to commence war at any time or place in the name of regional stability, by authority of the UN Security Council, or for any other reason the president ordains is in the national interest.[1] Congress, the mass media, the legal community, and the public once again showed little concern while Obama disregarded the Constitution (which always trumps a UN decision).

The system of checks and balances requires three vigilant branches, but Congress has disgraced itself on this front, starting at virtually the beginning of the Bush administration and continuing through the Obama administration. Their failure to act has enabled an extraordinary concentration of power in the executive branch—a development the founding fathers rebuked as the very definition of tyranny. In October 2001, a panicked Congress passed the USA Patriot Act, without proper congressional hearings, giving the Bush administration unprecedented powers over individuals suspected (and in some cases not even suspected) of crimes. Subsequently, Congress gave the president a virtual blank check to wage a costly war. The Patriot Act's provisions have either been routinely extended or made permanent under Obama without credible evidence that any of its awesome powers to eviscerate our privacy rights were needed to foil even one international terrorist plot. Dr. Erik Dahl, assistant professor at the Naval Postgraduate School who served twenty-one years as an intelligence officer, said, "When it comes to domestic attacks and securing the homeland, what works is really good, old-fashioned policing—law enforcement, tips from the public, police informants—and not so much spies overseas or satellites run by three-letter government agencies."[2]

The Patriot Act was followed by the Military Commissions Act of 2006. That debacle unconstitutionally suspended the great writ of habeas corpus for prisoners at Guantánamo Bay, as the Supreme Court held in *Boumediene v. Bush*. It also authorized the president to detain for life both citizens and noncitizens whom the president decreed held membership in a group affiliated or associated with al-Qaeda—elusive terms that could be stretched to include any dissident to the wars in Afghanistan or Iraq. The 2006 act also established military commissions, devoid of the trappings of due process, to prosecute and adjudicate war crimes that are also crimes under civilian law (for instance, material assistance to a foreign terrorist organization). Military commissions combine judge, jury, and prosecutor in the executive branch, an affront to the critical idea of impartiality.

Obama continued Bush's trampling of civil rights and reached new lows with the National Defense Authorization Act of 2012, which endows the president with powers beyond the monarchical or parliamentary excesses that sparked the Revolutionary War.

In these respects, and others, the war on terrorism has important parallels to the Cold War, which included unconstitutional presidential wars in Korea and Vietnam. Domestically, the Cold War was characterized by relentless focus on a bipolar world largely dictated by the iron triangle of giant defense companies, Congress, and the military leadership; by campaign contributions, lucrative contracts, new weaponry, and bureaucratic positions. A foreign policy responsive to that iron triangle produced some perverse results. The United States overthrew any number of governments (Prime Minister Mohammad Mossadegh in Iran, President Jacobo Árbenz in Guatemala) that were viewed as too congenial to similar reforms that our own ancestors fought for (land reform, worker's rights, neutrality toward foreign countries) and replaced such governments with brutal puppet regimes. We also used our armed forces to protect the interests of the oil, timber, mining, and agribusiness industries.

Indeed, such policies long preceded the Cold War. No one articulated this more clearly or candidly than Smedley Butler, a decorated early twentieth-century Marine general whose provocative eyewitness accounts were rarely noted in our history books:

> I spent thirty-three years and four months in active military service, and during that period I spent most of my time as a high class muscle man for Big Business, for Wall Street and the bankers. In short, I was a racketeer, a gangster for capitalism. I helped make Mexico and especially Tampico safe for American oil interests in 1914. I helped make Haiti and Cuba a decent place for the National City Bank boys to collect revenues in. I helped in the raping of half a dozen Central American republics

for the benefit of Wall Street. I helped purify Nicaragua for the International Banking House of Brown Brothers in 1902–1912. I brought light to the Dominican Republic for the American sugar interests in 1916. I helped make Honduras right for the American fruit companies in 1903. In China in 1927 I helped see to it that Standard Oil went on its way unmolested. Looking back on it, I might have given Al Capone a few hints. The best he could do was to operate his racket in three districts. I operated on three continents.

"War is a racket," Butler wrote, noting that it tends to enrich a select few, not those on the front lines. (The phrase was borrowed as the title of his memoir, republished at the start of the Iraq War in 2003.) "How many of the war millionaires shouldered a rifle?" he asked rhetorically. "How many of them dug a trench?"

Butler, a two-time winner of the Congressional Medal of Honor, devoted a chapter of *War Is a Racket* to naming corporate profiteers. He also recounted the propaganda used to shame young men into joining the armed forces, noting that war propagandists stopped at nothing: "Even God was brought into it." The net result? "Newly placed gravestones. Mangled bodies. Shattered minds. Broken hearts and homes. Economic instability."

Does this all sound familiar? The September 11 attacks opened the door to a corporate profiteering spree—including corporate demands for subsidies, bailouts, and waivers from regulators, tort immunity, and other evasions of responsibility. Before the bodies were even recovered from the ruins of the World Trade Center, the *Wall Street Journal* on September 19, 2001, was editorializing that President George W. Bush should seize the moment and increase defense spending, push through tax-rate cuts, and drill for more oil in Alaska.[3]

Our foreign policy should not amount to a neoconservative

strategy of permanent global war, always searching for new adversaries. It should offer a common defense to protect Americans on American soil, not a megabusiness opportunity for weapons and other contractors.

In the battle for budget allocations, what chance did the fix-America advocates have against the military-industrial complex? Which was the government more likely to choose: more B-2 bombers or repaired schools? F-22s or expansion of modern health clinics? More nuclear submarines or upgraded drinking water and sewage systems? Even before 9/11, those battles largely went to the warriors. And afterward it was no contest.

As the perceived threat shifted from the Soviet Union to stateless terrorism, the weapons programs still in the pipeline from the Cold War days moved toward completion. To those were added enhanced chemical and biological weaponry, surveillance, detection, and intelligence budgets to deal with the al-Qaeda menace. Everything was added, almost nothing displaced. We are constantly told by politicians and the anti-terrorist industry that 9/11 "changed everything." Even the militaristic evangelicals seemed to forget the words of Ecclesiastes 1:9: "there is nothing new under the sun."

This sentiment suggests the lack of proportionality of our new permanent global war. It's also a sentiment that must have made Osama bin Laden ecstatic, as we made him a figurative hero among many in the Muslim world. Bin Laden wanted to strike fear in America. He did so, and then watched as the first response to this fear was a sweeping crackdown on people with a Muslim name or Arab visage. Thousands were detained or arrested or jailed on the flimsiest of suspicions; mosques were monitored; police videos were developed demonizing Islam, opening the Bush and Obama administrations up to the charge of hypocrisy when we challenge Islamic nations about religious freedom and due process violations. All of this created more contempt for America among young people throughout the Middle East—no doubt helping the recruiting efforts of our enemies.

Bin Laden must have delighted in attempting to push America toward becoming a police state and sowing costly discord among us. He must have been thrilled by all the excessive expenditures draining our economy. Bush's invasion of Iraq prompted his own retired antiterrorism expert, Richard A. Clarke, to write in his book *Against All Enemies* that by invading and occupying Iraq:

> Far from addressing the popular appeal of the enemy that attacked us, Bush handed that enemy precisely what it wanted and needed, proof that America was at war with Islam, that we were the new Crusaders come to occupy Muslim land.
>
> Nothing America could have done would have provided al Qaeda and its new generation of cloned groups a better recruitment device than our unprovoked invasion of an oil-rich Arab country. Nothing else could have so well negated all our other positive acts and so closed Muslim eyes and ears to our subsequent calls for reform in their region. It was as if Osama bin Laden, hidden in some high mountain redoubt, were engaging in long-range mind control of George Bush, chanting "invade Iraq, you must invade Iraq."[4]

Bin Laden must have been pleased to hear the news about Bush's war of "shock and awe" and about Obama's self-defeating employment of Predator drones to kill innocent Muslim civilians in Yemen, Afghanistan, and Pakistan.

As all this suggests, America's response to 9/11 was not only disproportionate but also counterproductive. One Washington think tank member sensibly observed: "When you are fighting terrorism, you want to do it in a way that does not produce more of it." We should start by redefining national security and re-evaluating our relations with other countries, and redefining our mission as citizens of the world to include becoming a humanitarian superpower.

The failures of Congress and the judiciary to rein in the out-of-control executive branch in recent years have contributed to the emasculation of the rule of law—the authority of our constitutional system. If we are to protect ourselves against encroaching tyranny, we must begin to restore the rule of law. The new National Commission on Intelligence Misuse to Justify War, a citizen group, is dedicated toward reinstating these constitutional behaviors.

Our nation's history is marred by such sacrifices of civil liberties. We must learn from history not to trust rhetoric warning that the threats of the present day are greater than ever before; such rhetoric has been used throughout history to justify the curtailment of civil liberties. The disintegration of the Soviet Union has rendered the United States safer from external threats to its sovereignty than at any time.

The nation's first law that dangerously curtailed civil liberties—the infamous Alien and Sedition Acts of 1798, employed by the Adams administration to punish dissent—lasted only a few years. Contrary to conventional wisdom, it was not repealed by Thomas Jefferson's Democratic-Republican Party after he came to power in 1801. They didn't have to take action: the act was already set to expire after two years unless reauthorized. President Jefferson pardoned all who had been convicted, and Congress remitted all fines that had been imposed.

This is a model we need to revisit today. Congress should never impose a law that diminishes our freedoms without adding an automatic expiration in two or four years, not to be extended unless certain factors are met—namely, unless Congress determines, after meticulous hearings that (1) the act has been effective enough in protecting our security to justify its limits on our freedom, and (2) it remains necessary. Similarly, any executive order limiting our civil liberties should automatically expire unless renewed by the president or the legislature. We must be able to hold Congress accountable for the ongoing suspension of civil liberties if we are to prevent abuses of the system.

When Congress moved hastily in the aftermath of the 9/11 attacks to take measures enhancing security, without carefully considering the dangers of overreacting and overcurtailing civil liberties, it cleverly titled its legislation the USA Patriot Act. Senator Russ Feingold was the sole senator to oppose the act (because he saw certain provisions as needlessly authorizing the invasion of innocent citizens' civil liberties). Senator Feingold acted as a true patriot in a great American tradition.

As the story of the Patriot Act suggests, an attack on the United States can set in motion irresistible pressure for immediate action. The Patriot Act permits federal agents to search our homes and businesses without even notifying us for seventy-two hours simply by asking for a warrant from a court—a court that almost never says no. It entitles the government to command libraries and bookstores to reveal what we've been reading and prohibits librarians or store owners from telling us about the snooping. The act allows the government to listen in on conversations between lawyers and their clients in federal prisons and to access our computer records, e-mails, medical files, and financial information on what is essentially the whim of law enforcement. It eviscerates the great constitutional restraint called "probable cause." Without probable cause, government agents can covertly attend and monitor public meetings, including at places of worship. Anything communicated on the internet is fair game. Google receives six thousand requests monthly from government to turn over records of individual electronic footprints. With huge government contracts, Google complies with alacrity.

These enhanced government powers were not tailored to the narrow goal of preventing terrorist attacks. Rather, as Professors Laurence Tribe and Patrick Gudridge have observed, under the guise of preventing another 9/11, Congress took action that affected "the most commonplace bureaucratic and policing decisions . . . not only at obvious focal points of precaution like airports but also at other, seemingly unconnected institutions such as public libraries," expanding government power "in the everyday settings of general police procedures and criminal prosecutions of defendants charged with strictly domestic crimes."[5] We witnessed, in their apt phrase, the "bleeding of emergency into nonemergency, of extraordinary into ordinary."

Three days after the terrorist attacks on 9/11, Congress passed the Authorization for Use of Military Force (AUMF), permitting the president to "use all necessary and appropriate force against those nations, organizations, or persons he determines planned, authorized, committed, or aided the terrorist attacks that occurred on September 11, 2001, or harbored such organizations, or persons. . . ." At that point, the Bush administration and Congress did not know which nations had played a role in assisting those who attacked us. The U.S. government just wanted to do whatever was necessary to punish the perpetrators of the attacks.

The AUMF language contains at least two vague and open-ended words—"appropriate" and "aided"—and together they present an obvious risk. What would the resolution authorize us to do to nations that may have provided *minimal* aid to bin Laden? At one point or another, at least a dozen nations might have given safe haven to him or members of his organization— out of indifference, inertia, or domestic political calculation, not to help him launch an assault on America. Such assistance to terrorists may be something for us to condemn and actively discourage, and there are numerous diplomatic and economic means for doing so—but AUMF could be read as authorizing the president to wage all-out war against any nation that, in even incidental, inadvertent ways, may have "aided the terrorist attacks" of 9/11.

We needn't speculate about how loosely a president might interpret the authorization. Under its authority, the Bush administration engaged in extensive eavesdropping on telephone calls by and to American citizens. Such surveillance may be necessary to help capture terrorists or thwart specific attacks, but the Foreign Intelligence Surveillance Act (FISA) already exists for that purpose, and FISA courts have been overwhelmingly compliant with requests for warrants to wiretap. And FISA explicitly addresses how it should operate in times of war. Under the guise of AUMF's authorization of "necessary and appropriate force" to fight those involved in the 9/11 attack, the administration ignored FISA's requirement of a warrant, which is a felony under FISA's terms.

Can AUMF reasonably be read to trump FISA? Conservative columnist George Will notes that "none of the 518 legislators who voted for the AUMF has said that he or she then thought that it contained the permissiveness the administration discerns in it."[6] The argument that it nevertheless trumps FISA, observes Will, is "risible coming from [an] administration" that claims to demand strict interpretation of other laws. The Bush administration also cited a second legal basis for the eavesdropping program: the president's inherent war-making authority under Article II of the Constitution. On this interpretation, surveillance required no congressional authorization.

This amounts to a monarchical model of presidential power, one that completely disregards the crucial American value of separation of powers. Congress should not assist the executive in such power grabs by handing over additional war-making weapons that amount to a blank check. Admittedly, it would be difficult for any Congress to thwart a president hell-bent on expanding executive powers. George Will jokingly proposes that when Congress passes laws authorizing executive power, it should "stipulate all the statutes and constitutional understandings that it does *not* intend the act to repeal or supersede." More realistically, Congress should stipulate that any such grant of power is "subject to the limitations of existing law"—and attach a definitive procedure for consultation on whatever war-related powers the executive chooses to exercise. Congress should never authorize the president to use all "necessary and appropriate force" without a declaration of war.

All the laws in the world are meaningless to restrain a president, however, if they don't include a genuine risk of impeachment for disobedience. President Obama's war in Libya was so flagrantly unconstitutional that it raises the question of executive tyranny. Congress must be willing to contemplate impeachment and removal from office for any president who defies Congress or usurps the war powers of the legislature. Obama obtained no congressional authorization for the war and received no appropriations to fight it. As such, he flouted the express terms of the War Powers Resolution. Yet Congress did nothing to defend its constitutional prerogatives. Impeachment has a much-diminished profile today, thanks to the conduct of several recent presidents. As Benjamin Franklin sermonized, however, the resort of impeachment was intended as a substitute for violence against dictatorial tyrants. And the framers viewed any attempt to subvert the Constitution as impeachable offenses.

The Bush administration was listening to any conversations it wished without any need to show cause and would happily have done so indefinitely. And, the American people and most members of Congress were unaware of the surveillance program until it leaked. When we grant the executive branch exclusive power to define its own authority, we virtually guarantee that the rule of law will be supplanted by the rule of men. That this is happening in practice, as with the president ignoring or circumventing legal restraints on his drone strikes and cyber warfare, is no excuse for Congress to create the monster itself.

Vice President Dick Cheney claimed that the AUMF surveillance was solely a means of keeping tabs on known terrorists, not a matter of eavesdropping on ordinary Americans. Of course, if the president knew that a given target is a terrorist, he would have no problem getting an immediate judicial warrant for the surveillance. The Terrorist Surveillance Program was embraced precisely because the executive wished to spy indiscriminately without having to show probable cause. As the Church Senate Committee hearings revealed, presidents cannot be trusted to resist the temptation to spy on political opponents or critics, because the number one priority of the Oval Office is power and reelection. This is just the kind of abuse the founding fathers created the Fourth Amendment to prevent.

If the founders saw the need for protection against this sort of thing, history vindicated their judgment. Richard Nixon notoriously ordered illegal wiretapping of political groups and individuals he considered hostile, and his administration wasn't the first. It was a Democratic attorney general under Democratic presidents who engaged in illegal surveillance of Dr. Martin Luther King Jr. Of course, Nixon, John and Robert Kennedy, and J. Edgar Hoover did not see themselves as engaged in unjustified, undemocratic behavior. Rather, people in power tend to rationalize such misconduct, convincing themselves that their opponents are actually disloyal and dangerous to America. In other words, the risk is not that an administration will decide it wants to hear innocent conversations between citizens, but rather that it will seize the opportunity to invade the privacy of their political adversaries, convinced in their zeal that these opponents present a threat to the nation. The mind-set was captured by former national security advisor Henry Kissinger, who insisted on extending wiretaps on leak suspects long enough for the targets to establish a "pattern of innocence"—an egregious reversal of our nation's treasured presumption of innocence until proven guilty.

Moreover, as the framers well understood, government officials who abuse the power to search, seize, and harass tend to do so below the public's radar. Legal scholar John Hart Ely notes that the Fourth Amendment was motivated by "a fear of official discretion," a recognition that officials who are granted the power to violate an individual's civil liberties "will necessarily have a good deal of low visibility discretion" in exercising—or abusing—that power.

Of course, if all relevant decisions concerning these violations were made by elected officials, We the People would be able to use our votes to hold the officials accountable. But the reality on the ground is often different. Some of the worst abuses of civil liberties inevitably result from the clandestine actions of unaccountable, lower-level officials. We must avoid having the means of conducting such invasions fall unnecessarily into the hands of unaccountable government actors. Such violators are characteristically not prosecuted by the executive branch, which routinely cites national security or state secrets to thwart any attempts to investigate or punish wrongdoing. As a result, these lower-level officials risk nothing by flouting their oaths to support and defend the Constitution.

In the discourse on the tradeoff between freedom and security, the mantle of "patriotism" has been hijacked by those who are most willing to sacrifice civil liberties. Samuel Johnson famously considered patriotism "the last refuge of a scoundrel"; his biographer James Boswell, who passed along that judgment, clarified that Johnson "did not mean a real and generous love of our country, but that pretended patriotism which so many, in all ages and countries, have made a cloak for self-interest." If patriotism is the love of country, then making one's country more worthy is the mark of a true patriot. We must realize that blind obedience cannot help a country fulfill its promise. Thomas Paine defined a patriot as a person who saves his country from his government.

Affronts to the rule of law can come in a variety of forms. Congress has allowed presidents Bush and Obama to mislead Congress and to engage in unconstitutional wars. In a September 3, 2007, op-ed in the *Los Angeles Times*, former New York governor Mario Cuomo wrote:

> The [Iraq] war happened because when Bush first indicated his intention to go to war against Iraq, Congress refused to insist on enforcement of Article I, Section 8 of the Constitution. For more than 200 years, this article has spelled out that Congress—not the president—shall have "the power to declare war." Because the Constitution cannot be amended by persistent evasion, this constitutional mandate was not erased by the actions of timid Congresses since World War II that allowed eager presidents to start wars in Vietnam and elsewhere without a "declaration" by Congress.
>
> Nor were the feeble, post-factum congressional resolutions of support of the Iraq invasion—in 2001 and 2002—adequate substitutes for the formal declaration of war demanded by the founding fathers.

We must not allow the White House to make, or accept, questionable claims of executive privilege. And we must not accept the claim that government secrecy is almost always justifiable. Such positions undermine our country's moral authority. Bob Barr, a conservative Republican and former member of Congress, has said that the "state secrets privilege" should "be treated as qualified, not absolute." In his testimony before the House Judiciary Committee on July 25, 2008, he added, "Congress could assist the judiciary by holding hearings and drafting legislation clarifying the authority of judges, procedures to be used to adjudicate executive claims of state secrecy, and sanctions to be imposed for the executive branch's refusal to comply." This small, but consequential, suggestion would go a long way toward preventing the kinds of misdeeds that can occur when the executive branch seeks to escape judicial accountability.

Both the Bush and the Obama administrations have also tried to increase the power of the executive branch by using "signing statements" to circumvent Congress. This abuse has prompted even the normally reserved American Bar Association to condemn the repeated practice as unconstitutional in a resolution:

> That the American Bar Association opposes, as contrary to the rule of law and our constitutional system of separation of powers, the misuse of presidential signing statements by claiming the authority or stating the intention to disregard or decline to enforce all or part of a law the President has signed, or to interpret such a law in a manner inconsistent with the clear intent of Congress. . . .[7]

President Obama could act immediately to right the egregious wrongs by issuing appropriate executive orders to clarify government policies on abuses of civil liberties. But nothing in his record so far suggests he is likely to do so.

A number of prominent experts in constitutional law[8] have asserted that President Bush engaged in at least five categories of repeated, defiant "high crimes and misdemeanors," which separately or together would have allowed Congress to pursue impeachment under Article II, Section 4 of the Constitution. President Obama has also perpetrated undeniable impeachable offenses by initiating war against Libya without congressional authorization; fighting the war without appropriated funds;

flouting the War Powers Resolution; and assassinating American citizens based on secret facts and secret law with no postmortem accountability.

As citizens of a nation that depends on the rule of law, we must call upon our representatives to reclaim power from the executive branch. To date, Congress has been far too docile in dealing with the Bush-Obama era's abuses of power. It has meekly accepted subservience to the executive branch.

On July 25, 2008, Elizabeth Holtzman, a former member of Congress, made a compelling case for impeachment before the House Judiciary Committee. She said:

> The framers put the power to hold presidents accountable in your hands. Our framers knew that unlimited power presented the greatest danger to our liberties, and that is why they added the power of impeachment to the constitution. They envisioned that there would be presidents who would seriously abuse the power of their office and put themselves above the rule of law. And they knew there had to be a way to protect against them, aside from waiting for them to leave office.

If we want to prevent future administrations from trampling the Constitution and the rule of law, we must call upon Congress to use its impeachment powers when necessary. The Bush administration's criminal war of aggression in Iraq, in violation of our Constitution, statutes, and treaties; its arrests of thousands of individuals in the United States and their imprisonment without charges; its spying on Americans without judicial warrant; its systematic torture of detainees; and its unprecedented use of signing statements in defiance of Congress—all of these should long ago have prompted Congress to act. And it is not too late to do so now. Federal criminal laws still apply to presidents and vice presidents after they leave office. And if it is wrong to let smaller crimes go unpunished, how much worse is it to stand by and allow such monumental abuses of power?

Sadly, much the same can be said about the Obama administration. Its continuing, criminal war of aggression in Afghanistan, its criminal war of aggression in Libya, its assassinations of American citizens, and its refusal to faithfully execute the laws against torture or criminal violations of FISA all constitute grounds for the sitting Congress to commence an impeachment inquiry. President Obama's Bush-like conception of his constitutional powers have put our liberties at the indulgence of the White House.

On the heels of the constitutional convention of 1787 in Philadelphia, a woman asked delegate Benjamin Franklin, "Well, Doctor, what have we got—a Republic or a Monarchy?" He retorted, "A Republic, if you can keep it."

Our generation will earn eternal odium if we fail Dr. Franklin's challenge.

9

Use Government Procurement to Spur Innovation

According to corporate boosters, and more than a few presidential candidates, private business is the only real source of technological innovation. All we have to do is get government out of the way, and business will unleash its creative zeal. What these business mouthpieces don't want you to know, however, is that government spending also promotes innovation in a wide variety of ways. Since World War II, the government has financed at least half the nation's R&D budget, generating advances in aviation, containerization, electronics, pharmaceuticals, biotechnology, computers and the internet, medical devices, consumer safety, environmental technologies, and countless other applications.

The government is also a significant force for innovation because of its immense market power as a purchaser. In 2010, the U.S. Federal Government spent roughly $528 billion on goods and services. That represents over 3.5 percent of GDP spent on everything from office equipment, cars, drugs, food, energy, furniture, appliances, paper, building materials, and road pavement every year.

Yet our government uses too little of its immense market power to stimulate change.

For example, on both technological and economic grounds, the government has more than enough power to develop robust new markets for alternative energy. But government agencies, no doubt cowed by opposition from fossil fuel lobbyists, have failed to develop and deploy any significant new technology and failed to promote the growth of renewable energy by pioneering its use in federal projects. The General Services Administration (GSA), the Department of Defense, and the Obama White House have taken some steps forward on this issue but haven't gone nearly far enough. The government's overall shortfall in this regard has made our energy system less resilient and more vulnerable than it could be.

Government purchases can instantly create a large market for some new technology or service. This, in turn, improves producers' and vendors' economies of scale, lowering their unit costs and their risk in investing in new technology and resources. The government, in other words, can make it possible for producers to invest in innovations *before* a consumer market emerges— helping these new ideas and products reach the market more quickly and affordably, and thus making them available to a wider consumer public.

By mandating standards more advanced than those of the usual consumer products, government can stimulate innovation even more aggressively. When officials spend taxpayer money to buy computers, batteries, paper, or thousands of other products, they don't have to accept whatever choices an industry happens to offer. Instead, they can encourage that industry to produce more imaginatively, more efficiently, more responsibly. The government's massive pool of organized purchasing power can jump-start the adoption of new or dormant products and technologies to promote higher productivity, greater human safety, a cleaner environment, and taxpayer savings. This kind of aggressive procurement cannot take the place of government safety and quality regulations, but it can produce some of the same results—and often more quickly.

Government purchasing has long been a force for stimulating

technological advances. Standardized clothing sizes were first introduced during the Civil War when the Union had to obtain uniforms for its troops, and these standards helped lead to national markets for the clothing industry. Several decades ago, the U.S. Army gave generic prescription drug products credibility in civilian markets by buying generic for its military personnel and for Walter Reed Army Medical Center, frequented by presidents and members of Congress. The pharmaceutical industry was initially reluctant to introduce generic drugs to common consumers, and it sent lobbyists and campaign contributions to legislators who were sympathetic to its cause, while spreading misinformation that generics were of lower quality and less effective than brand-name products. When the military started purchasing large quantities of generics, however, not only did it save the military a lot of money, but it also paved the way to generic drugs being available to consumers. Making low-cost generic drugs widely available has been an amazing boon to less affluent consumers around the world.

Many of these early procurement success stories involve the military—including the internet itself, which began as a defense project. Other government agencies are only beginning to tap their vast potential to change the marketplace by strategic investment in emerging products.

One such idea was Buy Quiet, an initiative that began with the EPA thirty years ago, which encouraged state and local governments to issue procurement specifications for products like quieter compressors and lawn care equipment. The idea behind Buy Quiet was not just to buy quiet products but to prod manufacturers to develop new ones as well. Within two years after the program was initiated, some thirty different communities issued bids for quieter products, and another fifty municipalities were planning to follow suit. Much to everyone's surprise, quieter equipment cost no more than noisy equipment and sometimes cost less—a dynamic that often occurs when governments collectively demand such innovations. Even though the EPA's original Buy Quiet program was eliminated by early Reagan budget cuts, the idea lives on today in places like NASA and New York City's Department of Environmental Protection, which continue to prove how sophisticated government purchasing can stimulate the development of better technology.

Another example of government using its consumer dollars to jolt an obstinate industry into action is the air bag, now a highly popular (and prominently marketed) standard feature in automobiles. Even though patents on air bag–related technology were first issued in the 1950s and 1960s, the bags were not widely available until the late 1980s because of the auto executives' entrenched hostility to federal safety programs. This prejudice began to crack because we persuaded the GSA to issue a federal procurement specification for automobiles purchased for government employees with driver-side air bags. Ford submitted the winning bid for 5,300 Tempos, which prompted the company to offer optional air bags in Tempo and Topaz models. Chrysler soon outpaced Ford with standard driver-side air bags on several models, and other companies climbed onto the competitive air bag bandwagon.

Gerald Carmen, the GSA administrator responsible for the initial air bag–equipped purchase, was dismayed that the government even needed to get involved to push the technology.

> At first I did not see any reason why the government should have to put up any money at all, and to this day I do not see any reason why we had to subsidize the program because it was to the car companies' benefit, not just to the consumer's benefit. Plus, its pricing took advantage of the fact that the government was willing to subsidize it. The cost did not have to be as high as it was, in my opinion, and should have been done by the private sector on a willing basis.[1]

This is another example of how even businesses, in their quest to remain agile and profitable, will suppress basic technology because they believe it to be unprofitable or even just unsettling to their established business practices. Carmen's belief that the "taxpayer is entitled to a procurement process that . . . really is improving the product line" helped save lives and prevent injuries.

On the other hand, government has failed to use its influence to promote more crash-resistant cars. Although the Department of Transportation still has the NHTSA, that agency has done too little, beyond air bags, to protect the traveling public since 1981. Procurement officials could demand that the cars they purchase have a bumper that can withstand a 10 mph crash without damage, a body that can crash at 50 mph without injury to occupants, and roofs that support twice the vehicle's weight when overturned. These upgrades were proven effective by NHTSA's vehicle safety research project *thirty years ago*. If the government were to start requiring them on all cars it buys, they could move them into the general marketplace.

More recently, the federal government has begun initiatives to advance clean energy technology. President Obama has proposed a goal of delivering 80 percent of the nation's electricity from clean energy sources by 2035. This is an admirable goal, but one that will likely require legislative action to achieve—a pipe dream, given the makeup of the 112th Congress. However, there are smaller-scale efforts that the federal government has taken to promote clean cars, clean energy, and green buildings.

With skyrocketing gas prices, hybrid and electric cars are finally gaining a foothold in the United States. The average mileage for all U.S. passenger vehicles, including SUVs and light trucks, is about 21 mpg. The average for many hybrid cars is about 46 mpg—and the top of the heap among hybrids is the Toyota Prius, which claims 50 mpg. Based on a current gas price of around $3.52 per gallon, the average American who drives around 13,476 miles per year in a 46 mpg hybrid can expect to save $1,227.63 per year over a standard car. Owners of 50 mpg hybrids can expect to save $1,309.12. Over ten years the savings can add up to more than $13,000.

Critics of hybrid cars will point out that their sticker prices are often somewhat higher than their standard gas competitors. This may be true on its face, but the potential gas savings far outpace the marginally higher upfront costs of purchasing many hybrids. The average price consumers paid for a new car in 2011 was $29,817. Most non-luxury hybrids have sticker prices well below that, as low as $18,200 for the Honda Insight. But to compare apples to apples, we will look at two examples for comparison's sake: the Honda Civic and the Toyota Camry. The highest price for a gas-powered Honda Civic is $23,605. The highest price for a hybrid Honda Civic is $26,900. The difference? $3,295—paid off in less than three years' worth of gas savings. The gas-powered Toyota Camry XLE has a sticker price of $24,775. Its hybrid counterpart costs $27,500, just a $2,725 difference.

The federal government has begun to recognize the huge potential for cost savings that this poses and is beginning to purchase hybrid cars as a part of their fleet. In 2008, hybrids accounted for less than 1 percent of the government's purchases. Over the course of 2009 and 2010, however, the GSA bought more than 14,500 hybrids, which amounts to 10 percent of the total vehicles bought over the same period. In 2009 alone, the government purchased 64 percent of GM's Chevy Malibu hybrids and 29 percent of all Ford Fusion hybrids. This is a good first step, but there's lots of room for improvement. If the government committed to buy an even greater percentage of hybrid and electric vehicles for its fleet, it would enable these companies to achieve greater economies of scale and offer hybrid vehicles at lower cost—making the cars more accessible while increasing their benefit to consumers.

In fiscal 2011, the GSA piloted a small program of electric vehicles that it estimates will save agencies and taxpayers more than $100,000 annually on fuel costs.[2] The GSA also boasted that more than 80 percent of the vehicles it bought, or almost forty-five thousand vehicles, ran on alternative fuel. However, only about 5 percent of the total vehicles purchased by the GSA were hybrid or electric vehicles. The remaining vehicles were ethanol and biodiesel vehicles, low-emission vehicles, as well as traditional gas-guzzlers—most of which don't provide the same benefits to the environment or cost savings that hybrids do. Putting aside the environmental benefits, the potential cost savings on gas alone make it clear that the GSA should be buying such vehicles almost exclusively. The upfront cost may be slightly greater, but the fiscal and environmental benefits over time will more than repay the initial costs.

Similarly, the government could enjoy even more energy savings by converting to clean energy sources and using energy- and resource-efficient products. Former House Speaker Nancy Pelosi's Green the Capitol initiative, which she launched in 2007, installed 30,000 efficient lights and fixtures and 2,700 low-flow bathroom fixtures in House buildings, introduced local and organic food in the cafeteria, and introduced composting to the Capitol. The initiative reduced water consumption by 23.3 percent in the House Office Buildings, and slashed energy use in the Capitol by 23 percent in thirty months, constituting an annual savings of $3.3 million.

But these are just four out of the 9,600-plus buildings the GSA owns and leases. If we could only expand initiatives like Green the Capitol to all federal buildings, the results would include not only environmental improvements but huge savings. In 2009 and 2010, the GSA started moving in this direction, using $5.5 billion of stimulus funds to begin "greening" its portfolio of federal properties. At the end of fiscal 2011, the GSA owned thirty-four LEED-certified buildings and leased twenty-six

more. It's an admirable start, but these LEED-certified buildings represent only a little more than 0.5 percent of the agency's
federally owned and leased buildings.

Why are these procurement success stories so rare? Why isn't our
government investing in more creative procurement programs
when the potential benefits are so numerous and significant? Is
it because of ideological opposition, lack of imagination, short-
term thinking, political opposition, or the residual bureaucratic
caution that takes over in the absence of leadership?

A good case in point is the government's generally incoher-
ent approach to life-cycle costing—the analysis of a purchasing
decision based on a product's expected useful life rather than
its short-term budgetary impact. Life-cycle costing is a way to
measure a product's initial cost, its total maintenance and operating costs during its entire useful life, and its final disposal
cost. Life-cycle costing encourages the acquisition of products
that may initially cost more but save money over time because
of reduced energy and maintenance costs.

Congress has repeatedly mandated life-cycle costing in energy bills, but it has never become a government-wide practice. The Energy Policy and Conservation Act requires federal
agencies to use life-cycle costing analysis when considering all
energy-related purchases, but this is carried out only intermit-
tently and with little support from administration officials. Even
where life-cycle costing requirements are clearly mandated—as
in energy standards for construction of federal buildings—they
are often waived or ignored. Without using life-cycle costing as
a tool, the government cannot be a smart buyer.

Another obstacle to energy-efficient buildings is the high
proportion of federal office space and housing that is leased.
The GSA provides space for more than 1 million workstations
for federal employees in 1,500 government-owned and 8,100
leased buildings. GSA spends about $7.5 billion a year for real

estate management, including acquiring sites and buildings, construction, leasing, repairs, alterations, maintenance, and protection. But little attention is given to the energy efficiency of these facilities. In contrast, New York State requirements for energy-efficient leased buildings include window glazing, efficient lighting, and motion detectors to reduce unnecessary use of lighting.

The federal government does not use life-cycle costing analysis frequently enough for energy efficiency when purchasing office equipment, such as photocopiers, even though it pays hundreds of millions annually for electricity to power office equipment. Their use also adds significantly to building cooling requirements.

But life-cycle costing is starting to play a bigger role in the way some office equipment is being bought. Today, the U.S. government spends about $80 billion annually on information technology. This makes it the largest consumer of technology products in the world and gives it significant leverage to bring about changes and innovation in the field. This level of spending has helped to encourage technological advances ranging from record keeping, to encryption software, to even the internet, which, as noted, began as a federal defense project.

More recently, the government has been moving toward cloud computing, allowing private contractors to store agencies' computer programs and data through the internet, cutting down the taxpayers' digital infrastructure costs. Vivek Kundra, the White House's former chief information officer, estimated that this transition could save between $3 billion and $5 billion annually. Unfortunately, despite the huge cost savings, there are legitimate concerns about such technology—about the security of private information, the privatization of government infrastructure, and the reliance on outside contractors to provide basic government services. Though such reservations are legitimate, the idea is still worth study as an example of the kind of innovation government could be encouraging and stimulating with its spending.

But the federal government, and the states, should do more. They would benefit by emulating the government of Massachusetts. When procurement specialists there realized that substituting one single compact fluorescent light for a traditional lightbulb keeps a half ton of CO_2 out of the atmosphere over the life of the bulb (and lasts at least ten times longer), they saw an opportunity and introduced not only energy-efficient office equipment and lighting fixtures, but also a holistic plan to strengthen markets for recyclable materials and minimize the environmental and health impacts associated with products throughout their life cycle.

The reduction or outright elimination of toxic chemicals used in harmful cleaners and pesticides is an important goal. Chemicals used on a daily basis adversely affect both workers and the environment. Poor indoor air quality (IAQ) is one of the nation's greatest health risks. Furniture, carpeting, paints, adhesives, insulation materials, and general construction materials can all adversely affect the air we breathe inside the workplace or inside our homes.

Accordingly, Massachusetts has established minimum specifications for recycled content, energy and water conservation, and toxic waste for many products (including janitorial products), according to the Center for a New American Dream. The program has developed specifications for recycled antifreeze, traffic cones, carpeting, and content paint; re-refined motor oil; retread tires; remanufactured hospital equipment and vehicle parts; energy-efficient lighting; and non-mercury alternatives. All of this has saved the state money, trimmed lifetime costs, and improved the quality of life.

Santa Monica, California, also adopted an aggressive green purchasing policy in the early 1990s. Shortly thereafter, it started buying cleaning products with low amounts of toxins. This cleaning product purchase has eliminated altogether

3,200 pounds of hazardous materials annually and, in the process, saved the city approximately 5 percent on annual cleaning product expenses, according to the Center for a New American Dream. Santa Monica also committed to buy 100 percent renewable electricity for all its facilities. This combined strategy will reduce greenhouse gas emissions by 13,672 tons, nitrogen oxide emissions by 16.2 tons, and sulfur oxide emissions by 14.6 tons annually. Electricity generation produces 36 percent of all carbon dioxide emissions in the United States and generates 15 percent of all U.S. toxic emissions.

Federal buying decisions too rarely address such environmental and societal costs or benefits that aren't explicitly included in the purchase price of a product or service, such as the pollution an item produces or prevents.

It's the failure to consider such life-cycle costs that has led to systematic discrimination against one very promising technology: solar energy. For example, while the initial cost of a diesel-powered generator may be lower, maintenance and fuel costs account for a significant portion of the technology's life-cycle costs. Solar photovoltaic systems, on the other hand, have a relatively high initial cost but require little maintenance and no fuel. For many years the navy has installed numerous solar photovoltaics in remote locations—for economic, not just environmental, reasons.

Solar energy is a prime example of a technology that has been hurt by government's failure to take advantage of its purchasing power. Solar cells exist, but they are still more expensive than conventional power sources for most applications. The technology has matured, and photovoltaic cells are now more cost-effective when evaluated in a life-cycle cost framework. But they still won't receive the necessary investment for mass production until industry is assured of a market. A good analogy is the semiconductor, which rapidly coasted down the cost curve thanks to large purchases by the Pentagon.

Since the 1970s, environmental scientist and activist Barry Commoner has been urging the government to seed markets for solar power. If the government were to purchase solar photovoltaic panels in quantity, it would make solar energy cost-competitive with conventional fuels by speeding the pace of development, enabling producers to learn and economies of scale to grow. Unfortunately, the government has never stepped up to test this thesis. In the early 1990s, Commoner found that the federal government purchased about $123 million per year in standard dry cell batteries. If solar photovoltaic cells were used to recharge such batteries, he calculated, it would require 49.7 watts of photovoltaic capacity at a cost of $86 million, and the annual costs of operation would be $15 million—a considerable saving over the cost of dry cell batteries and an opportunity to speed the learning curve.

Solar energy can be used in countless other ways that are already cost-competitive or very close to it. In Sacramento, after a voter referendum shut down the troubled nuclear plant in Rancho Seco that had provided nearly half of Sacramento's power, investments in efficiency and new, diverse, often decentralized and renewable supplies replaced the plant's power output reliably and at lower cost. Five tract developers in the area now offer, as standard equipment, house roofs that make solar electricity. Moreover, according to physicist Amory Lovins, university researchers have found that "five years' investments in electric efficiency had boosted county economic output by $185 million and added 2,946 employee-years of net jobs."[3] Around the country, other forward-thinking homemakers are planning local solar-powered subdivisions, linked to the main power grid, to reduce costs.

According to the Solar Energy Industries Association (SEIA), by March 2012, the 1603 Treasury Program had awarded more than 4,700 grants for over 33,000 solar projects in 47 states. It has provided $2.09 billion in grants and supported more than

$4.87 billion in private investment. SEIA also cited a report from EuPD Research in October 2011 revealing that an extension of the program would have resulted in 37,000 additional solar industry jobs in 2012 and produced 2,000 more megawatts of solar installations above baseline by 2016—enough to power 400,000 homes.[4]

Although the federal government has provided tax credits for residential and commercial installations of solar panels, it has done far too little else to encourage innovation and market competition for renewable energy sources like solar, wind, and geothermal power. In the absence of meaningful federal investment, however, many states have been passing legislation requiring utilities to provide a certain percentage of their energy from renewable sources. Some of the states leading the way on renewable energy standards, for instance, range from the expected—Hawaii (40 percent by 2030) and California (33 percent by 2020)—to the unexpected—Colorado (30 percent by 2020) and Kansas (20 percent by 2020). It is especially puzzling that the federal government has not more fully embraced solar energy, given its tremendous potential to enhance American energy security in the twenty-first century.

For years, the government has also failed to make full use of its purchasing power to stimulate the recycled paper market. The rising demand for wood products in our society has been driving the destruction of the world's forests, and the United States, with only 5 percent of the world's population, consumes 27 percent of the world's commercially harvested wood. Our practices are clearly unsustainable.

But the recycled paper market has demonstrated some additional benefits to commerce and society as well. The recycling market creates jobs in the collection, sorting, manufacturing, and distribution of recycled waste. Recycling ten thousand tons creates thirty-six jobs, whereas landfilling or incinerating the same amount creates six jobs and only one job, respectively. And producing recycled paper causes 74 percent less air pollution and 35 percent less water pollution, while it creates five times the number of jobs as producing paper from trees.

The remarketing of post-consumer waste gives use to trash that would otherwise be landfilled or incinerated. With landfills and incinerators releasing toxic chemicals into the air and groundwater, reincorporating waste into the economy is an essential solution. Further, many recycled and ag-based papers are processed chlorine-free (PCF), which eliminates the harmful dioxins released into the environment when chlorine bleaching is used.

While we're looking at the effects of government initiatives, it's important to look at instances of *unsuccessful* leadership, because they illustrate the systemic resistance such good government practices can encounter. During his first year in office, President Bill Clinton issued an executive order requiring federal agencies to purchase products made from recycled materials. "It's time for the government to set an example and provide real leadership that will help create jobs and protect the environment, encouraging new markets for recycled products and new technologies," he said as he signed Executive Order 12873 on October 20, 1993.

According to Todd Paglia, then director of our Government Purchasing Project, within four years the example set by the government was "dismally clear. Few federal agencies are satisfying the legal requirements of Clinton's 'Buy Recycled' order— even when it saves them money."[5]

Clinton's presidential order didn't aim to tackle anything terribly complex. It simply said that if a recycled product could compete on price, performance, and availability with a product made from virgin material, federal agencies were required to buy the recycled product.

But getting government employees to carry out a president's

executive order proved to be no simple matter. Consider the record on purchases of one government staple: copier paper.

Every six months, the Clinton administration held something called the "White House Copier Paper Summit." This conclave of government employees, environmental advocates, and trade press did not usually yield good news. Despite the presidential order, "only 39 percent of the federal government's copier paper contained recycled material, according to figures released at the summit." All this happened even though the GSA was selling recycled copier paper to federal agencies at a lower price than virgin paper. When one GSA Federal Supply Service employee was confronted with the government's poor record, he replied, "Executive orders are executive orders. Big deal." Only when one of our lawyers called this to the White House's attention did the GSA move to adhere to the order.

But other agencies also ignored the presidential directive. The Smithsonian's order of recycled paper amounted to 7 percent of total copier paper purchased; the General Accounting Office's order was only 2 percent.

However, even when agencies complied, they were undermined either by inertia or incompetence. Several agencies requested that the GSA fill all orders with recycled paper because of difficulty with remote purchasing officials. The GSA took almost eight months to comply.

This executive order, if it had been properly applied, could have boosted the market for recycled products and conserved natural resources in the process. This end was finally achieved when a number of agencies instituted a policy to substitute recycled-content paper automatically when virgin paper was ordered. By 2000, more than 98 percent of federal agencies' copier paper purchases from GSA and the Government Printing Office contained 30 percent post-consumer content, though not chlorine-free. Today, when anyone in the country buys recycled-content copier paper, it most likely meets or exceeds the government's 30 percent standard. Now that compliance rates are up, the percentage of recycled content needs to be increased to reflect the high-quality papers being made from 50, 75, and even 100 percent recycled or alternative fiber content. The government can still do more. Even with a clear executive order, the policy is unnecessarily complicated and slow to administer. So imagine how hard it must be for even the best-intentioned federal purchasing agent when faced with a contradictory stew of congressional mandates and agency agendas.

And these problems aren't limited to old-fashioned physical products like batteries and paper. As mentioned, the U.S. government spends about $80 billion annually on information technology. If the government is looking for solutions to the enormous security and competition issues in the software market, it should consider using its own purchasing might to steer things in the right direction.

Microsoft, for instance, has an astounding market share for desktop operating systems and office productivity software. According to *Daily Tech*, in 2010 Microsoft Office had 94 percent of the office productivity market.[6] In that same year, Gartner Inc., one of the leading information technology research companies, reported that Microsoft had 78.6 percent of the operating system market.[7] The Department of Justice has spent years in court trying to restrain very modest elements of Microsoft's monopoly abuses. In the 1990s, the DOJ brought a suit against Microsoft asserting that the company's practice of bundling Internet Explorer with Windows was an anticompetitive practice; after a 2000 decision supporting the DOJ was overturned upon appeal, the government ended up accepting a settlement that required Microsoft to make its application programming interface available for license at reasonable prices. The settlement was intended to prevent Microsoft from engaging in anticompetitive practices that rendered competitors' products inoperable on its operating systems—and to give the DOJ oversight on this issue. But the DOJ never required Microsoft to change its code or prevent it from tying other software to Windows in the future, and its oversight authority expired in May 2011. The Microsoft monopoly has done immeasurable harm to innovation, security, and pricing within the tech industry. Instead of rewarding this performance, the government should have used its procurement power by issuing demands that Microsoft be more responsive to government and taxpayer needs. Instead, the federal government still spends billions of dollars on software purchases from this one company, which is continually raising prices, making its products incompatible with previous versions in order to force upgrades, and deliberately creating interoperability problems with would-be competitors. No business spending this much money would be such a passive consumer.

There are other novel ideas the government could implement to rein in Microsoft's anticompetitive practices. Some include auctioning off several licenses for Microsoft's intellectual property, which would create instant competitors for its main software products and give outside programmers the technical information they need to make products that work properly with Windows and other Microsoft products; stopping the use of discriminatory pricing to discipline computer manufacturers who offer software from Microsoft's competitors; supporting, or at least not interfering with, open or third-party protocols that run on top of Microsoft operating systems; and unbundling various components of those systems.

If we want to unleash government purchasing as a major dynamic force for market innovation, Congress and the executive branch must first recognize its vast potential power. We need either a presidential commission or a set of coordinated congressional hearings to launch a new era in strategic federal purchasing. Environmental and consumer groups could present problems that need redressing, and entrepreneurs, including small businesses, could present new products, technologies, and designs to replace the wasteful, environmentally destructive ones that currently dominate the market. Representatives from our national laboratories, such as the Oak Ridge National Lab, which specializes in energy savings, could discuss their research and explain how guaranteed government markets could move innovation rapidly into the marketplace. Procurement officials—not just top officials but representatives from all levels—could disclose impediments, technical and nontechnical, to innovative procurement. As MIT professor Nicholas Ashford argues, "There is a role for government from the direct support of R&D and incentives for innovation through appropriate tax treatment of investment; to the creation and dissemination of knowledge through experimentation and demonstration projects; the creation of markets through government purchasing. . . ."[8]

Congress and the president could then make technology-advancing procurement a part of the mission of all federal agencies, with appropriate support and funding adjustments. Agencies embodying national missions, such as the EPA and the NHTSA, can actively influence government procurement at the federal, state, and local levels by making their knowledge and expertise available whenever products within their purview are being purchased. For instance, every state, as well as in the federal government, has an office responsible for the purchase of motor vehicles. That office should regularly receive information from the NHTSA on safety features, beyond the present minimum standards, that can be purchased for their new vehicles. This is another way that government procurement can push the envelope, focusing on safety features not yet widely available and moving them from optional to standard equipment. Top-level administrators and members of Congress should be models of initiative, using the most environmentally sound paper products, energy-efficient lighting, and safer, fuel-efficient motor vehicles.

Unfortunately, after the 2010 elections, Congress chose to take a step backward instead of leading the way in advancing green initiatives. Despite the success of Nancy Pelosi's Green the Capitol initiative, the Republicans, upon retaking the majority in the House, canceled the program. This not only reversed significant progress in energy efficiency at the Capitol, but it actually cost taxpayers up to $50 million. Just another example of how our elected officials are failing to lead the way in government procurement, wasting taxpayer money while actively dismantling all efforts at meaningful progress.

We should also call on Congress to pass laws mandating new procurement quotas and compliance deadlines. Training and funding should pave the way for improved procurement spending and life-cycle cost analysis on all projects and renovations over a certain size. Such requirements are rarely enforced today, despite the occasional question from congressional oversight committees. It's time that we, the taxpayers who ultimately pay these bills, have a voice in these matters. The people should be given explicit standing to sue government executives whose agencies refuse to follow these laws in these areas.

We must also call on our talent-loaded national laboratories and procuring agencies to cooperate. All of our government agencies—and the general public—should be kept abreast of the laboratories' work and how they can use such discoveries. The agencies should monitor their progress in promoting and using innovative technologies. Individuals who show leadership in this area should receive recognition for innovative use of their facilities' purchasing dollars to benefit taxpayers, consumers, and the environment. Universities and relevant professional associations should offer procurement education programs focusing on giving buyers the skills necessary to make more creative and prompt procurement decisions. The government's potential to use its buying dollars to advance the nation's daily quality of life for most Americans should become a campaign issue, heralded by candidates who want their country to lead the way in both responsible spending and innovation.

In the spirit of John F. Kennedy's Consumer Bill of Rights, I would like to outline four basic principles that should govern future institutional purchasing decisions. If these four points are accepted as a broad framework, they will help ensure that the government transforms itself from a passive consumer to an active leader in the marketplace.

From this point forward, all responsible government procurement should:

1. Improve government employee health and productivity
2. Spark innovation and benefit society as a whole
3. Lessen our energy demands, advance consumer safety, and reduce environmental damage
4. Reduce long-term economic costs

If we can persuade the government to use its purchasing power for the greater good, not only will we induce industry to make its own products safer, more ingenious, more efficient, and more environmentally friendly; we will also help to create higher-quality, more competitive markets, while reducing costs to consumers, corporations, and the overall economy. Sound procurement policies represent a way for the biggest consumer—We the People—to say to the biggest sellers: *Here is what we want to buy. Take it or leave it.*

10

Reinvest in Public Works

On March 4, 1992, the *New York Times* carried a full-page message about rebuilding and replacing the real capital known as our public works. It was signed by a maverick capitalist, an exercise-equipment manufacturer named Jerry L. Wilson. The Soviet Union had recently collapsed, potentially freeing our country from decades of heavy investment in the military sector of the economy and allowing labor and capital to be redirected into our public works: schools, libraries, public transit, roads, bridges, airports, levees, ports, grids, water and sewage systems, even toxic dumps in need of cleanup. "Never in the history of Western civilization," Wilson noted, "has there been a broad improvement in private wealth and upward mobility without first being preceded by a *significant public investment!*" About a year later, President Bill Clinton sent a modest public works restoration bill to Capitol Hill—only to see Congress reject it because it wasn't being funded. The notion of public capital investment is apparently foreign to a majority of the professional law-blockers among our elected representatives.

That was the story of the 1990s: a great lost opportunity to take the "peace dividend" and reinvest it in modernizing our public works.

Now, in the midst of our current economic recession, public America is literally crumbling. Our roads and bridges are decrepit, school roofs across the nation are leaking or falling in, the public water system does not deliver safe drinking water to millions, and the reach of public transportation systems is not expanding. Even our great national park system is decaying while the weapons-of-mass-destruction industry is booming.

We are overdue to launch a major public works initiative to repair one of society's greatest storehouses of shared wealth: the basic infrastructure we all rely on for critical services, the physical plant that has historically enabled commerce to expand and thrive like no other feature.

In 2008, as his campaign gained momentum, presidential candidate Barack Obama promised to invest in our future, to direct unprecedented government resources to investments in human (schools, job training) and physical (buildings, roads) infrastructure. After his election, when the time came to bring about the "change" Obama had promised, he could have pushed seriously for a visible public works program producing domestic jobs in thousands of communities for improved public services. He could have directly challenged the Tea Partiers with cuts in corporate welfare. But he did not, except for reducing ethanol subsidies. He could have made a big deal of cracking down on corporate fraud on Medicare and Medicaid, liberating tens of billions of dollars a year. Yet Obama played a defensive game from the start, and he remained on the defensive deep into his White House years.

Many urged the president to seek a balance, at least, between the demands of Wall Street and sensible investments to spur future economic activity. But President Obama largely ignored this advice. Instead of delivering on his promises of public investment, he chose instead to continue to divert hundreds of billions of dollars to the defense budget. As the Center for American Progress has noted, defense spending has increased for thirteen straight years, since the end of President Clinton's term in office; today, it stands $100 billion above Cold War levels. Furthermore, our nation's share of global military spending has jumped from about a third to *nearly one-half*. President Obama recently signed a defense spending bill authorizing more than $660 billion in defense spending—not counting the special direct appropriation for the Iraq and Afghanistan wars, which total about $150 billion. This is more than double the amount authorized for defense spending in 2000 (roughly $295 billion).

Military spending in the United States now exceeds the combined military expenditures of the next twenty countries: China, France, the United Kingdom, Russia, Japan, Germany, Saudi Arabia, Italy, India, Brazil, South Korea, Canada, Australia, Spain, the United Arab Emirates, Turkey, Israel, the Netherlands, Greece, and Colombia.

But new times call for a new outlook. It is time—actually a decade late—for the United States to abandon the last vestiges of its Dr. Strangelove perspective, to put an end to the perpetual wars abroad in the name of a "war on terror," and to adopt a less constricted, but more precise, definition of national security. Our security rests not only on protection from foreign invasion or attack, but also on a well-functioning economy resting on a sound foundation here at home while waging peace abroad.

If our nation is going to fulfill its truly unmet needs, we must close the public investment deficit. It's not always helpful to compare the government with a corporation, but consider this: any corporation that collected healthy revenues every year but allowed its plant to deteriorate would be considered reckless, a bad prospect to investors. It's troubling to think that the same could be said for our government, which is recklessly failing to invest in the country's long-term prosperity and well-being, as determined both by traditional economic yardsticks and by more citizen-oriented standards.

The federal government needs to adopt a far-reaching public works agenda—building, repairing, and modernizing schools, courthouses, sewage facilities, libraries, public transit, water systems, parks, roads, bridges, and railways, as well as cleaning toxic environments—in order to serve the interests of all of society. In doing so, our government will only be fulfilling several of its grand and proudest functions: guaranteeing essentials to every member of society, laying the physical structural foundation for an efficient and dynamic economy, and filling roles the free market fails to fully address.

Surely every person in the richest country in world history has the right to expect clean water, structurally sound buildings for their children's schooling, and access to efficient public transportation. But thousands of communities around the country now suffer from unsafe drinking water, send their children to rickety and underfunded schools, and remain disconnected from metropolitan neighbors and employment because of mass transit shortcomings.

These are public deficits and at least as urgently worthy of government attention as the government's budget deficit. The market's current answers—bottled water, private schools, car ownership—have been unresponsive to the public needs of millions of Americans. It is the government's responsibility to satisfy these basic rights.

Happily, meeting these and other public demands—including building new roads, bridges, and public buildings—can only *strengthen* the economy. The economy benefits from a better-educated and healthier workforce and from the efficient transportation of goods and people. Public works projects also enable the government to achieve other important goals.

Despite the recent financial crisis, the economy has expanded significantly in the past several decades. Despite this expansion, however, poverty and inequality remain shockingly severe. Between 2000 and 2009, the number of children living in poverty increased by 33 percent. This trend has continued in the years since, with 3.8 million more children living in poverty today than in 2000. One-quarter of the nation's children under the age of six live in poverty, and 42 percent of the nation's children live in low-income families. Although the stock market has sky-rocketed, average real wages remain below 1973 levels. Income and wealth inequality is gravitating to the standards of Brazil and the other lopsided economies of the developing world. Bill Gates alone in 2000 was worth as much as the combined wealth of the bottom 40 percent of the wealth hierarchy in the United States—more than 120 million people.

Investing in public works helps to counteract poverty and inequality by creating good jobs that are not subject to competition from low-wage countries and by increasing productivity and mobility in the domestic economy. It also gives government the opportunity to address other market failures. A school construction and repair program, for example, can include the provision of solar heating panels and energy efficiency technologies and architecture as core elements, thus creating a market for solar and energy efficiency technologies.

If we undertake a dramatic effort to rebuild our nation's crumbling schools and inner cities, we can remake our most troubled cities as attractive places to work and live. Preserving green spaces and making new outlying communities pay their fair share for expanded sewer lines are important steps to help curb sprawl, but in the long term, sprawl can only be contained if families believe they can live safely and happily in inlying urban areas.

The benefits of public works are widespread. They are not confined to the corporate elite, but neither do they concentrate among the poor. Unlike the narrowly tailored subsidies of corporate welfare, whose benefits are captured by special interests, public works enhances the well-being of the entire society.

REBUILDING THE SCHOOLHOUSE

According to the National Education Association (NEA), one in three schools across the United States—a country that prides itself on its tradition of public schooling and puts education at the center of its "Only in America" and equal opportunity national narratives—is "in need of extensive repair" or replacement.

In 2006, a Healthy Schools Inc. national report called *Lessons Learned* confirmed the severity of the situation and indicated that things may even be getting worse. The report estimated that 32 million schoolchildren attended schools with self-reported facility environmental problems that could affect their health or learning.

Today, the American Society of Civil Engineers (ASCE) reports that an astonishing $322 billion would be required to bring our nation's schools into a state of good repair. Sixty percent of schoolchildren—that's 32 million kids—attend schools with at least one inadequate building feature. These include roofs; framing, floors, and foundations; exterior walls, finishes, windows, and doors; interior finishes and trims; plumbing and heating; ventilation and air conditioning; electrical power; electrical lighting; and life safety codes. Most of the schools with at least one problem suffer from multiple inadequate features in need of repair.

At the time of a 1995 GAO study, more than one in eight schools suffered from five or more unsatisfactory conditions. These numbers exclude numerous outstanding obligations for management or cleanup of asbestos, lead, underground storage tanks, and radon. The situation has not improved significantly since that time.

Does all of this really matter? Of course it does. In some cases, as has happened in Washington, D.C., in the past, school disrepair has prevented students from attending schools, with courts ordering that safety problems be addressed before students be allowed back into their school buildings. And the safety concerns can be far more immediate: In one Alabama elementary school, the roof collapsed just forty minutes after children left for the day. At a Chicago school, teachers were forced to use cheesecloth and mesh to protect students from flecks of lead-based paint flying into their classrooms through heating vents.

Students who are forced to sit for classes in hallways, closets, and other makeshift classrooms, to substitute for leaking or otherwise unusable classrooms, are not in an environment that's conducive to learning. Academic studies show that students consistently perform better in above-standard buildings than below-standard buildings, according to a literature review by Dr. Glen Earthman of the Virginia Polytechnic Institute. "Students who attend class in clean, safe, modern buildings receive a far more positive message about their self-worth than those in run-down, antiquated buildings," notes the National Educational Association. "Student behavior, staff morale, and overall attitude are positively affected by better environments."

The school building crisis is distributed throughout the country: schools in all regions—urban, suburban, and rural—all need repair. The 1995 GAO study listed nine states in which more than 65 percent of schools have one or more inadequate building features: Alaska, California, Delaware, Maryland, Massachusetts, New Mexico, New York, Ohio, and West Virginia, as well as the District of Columbia. The Healthy Schools report, more than a decade later, cited all the same states—and *added* Indiana.[1]

Although the crisis is distributed throughout the country, it is not distributed evenly. Not surprisingly, the problem is worst in poor, inner-city school districts serving minorities—meaning that the numerous disadvantages faced by children in these schools are compounded by decrepit public schools. Thirty-eight percent of schools in central cities have at least one inadequate building, 9 percent higher than suburban schools. Sixty-seven percent of inner-city schools—with 10 million students—report at least one building feature in need of repair, compared to the national average of 59 percent.

If we don't take fast and aggressive action to change this situation, our inner-city problem will only worsen. While urban schools spend about 3.5 percent of their budgets on facilities maintenance, 85 percent of this amount is allocated to emergency repairs, with only the remaining increment spent on preventative maintenance.

The sums needed for school repair are only part of the story. With a new baby boomlet under way, we're facing an urgent need for new school construction—though the medium-term needs could be alleviated if city schools are renovated to stay abreast of reviving city neighborhoods. Public elementary and secondary school enrollment has risen from 40.53 million in 1990 to 49.04 million in 2009, and this trend is only expected to continue.[2]

In the early 2000s, the NEA and ASCE estimated that $60 billion to $70 billion would be needed for new school construction over the next decade. In the midst of unrelenting budget cuts at the federal, state, and local levels, that figure has increased since then.[3]

More recently, the NEA reported that local public schools were in need of $268 billion for infrastructure and $54 billion to equip schools with modern technology. Improving education is on the lips of every politician in Washington, D.C. As we redouble our efforts to educate the country's children to be creative, inventive, intellectually engaged, and dynamic adults, however, we must first provide them with functioning physical facilities. After decades of slippage in this area, we need a concerted national effort to revive our schools, with hundreds of billions of dollars devoted to the campaign.

GUARANTEEING A CLEAN DRINKING WATER SUPPLY

In recent years, we've had plenty of warning signals about the consequences of failing to maintain the nation's water supply system. Milwaukee, Washington, D.C., Las Vegas, Austin, New York City, and many others have been forced to ask residents not to drink unboiled water because of microbiological and chemical contaminants.

In 2009, a *New York Times* investigation found that "more than 20 percent of the nation's water treatment systems [had] violated key provisions of the Safe Drinking Water Act over the five years."[4] From 2004 to 2009, water that contained illegal concentrations of dangerous chemicals, including arsenic, bacteria often found in sewage, and radioactive substances such as uranium, made its way to 49 million consumers. As the *Times* reported, regulators were aware of each of these violations. But the water systems that broke the law were fined in less than 6 percent of the cases.

A major part of the problem is the weakness of the Safe Drinking Water Act. More than sixty thousand industrial chemicals are used in the United States, but only ninety-one contaminants are regulated by this act and not a single chemical had been added to that list since 2000. And of those that are regulated, the levels of contamination are far too high. For instance, the *New York Times* reported that "the drinking water standard for arsenic, a naturally occurring chemical used in semiconductor manufacturing and treated wood, is at a level where a community could drink perfectly legal water, and roughly one in every 600 residents would likely develop bladder cancer over their lifetimes."[5]

It is one thing to travel to a poor developing country and be told not to drink the water. But to live in as highly developed a nation as the United States and be warned to boil water before drinking it is quite another.

The failure to provide clean drinking water to all of the nation's people is not only a disgrace, it is a public health nightmare waiting to happen—and one in which the poor, the young, the elderly, and the ill are especially vulnerable. The Milwaukee cryptosporidium outbreak in 1993 alone sickened more than 403,000 and killed over 100 people. In the late

1990s, the Centers for Disease Control estimated that a million people get sick every year from bad water, including about nine hundred deaths.

By 2006, the CDC estimated that about 16.5 million people became ill annually due to waterborne illnesses related to their drinking water. Continuing the downward spiral, in 2009 the *New York Times* reported that as many as 19 million Americans become ill each year because of parasites, viruses, and bacteria in their drinking water. The International Conference on Emerging Infectious Diseases estimated in 2010 that the cost of hospitalizations in the United States for just three common waterborne diseases was more than $500 million.

The wealthy tend to avoid these problems by buying bottled water, but that is an unreachable luxury for many. It is also something that any decent society, at least any decent society with the accumulated wealth of the United States, would not ask of its people. Given the nation's failure to invest sufficiently to protect drinking water supplies and systems of provision, we need to make substantial new investment to guarantee clean water to all.

The 2007 EPA Drinking Water Infrastructure Needs Survey and Assessment estimated that ensuring safe drinking water for those served by community water systems would require $334.8 billion over the next twenty years for water system investments to install, upgrade, or replace infrastructure. (Earlier estimates from the CBO and EPA ranged from $200 billion to $590 billion.) Of that total, the EPA found that $52 billion would be needed immediately to meet existing Safe Drinking Water Act requirements. Approximately 30 million Americans are not served by a community water system. While the EPA was unable to estimate the full cost of providing clean water for all these households, the agency estimated in 1995 that it would cost $6 billion to connect only some of those households that are close to existing community water systems to a safe water supply.

More than $130 billion of that $334.8 billion would go toward infrastructure improvements that are needed to protect public health. These needs include source, storage, treatment, and water main improvements that are necessary to minimize water supply contamination. Just over $50 billion is needed to repair or replace infrastructure in systems not in compliance with Safe Drinking Water Act regulations, including the Total Coliform Rule.

The EPA estimates that $200.8 billion of that $334.8 billion would go toward the installation and rehabilitation of transmission and distribution systems—critical elements in protecting the public from water contamination. This is about an 8.5 percent increase from a previous analysis in 2004. "Deteriorated distribution piping can allow water in the distribution system to become contaminated and can lead to interruptions in water service," the EPA explained in its report. "Transmission line failure can lead to interruptions in treatment and water service."[6]

Repairing these systems means, above all, replacing existing pipe. "In some cases, wooden mains that have been in service for more than 100 years must be replaced," the EPA reports. "In other instances, pipe that is severely undersized, or that has exceeded its useful service life, must be replaced. Such pipe often leaks and is prone to high rates of breakage, which can lead to contamination."

The second-largest category of need is treatment. In 1995, one in four systems were in need of improved treatment for contaminants. By 2007, the EPA estimated that twenty-year costs in this area had more than doubled since 1995, from $36.2 billion to $75.1 billion.

There is good news, however. Investment in our nation's water infrastructure has been shown to benefit the economy. A 2008 presentation at the U.S. Conference of Mayors revealed that "one dollar of water and sewer *infrastructure investment* increases private output (Gross Domestic Product, GDP) in the *long-term* by $6.35."[7] The presentation found that for every one job in water and sewer infrastructure added to the economy, 3.68 jobs would be created in the national economy to support that job.

That the water provision system has deteriorated to this point is a national disgrace. Earlier generations, seeking to advance the interest of public health and to better community life, gave us working water systems that should have lasted indefinitely. In our shortsightedness, we have failed to invest in upkeep. But further delay will only bring greater expense, severe damage to public health, and the deepening of an ugly class divide based on access to healthy living conditions. We owe it to future generations to correct this problem before it's too late.

ROADS, BRIDGES, AND HIGHWAYS

If one area of the nation's infrastructure is receiving the resources, funding, and national priority it deserves, it is the national highway system, which has received nearly $150 billion in annual investment at all levels of government. There is no mystery as to why this area fares so much better than other infrastructure demands: not only do the highways benefit the construction lobbies that support, though less vigorously, other public works investments, but they are integral to the well-being of the auto and oil industries.

In 2009, the ASCE estimated that it would cost $930 billion to bring the nation's transportation infrastructure into a state of good repair (triple what was already being spent). President Obama released a six-year transportation spending plan as a part of his FY2012 budget that would total $556 billion. In this plan he called for increasing annual transportation spending to $128 billion, up $51 billion from 2010's budget of $77 billion. This would primarily be split between roads, bridges, and transit. In 2011, the ASCE estimated that "in order to bring the nation's surface transportation infrastructure up to tolerable levels, policy makers would need to invest approximately $1.7 trillion between now and 2020. . . ."[8]

Though this amount might be sufficient to keep the highways in relatively good working order, it may also be used to support highway expansion, some of which may be ill-advised. Since the states have significant discretion over how they will spend the money, such investment in new roads could come at the expense of repairing existing roads and bridges. Leaving our existing highways and bridges in shoddy condition, or using low-grade materials to repair them, will only impose huge costs on car owners, impede efficient transportation, and pose safety hazards to drivers and passengers.

THE POTHOLE PROBLEM

Potholes are a consumer nightmare. The American Association of State Highway and Transportation Officials (AASHTO) estimates that poor roads cost American drivers $67 billion annually in wear and tear, repair expenses, and decreased fuel economy. As the Department of Transportation explains: "Rough pavement affects the cost of travel on the roadway. These costs include vehicle operating costs, delay, and crash or accident costs. Poor road surfaces cause additional wear or even damage to vehicle suspensions, wheels, and tires. Vehicles slowing for potholes can cause delay. In a heavy flow of traffic, such slowing can create significant queuing and subsequent delay. Inadequate road surfaces can lead to crashes when unexpected changes in the surface and reduction in the road surface friction due to age or wear affect the stopping ability or maneuverability of vehicles."[9]

The annual cost of driving on poor roads for the average motorist comes to about $335, according to AASHTO and TRIP, a national transportation research group. This means that driving on poor roads costs individual motorists about an extra

$31.30 per thousand miles driven. And the cost to motorists can be much higher if they live in an area whose roads are in poorer condition. Motorists in San Jose, California, pay an average of $756 annually for driving on poor roads. New Orleans? $681. Oklahoma City? $662. The New York metro area? $640. Omaha? $587.

Over the life of a car (an average of about twelve years), the average driver will pay $4,020 due to poor road conditions. In a city like San Jose, motorists will pay $9,072 over the life of their car. This "pothole tax" comes to $8,172 in New Orleans, $7,944 in Oklahoma City, $7,680 in the New York metro area, and $7,044 in Omaha, Nebraska.

Cities across the nation are pocked with craterlike potholes. According to the Federal Highway Administration, 45 percent of the nation's highways were in less than good shape— poor, mediocre, or fair—in 2008. More than one in four urban roads are in poor condition, and approximately two-thirds are in less than good condition.

The Department of Transportation has estimated that simply maintaining the condition of just the federal highway system would require $100 billion annually—which is about $30 billion above spending levels in 2008. The key to making this investment sound is to invest in long-lasting pavement technologies, so that new roads remain good roads for decades. Western Europe is ahead of the United States in this regard, using quality, longer-lasting highway pavement materials that diminishes pothole frequency.

In much the same way that investment in water and sewer infrastructure benefits the economy, a Federal Highway Administration study found that for each $1 billion of federal spending on highway construction nearly twenty-eight thousand jobs were generated annually. The FHA also concluded that each dollar spent on road, highway, and bridge improvements resulted in an average benefit of $5.20. These benefits ranged from reduced vehicle maintenance costs, delays, fuel consumption, emissions, and bridge and maintenance costs, to improved safety and traffic.

FALLING THROUGH THE BRIDGE
TO THE TWENTY-FIRST CENTURY

The Brooklyn Bridge is falling down. With pieces of concrete falling from the famous bridge, New York City officials have been forced to begin an emergency repair project, currently scheduled to last until at least 2014. Unfortunately, the Brooklyn Bridge is not an anomaly. In August 2007, the I-35W Bridge in Minneapolis collapsed into the Mississippi River. This horrific event killed 13 people and injured 145 others.

All across America, bridges are in states of near collapse—an issue that can't be put off or ignored. As U.S. PIRG, the Federation of State Public Interest Research Groups (PIRGs), noted in its report *Road Work Ahead*, the Minneapolis bridge was forty years old and the Federal Highway Administration had labeled it "structurally deficient." And yet, in the three years before the bridge collapsed, Minnesota had diverted more than half of its federal bridge funding away from bridge repair and maintenance.

The U.S. Department of Transportation reports that more than 162,500 bridges were deficient or functionally obsolete at the end of 2008. More than 72,500 were structurally deficient, meaning they have been restricted to light vehicles, need immediate rehabilitation to remain open, or are closed. Nearly 90,000 bridges were declared functionally obsolete, meaning that their deck geometry, load capacity, clearance, or approach roadway alignment no longer meet the criteria for their roadway systems.

While the bridge disrepair problem is serious even in the federally supported national highway system, the problem is extremely severe in cities. As recently as 2009, one-third of urban bridges were deficient—more than fifty thousand in total.

According to AASHTO, fixing the nation's bridges will require an investment of roughly $850 billion over the next fifty years, amounting to an annual investment of $17 billion. With President Clinton's phrase "bridge to the twenty-first century" still ringing in our ears, it is ironic that the nation's actual bridges are deteriorating so badly. Bridges bring people together; they facilitate commerce; they make it easier and more efficient for us to travel—and they must guarantee that that travel is safe. As we construct the bridge to the twenty-first century, we must also ensure that we care for and maintain the bridges of the nineteenth and twentieth.

THE PARKS

Almost a century ago, the National Park Service Organic Act established a clear mission for the National Park Service: "to conserve the scenery and the natural and historic objects and the wildlife therein, and to provide for the enjoyment of the same in such manner and by such means as will leave them unimpaired for the enjoyment of future generations." This is a noble mission. As a society, however, we are failing to make the investments required to honor that trust.

The twentieth century was a time of economic development—and that led to the plowing of the nation's forest cover, which declined by 30 percent from its original expanse.[10] From 2000 to 2005, forest cover in the United States has declined by about 6 percent, according to a report titled *Quantification of Global Gross Forest Cover Loss*.[11] The United States lost 120,000 km of forest cover in that time period. Could Teddy Roosevelt, John Muir, or the other conservationist founders of the National Park System ever have anticipated the overwhelming destruction of natural habitat that would occur in the century ahead? These pioneers bequeathed to us a truly invaluable resource, complemented by the nation's state and local parks. But as a society we have failed to honor and respect their foresight, failing to invest sufficient resources to maintain, let alone properly expand, the parks.

As a result, the National Park Conservation Association estimates that the National Park Service, which operates and maintains fifty-eight national parks, has an investment backlog of $10.8 billion for deferred maintenance and construction—of which $3.7 billion is for critical deferred maintenance and about $2 billion is for land acquisition—and a park operations shortfall of $500 million to $600 million. Among the resulting problems:

- Parks fail to monitor their wildlife. Indeed, most of the parks in our system have never inventoried their wildlife or plant life. This can result in loss of entire animal populations— since, as the Commission on Research and Resource Management Policy in the National Park System declared in 1989, "we cannot protect what we do not understand." Researchers have documented the loss of at least twenty-nine mammal populations in western North American national parks.
- The parks system relies on an old and declining physical plant, including: a network of old and leaky pipes, which waste water or fail altogether; park roads that suffer from gaping potholes; playgrounds that are closed or substandard; and other physical amenities that are antiquated and in need of repair or replacement.
- Many national historical artifacts under the Park Service's jurisdiction are in danger of being lost to posterity. Only 40 percent of parks adequately protect and preserve their collections, according to the National Parks and Conservation Association. Until recently, for example, the collections at Gettysburg National Military Park were stored without adequate humidity and temperature controls and suffered from mildew and rot.

Annual federal appropriations for the National Park Service totaled $3.16 billion in 2010; these were cut by about $140 million in 2011, but in real terms, this figure has fallen by about 15 percent over the last twenty years. Yet park visitation has skyrocketed, rising from 210 million in 1977 to more than 281 million in 2010, more than three decades later.

Underfunding for parks is so severe that, a couple years ago, Congress gave serious consideration to corporate sponsorships of parks. Happily, the public still appreciates the proper distinction between public and commercial, and support for the idea quickly waned.

We need to make the necessary investment in the Park Service—and in the "human capital" the National Parks Conservation Association (NPCA) needs to run the system responsibly. The NPCA has documented significant cuts in ranger staff at national parks across the country—cuts that prevent park staff from adequately managing large crowds, endangering the well-being and long-term viability of the parks.

And the same goes for the nation's great municipal parks. From monumental spaces like New York's Central Park to small single lots, these green spaces offer a public place for recline and reflection amid the city's asphalt, glass, and concrete, and a venue for public gathering. Across America, our once-glittering parks are now deteriorated, improperly maintained, and viewed by the public as unsafe.

In a society as rich as ours, is it smart that we refuse to invest in the parks—federal, state, and local—that bring us together as communities?

GETTING MOVING ON MASS TRANSIT

In a nation whose history has depended so heavily on transit and transportation, it is especially disturbing to see how badly we have failed to invest sufficiently in mass transit over the past century. One thing the statistics do tell us is that the need for mass transit is there. From 1995 to 2005, transit use increased by 25 percent. This increase was more than any other mode of transit, and the number of annual trips—10.3 billion—was the highest number in fifty years. The American Society of Civil Engineers reported that this occurred despite the fact that bus or rail transit is inaccessible to nearly half of American households, and of those with access, only 25 percent report having what they consider a "good option."

In 2008, the Federal Transit Administration assessed the nation's transit infrastructure as adequate, which according to their scoring system is 3 out of 5, or approximately 60 percent. Although most bus and rail vehicle and stations conditions have improved marginally since 1997, between 2004 and 2006, the conditions of tracks and structures declined.

Maintaining the public transit system at current levels, the Federal Transit Administration estimates, will cost $15.8 billion a year. Improving the infrastructure to the targets established by 2026 would require upping annual expenditures to $21.6 billion a year.

However, maintaining or slightly upgrading our public transit is not nearly enough. Unlike in most of the other public works programs mentioned here, our public transit system needs not just repair and restoration but a wholesale reinvention. We need to create a modern mass transit system designed to service livable cities, one that brings community residents closer together, combats the momentum toward sprawl, and guarantees lower-income groups the ability to travel safely and efficiently in metropolitan areas, along with reduced air pollution and what is called "seamless transportation" between different modes of travel.

Due to the concerted antitrust violations of GM and other highway lobbies, many cities abandoned the core urban mass transit systems they had created by the early part of the twentieth century, even ripping up tracks from the streets. Only a handful of eastern cities still maintain subway and light rail systems that provide efficient transport for urban residents, and even these systems have serious deficiencies. The relatively new D.C. subway system, built in 1976, was highly regarded until insufficient maintenance funds led to breakdowns and crashes.

Nonetheless, we have no choice but to start from where we are. Our first priority should be bus service. We need to call for much more frequent bus service to connect poorer urban areas to other parts of the metropolis, so that poor residents are not consigned, apartheid-style, to isolated ghettos requiring two hours of travel each way to areas where jobs are located. Bus travel must be a viable option to the middle class, which will opt out of the system in favor of private transport unless buses are frequent, well maintained, and reliable. And more bus service is needed to connect suburban commuters to train lines, so that they feel able to rely on public transit to take them to work and to downtown civic and social events.

We also need to invest in subways, trolleys, and light rail systems for our cities to ensure that such systems serve all our urban residents, including those in lower-income and minority areas—sections of town that are often left off the transit grid.

Ultimately, these investments must be complemented by a move toward free mass transit. And we must make a renewed commitment to Amtrak and efficient and affordable rail travel between cities. The social cost of moving people between cities by car is simply too high in terms of air pollution, greenhouse warming, and auto accidents, not to mention possible national security evacuation emergencies. Investment in rail should be given clear priority over investments in widening interstates.

These three elements—bus service, subways/light rail, and heavy rail—should be viewed not just as items on a checklist but as part of an integrated, seamless plan to make metropolitan and intercity travel safe, easy, efficient, affordable, and at least as desirable as most auto transport. It should be a central part of how we create livable cities, with reduced sprawl, pollution, and congestion and enhanced equity, mobility, and neighborliness.

The cost will be high, but as with the other areas discussed here, the cost of not acting would be much higher. A recent report released by the Center for Neighborhood Technology, Smart Growth America, and U.S. PIRG found that spending on renewable, energy-efficient public transit produced, at minimum, 2.5 times as many jobs as highway spending, with its traditional fossil fuel jobs. In the midst of an economic downturn, results like that make it too expensive *not* to invest in public transit.

THE PUBLIC WORKS AGENDA:
LET'S PUT AMERICA BACK TOGETHER

The public works agenda is a livability agenda. It will make our schools better, our drinking water safer, our roads less congested, and our communities stronger and more closely knit.

The public works agenda is also an environmental agenda. It will clean up and prevent new land and water pollution; cut down on air pollution and greenhouse gas emissions; deter sprawl and its encroachment on farmland, forests, and green space; and offer the government an opportunity to spur innovation by making smart, forward-looking procurement decisions in building and vehicle purchases.

The public works agenda is a pro-consumer agenda. It will lead to cleaner drinking water, less wear and tear on cars, and better schools.

And, finally, the public works agenda is a pro-worker, pro-economic development agenda. Its slate of public investment will help to improve the economy and make it stronger for decades to come. It will create productive and well-paying jobs in the United States, not subject to NAFTA-style race-to-the-bottom pressures to cut wages and benefits.

The conservative estimates of the cost of public works discussed here—almost all coming from cautious government reports from agencies like the GAO, which are not known for exaggeration—easily merit a federal public works investment, beyond current expenditures, of $100 billion annually.

In our current political atmosphere, such a figure might seem outrageous. But in fact it's quite modest. Rather than investing the Social Security trust fund in the stock market, those funds could be invested in government public works bonds. Like private or other government bonds, public works bonds will constitute a real IOU, with an assurance of repayment to the trust fund. However, unlike investment in the stock market, an investment in public works bonds would actually work to expand the economy—creating the social wealth to fund Social Security.

It is true that, with the exception of highways, the public works agenda does not have powerful special interests to lobby on its behalf. Its potential supporters range from local construction companies and labor unions to chambers of commerce, city halls, and the people themselves, but these have yet to be pulled together in an organized fashion to fight for change. And yet investing in our nation's physical plant has inherent broad appeal; We the People can, and should, rally around the cause. Ending the Afghan and Iraq wars, putting a stop to corporate welfare, and closing corporate tax loopholes will provide more than enough public savings to rebuild our country's crumbling public works.

It's time to put America back together.

11

Reduce Our Bloated Military Budget

As I write this, I'm holding in my hand a special pen sent to me more than a decade ago by a group with a unique name: Business Leaders for Sensible Priorities. This "Priorities" pen has a pull-out shade with a graph portraying federal spending on selected programs during the 2000 budget period. The Pentagon budget came in at $291 billion, children's health at $36 billion, housing at $29 billion, education at $35 billion, EPA at $7 billion, and Head Start at $5 billion. Ten years after the fall of the Soviet Union, that is where your budget dollars—the mythical peace dividend—were going.

Compare this 2000 budget with our budget priorities today, and the results are jarring. The U.S. budget for 2012 allocates just under $806 billion to the military budget, including the wars in Iraq, Afghanistan, Pakistan, and elsewhere. This sum does not include the spending of tens of billions of dollars for the vast, supersecret National Security Agency or the Central Intelligence Agency, which has its own military arm. It doesn't include our veterans' disability payments, which will roll out for many years to come. The overall military budget in the Pentagon, Department of Energy, and related programs in other federal agencies now amounts to a staggering 56 percent of all federal discretionary spending (which excludes Medicare and Medicaid).[1]

All this military spending—and yet we have no major enemy in the world.

Justifying this massive expenditure, at the expense of major public works to repair and upgrade our infrastructure, means desperately seeking enemies, then exaggerating and overreacting to them so as to expand our military reach overseas. September 11, 2011, provided the perfect storm for this historically tragic overreaction, which is now recognized by more and more clear-eyed observers as an expansion of the American Empire.

As history teaches us, all empires eventually devour themselves.

After World War II, no one knew better than President Dwight Eisenhower about the multiple dangers that our country can inflict on itself from an out-of-control military, manipulated shamelessly by its corporate contractors. Speaking before the American Society of Newspaper Editors on April 16, 1953, on the "Chance for Peace," President Eisenhower depicted this military-civilian tradeoff more openly than any president has done since. Even as the United States and the Soviet Union were busily arming themselves to their nuclear teeth, and Senator Joe McCarthy was whipping up a frenzy of anti-Soviet fear and hysteria, Eisenhower asserted that:

> Every gun that is made, every warship launched, every rocket fired signifies, in the final sense, a theft from those who hunger and are not fed, those who are cold and are not clothed. This world in arms is not spending money alone. It is spending the sweat of its laborers, the genius of its scientists, and the hopes of its children. The cost of one modern heavy bomber is this: a modern brick school in more than 30 cities. . . . It is two fine, fully equipped hospitals. It is some 50 miles of concrete highway. We pay for a single fighter with a half million bushels of wheat.

We pay for a single destroyer with new homes that could have housed more than 8,000 people. This, I repeat, is the best way of life to be found on the road the world has been taking. This is not a way of life at all, in any true sense. Under the cloud of threatening war, it is humanity hanging from a cross of iron.

The country heard the five-star general's words—and promptly forgot them. The McCarthy frenzy kept building; the Pentagon kept buying bombers, destroyers, and rockets. As America's consumer production lines were turning out junk cars and shoddy toasters, the nation's best scientists and engineers were working on weapons of mass destruction. The nation's military expansion was so all-encompassing that Eisenhower literally had to use the national defense argument to get the Interstate Highway System approved by Congress.

Meanwhile, auto companies overseas were starting to notice the potential market opening up on our shores. Unburdened by the diversion of civilian technical talent into weapons programs, they were able to pour their resources into making new and better cars—an investment that would pay off in the decades to come as Japanese, German, and other cars came to dominate the U.S. auto market.

The U.S. military budget flourished as the nation militarized its foreign policy, planting bases in more and more countries around the globe. Not surprisingly, the economic momentum behind larger military budgets turned the Pentagon into the nation's largest jobs program. The weapons manufacturers started a routine that continues to this day, providing members of Congress with jobs for their constituents through prime and subprime contracts in each of 435 congressional districts. With their ample campaign contributions, these corporations gave rise to an unspoken maxim on Capitol Hill: "Money talks, jobs decide."

President Eisenhower revisited his concern in his celebrated farewell address to the country on January 17, 1961. His warning was resoundingly prescient:

> This conjunction of an immense military establishment and a large arms industry is new in the American experience. The total influence—economic, political, even spiritual—is felt in every city, every State house, every office of the Federal government. . . . Our toil, resources and livelihood are all involved; so is the very structure of our society.
>
> In the councils of government, we must guard against the acquisition of unwarranted influence, whether sought or unsought, by the military-industrial complex. The potential for the disastrous rise of misplaced power exists and will persist.
>
> We must never let the weight of this combination endanger our liberties or democratic processes. We should take nothing for granted. Only an alert and knowledgeable citizenry can compel the proper meshing of the huge industrial and military machinery of defense with our peaceful methods and goals, so that security and liberty may prosper together.

Compare these words from an experienced war general with sentiments George Washington expressed in *his* farewell speech. Be wary, he advised, of "those overgrown military establishments, which, under any form of government, are inauspicious to liberty, and which are to be regarded as particularly hostile to republican liberty." It's important to note that there was no "overgrown military establishment" in the young United States. And yet Washington, another of the nation's greatest generals, could see how militarism in Europe was undermining its people.

Though Eisenhower did not make the point explicitly, he was

reacting to his interaction with militarists, inside and outside of government, during his presidency. As Eugene Jarecki writes in his book *The American Way of War: Guided Missiles, Misguided Men, and a Republic in Peril,* the Democrats accused Ike of being soft on the Soviets and falling behind in the arms race: "These accusations took shape in two successive lines of negative propaganda: the 'bomber gap,' which plagued the president's first term, and the 'missile gap,' which plagued his second."[2] The president knew these charges were outrageously false, politically motivated (John F. Kennedy used the "missile gap" as a major theme of his 1960 presidential campaign), and was corporately backed. Kennedy himself admitted in 1962 to his secretary of defense, Robert McNamara, that he was "one of those who put that myth around."

Once in the White House, Kennedy, like all presidents, was overcome by the sheer global destructive power that the omnipresent black box placed in his hands. Never in human history could two men—one in the United States and the other in the U.S.S.R.—give orders that could literally destroy the planet. This awe of the sheer lethality and insanity of nuclear war probably explained a lot of the mutual restraint between the two superpowers, notwithstanding their belligerent language and accusations toward each other.

Our presidents have generally been reluctant to convey the extent of our destructive power to the American people—a hesitation that doubtlessly reflects both an aversion to being attacked in the political arena for some perceived weapons gap and a fear that the public might finally rise up and decide that enough is enough. Industrial engineering professor at Columbia University, Seymour Melman, used to calculate the total TNT equivalence of the massive atomic weaponry—by air, sea. and land—that the United States possessed. Before he passed away in 2005, he estimated that if the atomic weapons were all fired over the world, such massive throw-weight would destroy the planet many times over and make the rubble bounce. One Trident nuclear submarine could destroy 200 cities around the world with its multiple warheads before reloading. Keeping Americans in the dark about the potential scale of nuclear annihilation is in the interest of the military-industrial complex, which recognizes no limits to its demands for ever more and newer weapons of mass destruction. Defense Secretary James Schlesinger, walking out of his office with guests from the Massachusetts Institute of Technology, was heard to say that it was fortunate that the American people did not know the full destructive capability of the nation's weapons. One of MIT's scientists thought Schlesinger's comment spoke volumes about how autonomous the complex is from effective democratic controls.

Eisenhower believed in the deterrent effect of the threat of mutually assured destruction (MAD), which in his view had the economic benefit of reducing the need for large standing armies of conventional forces. His son John emphasized how strongly Ike felt about the tradeoffs between an ever-larger military budget and food and shelter for the hungry and homeless. "He was fighting with the Pentagon all the time for asking for too much and with Congress for giving in to them," the younger Eisenhower recalled.[3] Indeed, Ike's granddaughter, Susan Eisenhower, remembered that the original draft of his farewell address cast a wider net, warning the American people about the "military-industrial-congressional complex." The "congressional" part was dropped, she told Jarecki, because Ike prided himself on the strength of his relations with a Congress of the opposing party. Nonetheless, Eisenhower was long aware of the triad known as "the iron triangle" by Washington insiders. His decision to exempt Congress from blame deprived the American people of his insight into the power matrix within our government—and of the one segment we can actually influence from back home: our elected representatives.

The effects of this military-industrial-congressional complex go beyond the nonstop torrent of multibillion-dollar defense contracts. They underlie the mind-set that sociologist C. Wright Mills called "military metaphysics," in which our government tends to view situations abroad as military challenges instead of preventive, diplomatic, and assistance missions. In his book *The New American Militarism: How Americans Are Seduced by War,* retired career Army Colonel and professor Andrew Bacevich put it bluntly: "Americans in our own time have fallen prey to militarism, manifesting itself in a romanticized view of soldiers, a tendency to see military power as the truest measure of national greatness, and outsized expectations regarding the efficacy of force. To a degree without precedent in United States history, Americans have come to define the nation's strength and well-being in terms of military preparedness, military action, and the fostering of (or nostalgia for) military ideals."[4]

The modern American mind-set has given rise to a new kind of empire: an empire not of conquered territory, but of control, immediate intervention at will, and occasional, indefinite land occupations. Such conditions can only be maintained when their propagandized presentations enjoy popular consent—or, at the very least, the absence of dissent. One reason our imperial era has not suffered more widespread criticism is that young Americans are no longer subject to the draft. When millions of young people are no longer required to enter the armed services, over time they become isolated from the military's effects on the world at large—and come to see it as a glamorous alternative to more usual employment. When millions had to go through boot camp and see the army, navy, air force, and marines from the inside, the American people as a whole were more realistic about the downsides of the military. Under pressure from women's advocates, the Pentagon has issued data that one-third of females in the armed services have reported being sexually harassed.[5] Our soldiers are publicly known to have engaged in a disturbing number of brutalities in Iraq and Afghanistan, involving both personal outbursts and nighttime raids against homes. But the embedded news media rarely witness these incidents; indeed, the number of journalists reporting on these wars is at an all-time low.

Our adversaries in Iraq, Afghanistan, and Pakistan have no air force, no navy, no artillery, no tanks or armored personnel carriers, no elaborate logistics, no battlefield communications, and no nighttime vision. They have little training, and their principal weapons are roadside rifles, improvised exploding devices (IEDs) and suicide belts. With a U.S. estimate of some 25,000 to 30,000 Taliban fighters in sandals holding at bay the world's most powerful military force—one that has deployed more than 130,000 soldiers plus an equal number of contractors in the field—it is hard to convince people that U.S. soldiers are there to fight for *our* freedom and safety here. But between the fear mongering of government propagandists and the incessant advertisements by Lockheed Martin, Boeing, and other contractors, too many Americans have felt that it's impossible to be patriotic unless they support these wars.

We need to organize a new opposition to this ruinous runaway militarism. There are many among us who count ourselves as peace advocates and many just plain folks who agree with Eisenhower's warnings about the military, who are wary of runaway budget waste, and who see that the wars we have started are draining our nation in countless ways. There is a general feeling of "Come Home, America": come home and start tending to our problems—to our rampant unemployment, our aging public facilities, our declining standard of living, our epidemic of outsourcing, our cowardly politicians, our huge gap between the rich and the rest of us. No fundamental reordering of our priorities can happen until these Americans finally make themselves heard.

We need to reduce the defense budget and to change the way we use our military around the world, so that its only real role is the authentic defense of our people and our shores. But none of that will happen until we get the attention of the electorate. In all the exposés of waste and corruption in military contracting by the Pentagon, none is remembered more by people than the payment of $120.40 for a stainless-steel cup dispenser (retail: $25) and $1,868 for a toilet seat cover. The billions upon billions of contractor looting that has been exposed by Pentagon audits, investigations by the GAO, and the best media reporting has failed to impress themselves onto our collective memory as powerfully as one $436 claw hammer. To this day, Pentagon procurement officials agree that these anecdotes were the worst humiliation they have felt. There is a lesson here: We the People are most powerfully moved when stories are told through everyday incidents—even stories—we can recognize from our own lives.

Inevitably, the military responds to any potential budget cuts by circling the wagons. President Obama had barely signed the deficit reduction debt-limit-raising bill than his new secretary of defense, Leon Panetta—a former budget director under Clinton, now fresh from his covert assassination warfare at the CIA—threw down the gauntlet. Confronting the unlikely possibility of $600 billion in reductions over ten years if a bipartisan congressional panel could not reach an agreement on $1.2 trillion in budget cuts, Panetta launched a preemptive strike, calling it "unacceptable" and claiming "it would endanger our national defense." Later at his first news conference, defying his own president's position, Panetta released a letter to department personnel declaring his opposition. "I promised in my first message as Secretary that I will fight for you," he wrote. "That means I will fight for you and your families as we face these budget challenges." And so the WMD manufacturers joined their suppliers, consulting firms, and think tanks in jeremiads about job losses, while their dutiful allies in the House and Senate Armed Services Committees took their customary stand against any cuts, having consistently supported some of the most expensive, ill-conceived, strategically obsolete weapons systems in history. And their complaints received top news coverage—sandwiched in between large ads by the same corporate contractors Eisenhower warned us about in 1960.

Let's take a closer look at what Panetta and his corporate allies are fighting to preserve.

The Department of Defense budget is un-auditable and has been for years, according to the GAO. An un-auditable budget is, by definition, a budget no one can control for waste, redundancy, corruption, cost overruns, complex billing frauds, or poor quality control. This is something secretaries of defense don't like to talk about, because it reflects their inability to run the organization, so mum's the word—except at the GAO, the investigative arm of Congress.

When the DOD budget is in such a mess that it cannot provide the data for a thorough annual audit, anything can happen—such as the air force buying billions of dollars' worth of spare parts when it has identical parts sitting *in its own warehouses.*

The GAO released a report in July 2011 illustrating how the Pentagon handles surplus equipment. Between 2002 and 2005, for example, the department got rid of $33 billion in excess equipment; $4 billion worth was in new or excellent condition. These products were given away, sold for pennies on the dollar, or destroyed. According to the Pentagon citizen watchdog group Taxpayers for Common Sense (TCS): "The DOD's problems with excess property are systemic and extensive. In 2002, the DOD continued to sell top-grade chemical protective suits for $3 on the internet while military units were waiting to procure exactly the same suit for $200."[6]

Un-auditability means that one hand of the department doesn't know what the other hand is doing—in spite of wall-to-wall computerization. The well-regarded GAO looks for ways to get its message of prudence and frugality home. So it legally spending by the Pentagon as easy as fishing off the grand banks of Newfoundland in the nineteenth century.

Here are a few of the items on Korb's list of potential savings:

1. Cancel the V-22 Osprey program and save $9.15 billion through 2015. The V-22 Osprey helicopter has already killed more than thirty Marines due to its "technical problems." Cost overruns are astronomical. Each V-22 now costs more than $100 million each but lacks the payload of comparable helicopter systems such as the MH-60S or the CH-53K aircraft. The GAO found that the V-22's mission capability fell significantly below other helicopter models in Iraq that cost one-fifth of the V-22's price tag.

2. Reduce the 150,000 active-duty troops in Europe and Asia by one-third and save $42.5 billion through 2015. Korb is being too restrained here. Why do we have any soldiers in Western Europe, Japan, and Korea—firm allies and prosperous nations that are fully capable of defending themselves against nonexistent enemies post–Soviet Union? The exception is North Korea, whose leadership talks tough, but is unlikely to engage in a suicide mission by crossing the southern border, given the formidable, supermodern South Korean military capability and the aerial cover of the United States.

3. Limit the procurement of the Virginia-class submarine and the DDG-51 destroyer to one per year and save $20.04 billion through 2015. Korb supports this position by noting that "the U.S. Navy currently possesses more firepower than the next 20 largest navies combined—many of which are U.S. allies."

4. Cut back on the ballooning navy and marine F-35 Joint Strike Fighter variants and save $16.43 billion through 2015. These two branches of service have other fighter jets that can do the job. The air force would get to keep its "entire buy" and grapple with the lifetime operational costs of the F-35,

purchased numerous items anonymously from the DOD, including tents, boots, and medical supplies, for a total of $3,000. The value of the items they purchased cost the taxpayers about $80,000. The GAO report identified material reported lost, damaged, or stolen, including sensitive military items, totaling hundreds of millions of dollars. TCS concluded that "this isn't just a matter of bad bookkeeping, lax management or weak inventory controls. These numbers measure major weaknesses in critical combat support machinery. . . . Once dropped into the multibillion dollar black box of the excess property system, good equipment can mix with bad, or disappear altogether."

Two things leap out about this one report of Pentagon expenditure, exposed by a GAO that produces reams of reports about waste across the spectrum of the military budget. One is that no matter how many investigations the GAO does, the results fall on deaf ears among both the Pentagon leaders and their patron—Congress. The other is that almost no one ever gets fired or otherwise punished for such irresponsibility or dereliction of duty. Every now and then the Pentagon faces budgetary reform commissions, which dutifully issue lists of recommendations. In August 2011, for example, the Commission on Wartime Contracting in Iraq and Afghanistan reported that the U.S. government has wasted or misspent $34 billion contracting for services in those two countries. At least that's as much as they could trace in a search through chaotic spending—not including billions in disappeared hundred-dollar bills. The Pentagon periodically announces its own systemic changes, like the much-heralded "acquisition reform" program under the Clinton administration. Before that effort dissolved into the Pentagon's archives, the DOD's acquisition experts viewed "acquisition reform" as delegating even more of their authority to private contracting corporations—right down to contracting out "live wire" testing standards for weaponry compliance to the same companies that were selling the weapons.

For anyone who doubts such reports of out-of-control spending, the documentary *Iraq for Sale: The War Profiteers* should prove an eye-opener. One memorable scene reveals the outrageous costs KBR charged for laundry services as told through an interview with former KBR/Halliburton truck driver Shane Ratliff: "Halliburton charged the government one hundred dollars for every bag of clothes they washed. Whenever we got our laundry back, it felt worse than when we turned it in; everything was still grimy. I stopped taking my laundry into KBR and instead I was washing it in the sink."[7] Another interview in the film features a complaint about the Halliburton/KBR charging $45 for a case of soda.[8] Meanwhile, Pentagon officials trade chairs with corporate officials in the defense business in the Washington merry-go-round, a game that's now so entrenched that it's taken for granted. Neither Congress nor the mass media shows any outrage over these outrageous conflicts of interest. Leon Panetta's predecessor as defense secretary, Robert Gates—a seasoned poster man for the military-industrial complex—has decried the orgy of military spending after 9/11: "What little discipline existed in the Defense Department when it came to spending has gone completely out the window." By this point, each piece of military equipment has its own corporate lobbyists on Capitol Hill and its own champions among the senators and representatives. No matter how obsolete, unnecessary, hazardously designed, or redundant (each military service craves its own specially designed vehicles and aircraft), contracts keep getting renewed and overruns reimbursed year after year. After all, it's not their money; it's just the people's money.

TCS has called on Congress to save billions of dollars by canceling the Expeditionary Fighting Vehicle (EFV). The marines haven't stormed a beach in nearly half a century, but the amphibious vehicle apparently satisfies some nostalgic need. As customary with military white elephants, the cost of *each* EFV

has more than doubled—to $24 million. And yet TCS has documented that the prototype of this EFV "still breaks down every eight hours on average and is more than 10 years behind schedule for delivery."[9]

Think of Eisenhower's lament: How many community health clinics could be built in poorer areas of America with the money we'd save by junking just this one vehicle? And that's small potatoes compared to another judicious recommendation by TCS and other solid critics. We could save *$35 billion* by reducing our nuclear weapons arsenal—a move Russia asserts it will match. The wide bipartisan support from current and former military and civilian leaders for the New Strategic Arms Reduction Treaty (New START) with Russia revealed an uplifting political consensus for further mutual reduction of existing missiles, submarines, and bombers. Such reductions would also give rise to major savings by saving on operations and maintenance costs—an underrecognized and huge portion in the Pentagon expense account.

In 2001, former Air Force Chief General Merrill McPeak was quoted by the *Washington Post* saying, "If we can't defend this country for $300 billion a year, we ought to get some new generals." His words made hardly a ripple in the tight world of military budgeting and contracting. Nevertheless, it was an important move: a veteran military figure lending his cause and authority to a growing focus on cutting excessive military expenditures in an age of large government deficits. For more than twenty years, Lawrence J. Korb, former assistant secretary of defense under President Reagan, has been arguing in detail about how to hold down this "gusher" of defense spending, as Secretary Gates characterized it. Korb believes that the Obama administration and Congress "can cut $150 billion in defense spending annually and still keep our military budget at the Reagan administration's peak Cold War levels."[10] Analysts like Korb catch unnecessary

which have doubled since 2002, amounting to $1 trillion and expected to rise to $1.45 trillion over the next fifty years. The Pentagon is pressing allies in Europe and Canada to take more of this technically and monetarily troubled aircraft in order to spread out the frightening, mushrooming cost of these planes. The current estimate for just one F-35 is about $300 million. One is reminded that the super World War II fighter, the legendary P-38, cost $38,000 each—around $600,000 in today's dollars. Astounding!

5. Stop building aircraft carriers. Korb notes that the navy "fields 11 aircraft carriers, while no other country has even one of comparable size and power." He urges a stop to new carrier construction, "which costs $15 billion a pop," and "re-tiring two of our existing carrier battle groups." Even modern aircraft carriers would be sitting ducks to modern missile weaponry; the fact that this threat deters no one in the military from building more carriers only furthers the argument that we have no major enemy in the world. These carriers are the killer whales of the military, sailing the seven seas each day with no predators in sight.

6. Reduce ground forces and civilian DOD personnel and save $39.16 billion through 2015. Korb was a manpower specialist in Ronald Reagan's Department of Defense. He believes that "the United States is unlikely to deploy large land armies in the near future due to the tremendous cost of these wars in both blood and treasure," and argues that we should shift to ad hoc deployment of more efficient special forces.

Korb's ideas offer a glimpse of the vast world of Pentagon spending cuts—which Congress knows are needed but refuses to make. Even areas like what Korb calls "overutilization and double coverage" in the Pentagon's Tricare health care plan don't interest the congressional overseers.

For more information on resources that could be better

saved (and then used in our civilian sector), go to the Center
for American Progress website (www.americanprogress.org) to
view potential reductions in other areas, including the $9 bil-
lion a year boondoggle missile defense program. The Project
on Government Oversight (www.pogo.org) and Taxpayers for
Common Sense (www.taxpayer.net), two meticulous groups,
have jointly released a partial, conservative recommendation on
reducing national security spending by $586.112 billion over ten
years or less. These groups identified $72.54 billion in fat that
could be cut from private contracts with non-DOD national security agency entities, including the Department of Homeland
Security, the State Department, and the U.S. Agency for International Development. In 2011, the White House itself proposed a 15 percent reduction in service contract spending after
media reports revealed some of the waste involved. The POGO
and TCS recommendations demonstrate that reducing the lard
from DOD's service contracts by just 15 percent could save the
country $300 billion over the next ten years. These cuts also
expose the myth that outsourcing or contracting out to large
companies is more efficient and saves the taxpayer money.

Several years ago, I had an extended conversation with
weapons specialists who worked in the Office of the Secretary
of Defense (OSD). They were opposed to the F-22 from the beginning, they told me, in light of the similar role played by the
F-35 fighter. The F-22 was chronically rising in cost and presented risks to pilots, who frequently blacked out from gravity
adjustment while flying it. Lockheed Martin's estimated unit
cost for 648 F-22 planes was $125 million per plane;[11] when
the Pentagon cut its order of F-22s, however, saying it planned
to phase out the program after 187 F-22s were produced, the
unit cost rose to *more than $410 million.*[12] The F-22, which is
small enough to fit on the stage of a large college auditorium,
benefits from organized corporate boosters and susceptible
members of Congress, who have kept this project going year

after wasteful year despite the better judgment of smart public servants in the Pentagon.

The Department of Defense harbors many such honest and frugal analysts, who have opposed many such expensive programs often to little avail. One of these was a southern good ole boy named Ernie Fitzgerald, who fought the C-5A cargo plane in the mid-1960s because of its tendency to lose its wings in flight. Lockheed's executives and their Pentagon allies tried to silence Fitzgerald, but he attracted the attention of Senator William Proxmire, who made his campaign a cause célèbre for the few overt reformers on Capitol Hill. In the 1980s, Pentagon analyst Franklin "Chuck" Spinney testified before Congress that the $1.6 trillion military expansion under President Reagan was underfunded by at least 30 percent. Spinney's 1980 report reached a broad conclusion that still resonates today: "Our strategy of pursuing ever-increasing technical complexity and sophistication has made high-technology solutions and combat readiness mutually exclusive." He did not mention the corollary—that the real beneficiaries of such complexity are not the American people but the weapons manufacturers, which are only too happy to rise to each profitable new challenge.

Shortly before he died in 2006, Harvard economics professor John Kenneth Galbraith noted in his book *The Good Society: The Humane Agenda*: "the American military establishment effectively and independently decides on its own budget, on the extent and the use of the money it receives."[13] He viewed our country as "trapped by military expenditure unrelated to military need."[14] Galbraith zeroed in on the central issue: What national security or other purposes could be served by devoting 55 percent of the federal operational budget to military prowess against no known national enemy? The answer cannot be an assortment of military gangs in various third-world countries. More lives would be saved simply by not having our soldiers patrol the world and provoke the populace into adverse responses that they would not otherwise have engaged. Galbraith described this prescription: "the military and its needs must be recognized as the special case. For all who seek the good society the primary concern must be that the autonomous military power that now exists be brought under effective democratic control. To this end, the strongest political voice and action must be directed."[15]

As Galbraith would have been the first to admit, such a general recommendation is easier said than done. The key is to figure out how to get the process back under democratic control.

The first thing to know is that little can be done without the involvement of determined, knowledgeable people, adequate resources, and a commitment to an ongoing organization or coalition. Such a gathering must start by recognizing that public fear, stirred by manipulative politicians and amplified by the media, leads to the militarization of foreign policy—and that greed leads, or has led, to the corporatization of the military.

Such a group must include not only everyday citizens but retired officials from the military, diplomatic and national security services, taxpayer groups, labor leaders, scientists and technologists, elected and retired politicians, mayors and former mayors, foreign humanitarian assistance leaders, businesspeople for sensible priorities, religious leaders, university professors, veterans of past and present wars, veteran peace advocates, outspoken philanthropists, student leaders, neighborhood organizers, media and documentary filmmakers, and specialists in foreign cultures and history. People in the thousands from these backgrounds have already individually spoken, written, organized, and protested against the ravenous military, year in and year out, with only minimal media coverage. What they haven't done is get together to make their case as a unified whole—and start proving, once again, that a passionate whole is greater than the sum of its parts.

Such a group should then organize into focused groups, or workshops, to bear down on specific aspects of the problem that need correcting. To that effect, there are seven categories of workshops which, together, focus on the different areas. They are envisioned as follows:

Workshop I could concentrate on the array of widely recognized ideas for Pentagon reforms that have been ignored. These include reversing the outsourcing of services, enforcing wider competitive bidding, and stopping the rampant merging of defense contractors, which has led to some major contracts being automatically handed to one monopoly bidder. It could work to stop the revolving door between military and defense contractors (especially when Pentagon officials go to work for the companies formerly under their purview); it could work to transform today's one-sided corporate boilerplate military contracts until they can accurately reflect the costs of holding accountable contractors, who are so often responsible for cost overruns; it could call for the separation of procurement offices from testing offices, to prevent conflicts of interest in the assessment process. It could call for the military to make clear declarations of need, effectiveness, and purpose before issuing new procurement contracts; to enforce the sharing of weapons among the different armed services (instead of them insisting on their own special weapons, such as the Marine Corps' Osprey helicopter and the navy's gigantic white elephant aircraft carriers). And, finally, it could call on Congress to require that the Pentagon supply the GAO with the accounting data to make the deliberately slippery and evasive Pentagon budget auditable before next year's budgetary cycle.

Workshop II could focus on short-term progress by listing the items in the Pentagon's direct and contracting expenditures that could be cut. I have noted the good work being done by nonprofits such as POGO and TCS, which specialize in monitoring the mismanagement of the defense budget and the weapon-by-weapon, service-by-service expenses that can be eliminated or significantly reduced. This initiative has the added advantage of shifting the burden of proof more insistently onto private contractors. This workshop would expose the Pentagon's practice of defending indefensible programs by farming subcontracts out to providers in forty-seven states and four hundred congressional districts—and then justifying the expenditure because of the jobs it created, as Congress did with the B-1B bomber. No defense contract should be justified as a jobs contract; it must stand or fall on its own merits.

Workshop III could study the bigger picture of how the overall security budget should be allocated. In a June 2011 report from the Task Force on a Unified Security Budget for the United States, Lawrence Korb and Miriam Pemberton argued that U.S. security resources should be rebalanced more rationally between offense (military forces, which currently account for 88 percent of overall resources), defense (homeland security, currently 6 percent), and prevention (nonmilitary international engagement, currently 6 percent). The task force called for a modestly rewritten security budget—one that would reduce the offense allocation in FY 2012 to 79 percent and up prevention to 14 percent and defense to 7 percent. In the words of the report: "the goal is to strengthen our capacity to prevent and resolve conflict by non-military means. . . . Our top military and civilian national security leaders have all expressed support for repairing the extreme imbalance in our security spending to strengthen our non-military security tools. Their actions to get it done, however, have mostly lagged behind these fine words."[16] Obviously, narrowing the gap between fine words and real action requires the kind of jolt that could only be generated by exactly the kind of organized public protest we are calling for.

Workshop IV could seek new ways for the United States to become a humanitarian superpower, to help alleviate the conditions of poverty, destitution, and hopelessness that even George W. Bush and his top officials recognized after 9/11 had helped foreign extremists find new recruits for violent action. Our country has many resources available for humanitarian deployment abroad at a fraction of the costs of military deployment. We can provide assistance on a wide scale to address problems from securing clean drinking water—which alone can save millions of lives per year—to providing simple but effective shelter; to offering training in basic nutrition and health care; to teaching food preservation skills to reduce large losses of produced food from rodents, insects, and fungi; to building institutions like agrarian cooperatives and agricultural extension programs. Organizations like Doctors Without Borders and Engineers Without Borders have proven themselves capable of major change. We have the most advanced rescue technologies to deal with natural catastrophes and famine. We could eliminate mass famines with easily deliverable stopgap rations. And we could harness the pent-up idealism of American youth, which has fueled political change in our country for decades.

The Pentagon is capable of real positive action in this area—though the results have not always been well-publicized. Schoolchildren in the early 1940s learned about the army's valiant fight against yellow fever in Central America. In the 1950s, when the Air Force realized it was losing more men on U.S. highways than in the Korean War, it spent several million dollars funding university research on more crashworthy cars—research that helped me write *Unsafe at Any Speed*. During the Vietnam War, the Pentagon's drug development program at Walter Reed and Bethesda produced three out of the four leading antimalarial drugs in the world. So there is a tradition to reconnect with, one in which the U.S. military took unilateral action to advance humankind and change our role in the world from that of an aggressive, drone-driven military power to that of a power for worldwide good. Such action can only advance our national security and help prevent revenge-driven blowback, here and abroad.

Workshop V could apply itself to mobilizing the people to call for reform. Its members could focus on developing new tools, tactics, and strategies, including enlisting dedicated citizens to meet extensively with their senators and representatives in their home districts for change. Special attention could be given to the reformers in Congress—such as the left-right alliance between Representatives Barney Frank and Ron Paul, who together worked on reducing the bloated military budget—as a way to establish a beachhead on Capitol Hill. This workshop would be driven by the conviction that our military budget and strategy can be transformed through insistent enlightenment and relentless civic pressure. Its goal would be to make Congress recapture the constitutional reins, which it has abdicated to the White House in so many ways—from its war declaration power, to its appropriations power, to its all-important power of oversight.

Workshop VI could convene the veterans of past wars, along with those in ongoing wars, drawn from the armed services, the reserves, and National Guard. Again, the precedents are impressive: during the Bush/Cheney era, scores of retired high-ranking military leaders, diplomatic leaders, and seasoned former intelligence agency officials stood tall in opposition when the administration, as Congressman Ron Paul put it, "lied their way into the Iraq war." This workshop should benefit from the fact that frustrated insiders are often the most passionate reformers. Countless veterans have watched these decade-old wars in Afghanistan and Iraq, quagmires from the start, as they've devastated countries in so many human and material ways for no measurable gain. For what have seven thousand of our soldiers lost their lives? For what have more than one hundred thousand been harmed for life? For what have those two forlorn countries endured millions of casualties? Coming back home, the veterans saw the neglect in their own communities—jobs disappearing; the unemployed everywhere; their children in rundown schools; doctor bills piling up; wages slipping. . . . What are we doing blowing up impoverished, tribal-run countries that just want us out of their backyard, when we need all that money and more to rebuild America? A retired senior diplomat recalled that our country demobilized after every war. No longer. There is a permanent state of war now with huge military budgets being contemplated.

Workshop VII could be populated by mayors and other city officials who see the potential of redirecting funds from military expenditures back into their communities. A dozen U.S. mayors recently put out a joint statement calling for an end to the wars in Iraq, Afghanistan, and Pakistan, which they characterized both as tragic misadventures and as a terrible drain on public investment in the United States. Each of these mayors stood and emphasized that military savings should be redirected at once to cover specific municipal needs. One mayor gave this example: if the Pentagon should decide to cancel two superfluous aircraft carriers costing $25 billion, the savings could be applied directly to job-producing public works in cities and towns around the country. Add more and more such savings by canceling vastly overpriced new weapons, which defense experts can prove are merely unnecessary gold plating for the corporate complex. Pretty soon, you're funding the roadmap presented to America by the American Society of Civil Engineers to rebuild our public infrastructure.[17]

This kind of argument can give people in our communities a concrete way to envision the kind of changes that can come of an effort to remake our military budgets—and demonstrate to them that they have an ever-expanding stake in the outcome. It's the kind of campaign that could be backed by local chambers of commerce, trade unions, teachers, health care workers, construction workers, municipal workers, and small businesses. The mayors have said they will work through the Conference of Mayors to create a list of public works needs from municipalities all over the country. Congress has ignored the problem of military overspending for decades—but could our representatives really turn their collective back on a passionate, well-publicized campaign launched by their own constituents?

The workshops would return for the plenary session on securing the resources to fund such elaborate activation of the people. This would be called the philanthropy session, in honor of the two dozen very rich people who eagerly came to this convocation, having contributed the budget for the gathering in the first place. They represented $460 billion in familial assets. Many were elderly, having served in World War II, but they had turned against the Vietnam War in the 1960s. Many were troubled by the prospect of seeing their beloved country slip into the abyss of a de facto dictatorship on these momentous issues—this was not something our democratic republic was formed to allow. These people knew their only course was to provide the funding so people could organize and take back the power that had been surrendered by indifference to Washington.

To imagine such a congregation is to envision its real possibilities. Megabillionaires such as George Soros, who strenuously opposed the invasion of Iraq and has funded many civic action organizations in other countries, can bring these constituents together for such a mission-focused meeting. The immense, latent influence of the retired military, diplomatic, and national security officials who served under both Republican and Democratic presidents would respond to his call. George Soros is not the only potential wealthy galvanizer; there have never been so many billionaires who care for the country and the world, even though they are less than one percent of the population. But that is more than enough, given the supportive public sentiment and its committed citizenry.

In his book *The New American Militarism*, Professor Andrew Bacevich sums up present-day American militarism and its illusions: "If it persists in these expectations, then America will surely share the fate of all those who in ages past have looked to war and military power to fulfill their destiny. We will rob future generations of their rightful inheritance. We will wreak havoc abroad. We will endanger our security at home. We will risk the forfeiture of all that we prize."[18]

Bacevich leaves the last words to James Madison: "Of all the enemies of public liberty," wrote Madison in 1795, "war is perhaps the most to be dreaded, because it comprises and develops the germ of every other. War is the parent of armies. From these proceed debts and taxes. And armies, debts and taxes are the known instruments for bringing the many under the domination of the few. . . . No nation could preserve its freedom in the midst of continual warfare."[19]

Imagine what Madison would say today.

12

Reengage with Civic Life

We live in a golden age of exposés revealing the vast abuses perpetrated against We the People by unaccountable corporate and governmental powers. They emerge in the hundreds every year, in books and articles, magazine features and online investigations, films and TV reports.

This could be their missing chapter.

These muckraking works all perform an important service for our democracy. Yet they all fall short in one way: their final recommendations. After each blistering catalog of evils and injustices, harms and the repressions, what do the authors of such critiques offer as an inspiring path forward? Here is a random sample from my bookshelves:

An exposé of the giant coal companies ends: "We have reinvented our world before. Why can't we do it again?"

A book on how our politics have been captured by powerful economic interests ends with a timeless quotation by Dr. Martin Luther King Jr.: "We are tired. . . . We have no alternative but to protest."[1]

An investigation of the concentrated power that has entrenched millions in permanent poverty ends: "Ultimately, all that is required is the depth of commitment born of the recognition that our nation's future and our own depend on effective action."

An exploration of the nature of the good society beset by greed and corporate power wraps up by declaring: "With true democracy, the good society would succeed, would even have an aspect of inevitability."

Michael Moore's documentary *Sicko*, on the ravages suffered by millions of Americans at the hands of the corporate profit-driven health care industry, ends with the filmmaker himself carrying his dirty laundry up the steps of the U.S. Capitol.

These social critics certainly showcased a host of proposals and models that could be adopted by a humane, just society. But their final words fell short—because there was no civic or political infrastructure at the ready, no viable machine they could use to bring about action, to help replace the bad with the good.

Our nation has millions of skilled bikers and joggers, bird-watchers and bowlers, stamp and coin collectors, dancers and musicians, gardeners, card and chess players—and more power to them. But we are poor in existing action groups. We have no masses of skilled citizens who know how to practice the democratic arts, to use the power of numbers to bring about change.

We need more Congress watchers, more democracy builders, more sentinels over the industries or government agencies that affect us so seriously. We need to close our gigantic democracy gap, a people-power vacuum so noticeable that it serves as an open invitation for commercial and bureaucratic rascals. The corporations know that the few valiant civic groups and individually active citizens are so short in staff, resources, and media platforms that no significant corporate body is in danger of being stopped by their small efforts. Indeed, most of the larger corporations and government agencies—federal, state, and local—have no dedicated outside monitors at all.

Is the American revolutionary saying "Eternal vigilance is the price for liberty"?

We've forgotten how to pay that price.

Take any residential street in America—say one with a

hundred or so homes. Chances are that only half its inhabitants vote with regularity; maybe one or two make the local government a regular civic hobby. The rest take what is dealt them, grumble, adjust, and continue with their private lives. Once in a while, when an issue gets emotionally hot, local residents may become temporarily active—collecting protest petitions, attending strategy sessions, showing up at city council meetings, getting media to pay attention.

(This is what happened in my hometown when the hundred-year-old mismanaged local hospital went bankrupt, leaving an area of more than thirty thousand people without a facility. Twelve thousand people quickly signed a petition aimed at maintaining an emergency health care center at the same location. Hundreds buttonholed their neighbors and selectmen. Others wrote opinion pieces in the local newspaper. They won. It helped that they had a free community lawyer, Charlene LaVoie, to advise and guide them, to jump-start various initiatives reflecting the legitimate self-interest of the local populace. Her office was a steady base for what was often a rocky struggle. Very few communities have this kind of asset. In fact, very few ever manage to accomplish anything as concrete as restoring a threatened health facility.)

Out of those one hundred homes, perhaps twenty would say they'd like to become engaged but just don't know how to go about it. In this age of the internet, that feels more and more like a thin excuse, but such protests can still be sincere. Civic engagement for the vast majority of Americans is terra incognita. They've never been there. So they give their excuses: "I don't know what to do." "I don't have the time." "I don't want to risk the backlash." "Would it really make a difference anyhow? The Big Boys will get whatever they want."

There you have it: the conceptual basis for the Great American Society of Apathy. But the real reason for apathy is usually a feeling of powerlessness. The first step to changing this is getting people in small groups around the country to spend time in a civic space, just talking with one another. Every civic movement starts with one-on-one conversations, or with an experienced citizen activist offering guidance and support. Such conversations always start with what the people think is wrong and should be changed in the community. Although they may begin in living rooms or around conference tables, they lead to action at state and federal levels.

Such meetings should end with participants taking home some information about other instances where people just like them have righted civic wrongs—stories that can be found in books, newspaper and magazine articles, and online. The popular struggles in American history are what made America what it is—what gave rise to the many laws on our books that protect workers, consumers, the environment, and the elderly. We rely on these laws daily: on Social Security, Medicare, Medicaid, unemployment compensation, motor vehicle safety laws, consumer product protections, drug and drinking safety standards, and air pollution controls, but also on the right of worker collective bargaining laws, civil rights laws, and worker safety regulations in mines, factories, and foundries. We can thank popular uprisings for forty-hour workweeks, fair labor standards, the secret ballot, progressive taxation, abolition of child labor, creation of credit unions, and mutual savings banks. Going back further, we have citizen protesters to thank for the abolishment of slavery, for giving women the right to vote, for the creation of cooperatives and public schools. Each of these struggles entailed controversy and conflict. But the results came about not because of the ninety-eight out of a hundred people who stayed on the sidelines, but because of the two brave outliers who showed up, stood tall, and drew on the sentiment of many of their fellow citizens in fighting for change.

This kind of example is necessary to motivate people today. If people back then could change the world through activism—without electricity, telephones, radio/TV, motor vehicles—how can we *fail* to change it when we have accessible state-of-the-art communications, the internet, and other modern facilities on our side?

The follow-up meeting could be reflective. Motivation can come not just from historic examples of ordinary people doing extraordinary things but also from our concern with posterity—with the welfare of our descendants. This, beyond a doubt, is what drives many active environmentalists. Talking with your fellow citizens about your role in society—and measuring your contribution in terms of actual deeds—can be a sound basis for the kind of camaraderie it will take to launch a successful reform movement.

Sometimes it helps to ruminate a bit on the wisdom of the ancients. An ancient Buddhist proverb says, "You cannot travel the path until you have become the path." More recently, philosopher Theodore Roethke advised: "We learn by going where we have to go." Thoughts like these tend to help people view their civic endeavors in a more transcendent light. It was Supreme Court Justice Felix Frankfurter who used to refer to citizenship as the "highest office in the land." Certainly the stories of citizen-driven change that punctuate our history suggest that ordinary citizens deserve an extraordinary level of admiration for their role in fighting for liberty and justice.

As you get more informed and motivated about civic engagement, start thinking about the kinds of skills that can lead to success. Like any other human endeavor, the more skilled one is, the more likely one is to pursue it. There are lots of resources offering guidance for aspiring citizen activists: good books, pamphlets, tip sheets, how-to guides, and videos, many of them available online. Want practical, useful, good advice on how to pull off a successful press conference? Form a working coalition? Start a petition for a candidate or a ballot proposal? Access city hall and other agency records? Research and publicize the voting records of lawmakers? Want to learn how to use small claims court? Run a meeting? Locate talent? Build a neighborhood or community group? Use government documents? Research corporations? Use the freedom of information laws? How to do tactical research? To lobby? To petition regulatory agencies? To fund-raise? You can learn all these, and just about any other techniques you need to advance your cause, with the click of a mouse or at your local bookstore or library. In fact, there are so many such guides that it's astonishing that no entrepreneur has tried starting a chain of storefront civic schools where people can go to learn how to fight for their legitimate interests and improve their community and country. Pick an interest or hobby—cooking, dancing, sewing, public speaking, music, yoga—and there are plenty of classes available online or in person. Want to learn how to buy and flip real estate? There are expensive weekend events with materials piled high to take back home with you. But no such storefront operations exist for activism—even though there are zillions of empty and cheap storefronts on Main Street, USA.

The trouble is we live in a culture where self-improvement and instant gratification are king—and civic work requires selflessness and patience. This is the key challenge in developing one's civic personality, in developing a thirst for righting a wrong or achieving justice to the point where your goals become the principled equivalent of self-improvement. Candy Lightner, the founder of Mothers Against Drunk Driving, was so profoundly self-motivated by the loss of her own daughter that her passion for the cause led her to campaign, successfully, for tougher anti–drunk driving measures all over the country. There are many stories of passive people, absorbed with their own daily lives, who are transformed after encountering a horrific tragedy and respond by confronting the situation head-on. Lois Gibbs, a mother, was living with her children near Niagara Falls when the news of contamination of the nearby Love Canal hit the headlines. After she saw symptoms of the toxic environment in her children and her neighbors' children, she wrote extensively on the subject, and her successful struggles with the corporate polluters led her to start the nation's most extensive grassroots coalition of local antipollution activists.[2]

From time to time, well-attended training assemblies have gathered to focus on a particularly hazardous intrusion to the community. In 1973 and 1974, we convened in Washington, D.C., with one thousand people from all areas of the country where nuclear power plants were operating or being planned. For several days, through workshops and lectures, we talked about how to stop or close these plants. The attendees listened, learned, and networked for their return home. They made direct contacts with the scientists, engineers, lawyers, and doctors who could present their distinct viewpoint on the entire nuclear fuel cycle. As a result, these "trainees" became the leaders of the opposition to nuclear power and the promoters of alternative energy and energy conservation. The knowledgeable defiance at the grassroots level, together with the fast-rising costs of nuclear plants, meant that not one nuclear plant has been built since those years.

In the fall of 2011, the Occupy Wall Street movement, standing for the "99 percent," spread into scores of communities to put the inequities of the big business–dominated political economy on the media front burner. Still a work in experimental progress, Occupy is networking, training, and motivating more people every day with demonstrations, workshops, collaborations, and democratic assemblies; eventually, its outside supporters hope, it will have a sound agenda for long overdue changes in our beleaguered country.

We need more grassroots efforts to train aspiring activists around the country. Any issue involving mass injustice, abuse, invasion of constitutional rights to privacy, or deprivation can be addressed if private citizens transform themselves into public citizens and demand it. People who have gone through activist training exercises find they are genuinely fun, energizing, and empowering. Most people who are powerless don't feel good about being powerless; they just accept it. Over time, though, feelings of powerlessness can gnaw away at one's sense of self-worth—even for those who are leading the so-called good life. So when they start meeting other powerless people like themselves who want to learn how to take a hand in shaping their own futures—something wonderful is created: a small community with a serious purpose. As the great midcentury activist Arthur Ernest Morgan wrote in his book *The Small Community: Foundation of Democratic Life,* small communities are often not only the best places to get big changes started, but they can also be nimble enough to start implementing these changes.

In 2010, the organizer and musician Si Kahn wrote a political memoir called *Creative Community Organizing: A Guide for Rabble-Rousers, Activists, and Quiet Lovers of Justice.* In the book Kahn recalls some of the great social justice campaigns in recent American history in which he played a part, from the civil rights movement, to the Harlan County coal miner's strike, to the fight against privatized prisons. From his experiences, he has distilled twenty principles for successful community organizing. Kahn's principles are much more down-to-earth and galvanizing than the dry civics textbooks that have bored millions of students over the years. His pithy pointers are full of insights about what motivates people to become stakeholders for justice—and full of advice on how to get a movement going while anticipating the kinds of obstacles that often crop up along the way:

1. Most people are motivated primarily by self-interest. As a creative community organizer, you are always trying to figure out people's common self-interest, the glue that binds political organizations and movements.

2. Institutions and people that hold power over others are rarely as united as they first appear. If you can't get a person or institution to support you, you want to do everything in your power to convince them that it's in their best self-interest to stay out of the fight.

3. Start the process of strategy development by imagining that instant just before victory. Then, working backward, do your best to figure out the steps that will lead to that moment.

4. It is generally useful, as a part of any creative community organizing campaign, to advocate for a positive as well as to oppose a negative.

5. The more complicated a strategy or tactic, the harder it is to carry out, and the less likely that it will be successful. You can ask a few people to do a lot of things, particularly if they're committed activists. If you want hundreds or thousands of people to participate in a campaign, you need to ask the great majority of them to do one thing, and only one.

6. You need to believe that human beings, no matter how much they may hate each other, can somehow find some common connection. To do that, leave your stereotypes at the door.

7. In real life and in actual campaigns for justice, the people are always partly united, partly divided. It's up to you to reinforce unity and to compensate for the divisions among the people with whom you work.

8. Don't ever let anyone tell you that demonstrations were only effective in the 1960s—that in the twenty-first century, we need to find other, less confrontational ways to make our voices heard.

9. Be absolutely certain that the people you work with truly understand the risks they're taking, the things that could go wrong, the losses they might suffer, before they make the decision to act, individually or together.

10. One of the greatest skills an organizer can have is the ability to frame and ask questions in ways that make people not only want to answer them, but also to think deeply, and in unexpected ways, about what the answers might be.

11. Laughter really is therapeutic, and hope does heal. Be cheerful in the face of adversity, and help others feel that way.

12. The more sure you are of yourself, of your experiences in other communities and campaigns, the more you have to struggle to avoid the arrogance of thinking you know what's right for other people.

13. When an institution that has a responsibility to everyday people fails to do its job, one option is to build another organization to challenge the first one and force it to do the right thing. The other option is not only to build an alternative organization, but to use it as the base for a campaign to take over the original one.

14. When those who have been without power gain it, there is no guarantee that they will exercise it more democratically than those who have had it before.

15. The power of culture can be an antidote to people's inability to see beyond their "own people" or situation. Culture can transform consciousness and make social change transformative rather than merely instrumental.

16. Organizers are often unjustly accused by those in power of inciting violence. That's a lie, and it needs to be put to rest. It's just a tactic the opposition uses to discredit your organization. To shut down a prison; to drive an exploitative enterprise out of business; to make sure a sexual harasser is fired—that is not violence. It's justice.

17. Go not only with what you know, but with whom you know. Even in the Internet age, personal relationships still count, especially when you're asking people to do something. When recruiting volunteers, give them a specific list of campaign needs from which they can choose.

18. It's quite easy to slide from helping organize a community to becoming its leader and spokesperson—even though you're not really a member of that community.

19. We can never truly predict what human beings working together can accomplish, and therefore we can never compromise with injustice.

20. The beloved community of which Dr. King spoke, rather than something we reach some day in the future, may be something we experience a little bit every day while, as creative community organizers, we walk and work towards it.[3]

Kahn's principles can apply to any level of civic involvement: local, state, regional, national, or international. Beyond guiding the nuts and bolts of civic skills, they offer a path toward a larger goal: forging your own civic personality.

In the sports world, athletes of equivalent, excellent talents tend to perform differently, especially at crucial times in the games, because they have different athletic personalities. Staying cool under intense pressure, not getting ruffled, having a driving will to win, maintaining focus—these are some of the traits that help great athletes prevail over their competitors.

A civic personality shares some of these characteristics. Sharing credit with others, refusing to get discouraged, viewing your last mistake or defeat as your best teacher, continually absorbing new information and old precedents, being honest and consistent, exercising self-control, and practicing resiliency are all key elements in a mature civic personality. As in sports, working consciously to develop these traits—through study, reflection, and feedback from others—is the best way to up your chances of success.

Personality and ego conflicts between people on the same side of a struggle are always potential obstacles to a movement's success. Such friction can corrode the spirit and set the stage for failure. It's important to try to anticipate such personality conflicts rather than be surprised or discouraged by them. The more activists learn to view a regular civic life as an essential part of their daily lives of work, family, play, and leisure, the more it will nourish their commitment to the cause—and the more their example will encourage others to adopt the same perspective.

I recall an exchange in Sydney, Australia, with a cabdriver. It was a long ride, so I started some not-so-small talk. I was fascinated with the Australian voting system, I told him, which is mandatory, not voluntary. "Unlike us in the United States," I said, "you're *compelled* to vote—and if you don't have a proper excuse, you're fined a few dollars. How do you feel about that?" He turned to me and almost dismissively replied: "Why, mate, it's a civic duty." In other words, this cabdriver accepted voting as a way of life, as part of living in an electoral democracy that makes you obey many laws but also wants you to weigh in on who you want your lawmakers to be.

It is obvious that the earlier in life we start developing civic interests—and basic civic skills—the richer the civic life of our society will be. The responsibility here, of course, rests with schools and with parents. Yet the study of civics in our schools has long since been absorbed by the broader category of social studies—one of the most troubling, and least examined, failures of organized education, despite some very committed social studies teachers. As a result, our young people display a staggering ignorance of "civic affairs" and any understanding of what those words even mean. They know plenty about the electronic gadgets they use, the shopping malls and McDonald's they frequent, the social media universe they increasingly inhabit. But ask them if they've ever visited the local courthouse, or attended a local city or town council meeting or a public hearing, and they'll look at you like you've just suggested a trip to the moon. Such remoteness from the public decisions made in these forums, which affect their families and neighborhoods, is part of a larger ignorance about their own towns or cities where they live—an unfamiliarity that includes their history, their geography, and how their public services are delivered: where their drinking water comes from, where their sewage is dispensed, and where emergency public health assistance is available in their area. More than ever before, youngsters live in an enveloping virtual video reality that disconnects them from the natural world and often their own families.

To this state of affairs, teachers and parents can be crucial in turning this experience around—yet, in most areas, there are at least two obstacles to overcome. First, most debates over education revolve around questions like testing, class size, teacher pay, and budgets—not on the student experience, not on bringing the classroom into closer contact with the community. The supremacy of multiple-choice standardized tests, forcing teachers to "teach to the test," is the latest grand illusion of educational "reform." Prepared by commercial consulting firms, these tests fail to measure the most important factors for success—such as diligence, stamina, curiosity, creativity, even idealism. Unlike assessment tests, they fail to measure much factual knowledge. Rather, they measure quickness in completing a time-pressured test, one that often resembles a puzzle with one definitive answer. Pressed by politicians and administrators looking for a quantitative measure—a number they can trumpet—teachers now are cut off from the ability to use their judgment, their personal initiative, and their individual focus on the individual child in the interest of serving the political objective of a standardized test.

Here is where civic-minded parents must step into the breach. Beyond their interest in how their own children are doing, parents should ask the more important questions that tests never address: Are their schools helping their children understand their community? As noted earlier, lessons in civics can offer pathways into other, more traditional subjects; learning about drinking water testing and purification, for instance, helps children learn about chemistry and biology. Parents should ask: Are my children glued to their computer screens, or are they being challenged to understand how societies can change for the better? To understand our political and electoral systems? To understand the pluses and minuses of new technologies or the consumer content they interact with every day—from ads for processed foods to credit card solicitations to political advertisements? Are they learning how to engage in serious conversations with adults, to share the often-astonishing products of their imagination in their preteen years and the products of their intellectual curiosity in high school? Some of the most pointed questions seasoned politicians have ever faced have come from nine- and ten-year-olds. Candidates for office would much rather have town meetings with adults, I've been told, than with preteen kids.

One important way to get kids interested in civic life is to allow them to learn by doing. Experience motivates; it connects youthful idealism with imagination and can feed any child's thirst for knowledge. Bring your children to a town meeting, and you'll start to show them how societies try to solve problems and turn around entrenched patterns of misbehavior. Throughout our history, corrupt city halls and police departments have been reformed; a visit to a courtroom or a police station can be a useful occasion to explore the forces that were responsible for some important reform in your own community. It can be a good moment for them to learn how civic activity shapes political behavior. It's important for young men and women to understand that, without civic culture, our government and politics will be controlled by corporations or groups whose interests don't always coincide with those of the people.

These lessons must be calibrated to work for appropriate age groups, obviously. But don't underestimate your children: they can rise to remarkable challenges when their minds are sparked by new ideas. In the book *Civics for Democracy: A Journey for Teachers and Students*, which I published with writer Katherine Isaac, we give examples of such successes. One of my favorites involved a fifth-grade schoolgirl who appeared in her Salt Lake City classroom one day and announced that she'd discovered a waste dump nearby. Incredulous, the teacher asked her to lead her to the site. The girl brought her to an area overgrown with shrubbery and surrounded by sidewalks. Sure enough, the student was right. So the teacher got the class to take on the project of getting the dump cleaned up as its own personal mission. The students contacted the mayor and the press, called attention to the problem, and got it done. They were even invited to testify at the state legislature regarding a state superfund law. The teacher was so taken by her transformed group of students that she wrote a book called *The Kid's Guide to Social Action: How to Solve the Social Problems You Choose—and Turn Creative Thinking into Positive Action*. I visited another teacher, Brian D. Schultz, who worked in a low-income area of Chicago. He had scrapped his lesson plan and took the suggestion of his students to study their own rundown school—complete with broken furniture, cafeteria service relegated to the corridors, gym class being held across a busy street, and classrooms that were freezing in the winter—all within the sight of the gleaming skyscrapers, some tax-abated, of the self-styled "City that Works." The creativity, initiative, diligence, and excitement of his students proved how reliably good teaching leads to self-education. He too wrote a book about his students' success, entitled *Spectacular Things Happen along the Way: Lessons from an Urban Classroom*.

Everyone celebrates good citizenship among students. Yet community-based civics education is agonizingly sparse. Why? Because turning students on to the community as a "laboratory for social studies and civic training" tends to upset those who work at maintaining the scripted status quo. Students who ask "impertinent" questions may discover inconvenient conditions and probe into areas where the sun doesn't shine around city hall, supermarkets, factories, and public works facilities. Exploring their own hometown may lead kids to unsettling discoveries. Besides, the schools complain, turning kids into free-roaming civic activists comes with problems: insurance may not cover activities outside the school grounds; finding safe modes of transportation can be difficult. Except, that is, when they take their wards to airports, museums, theaters, or sports arenas—none of which teach youngsters how decisions are made in a society.

A school doesn't require expensive facilities to teach civic skills and engagement. The laboratory is the community. The materials are plentiful and inexpensive. Newspapers are often pleased to supply free copies on request, so desperate are they to stop the loss of younger readership. Of course, many papers are also available for free online, which can be helpful for limited budgets—but a little time away from the computer screen might come as a relief to students, who might find they prefer interacting with each other and with real people on real subjects in real time. To switch from memorizing fictitious history to an exercise in defining and detecting propaganda just takes an honest, forthright change in attitude to develop critical minds with self-generating critical capacities.

This approach to civic education—one that synthesizes many disciplines toward an overall comprehensiveness—should be even more robust at the college/university level. But many institutions of higher learning operate in their own world of vested interest pressures, censorship, self-censorship, and perverse incentives. Consider this: university faculty are subject to pressure from alumni, past and potential contributors, foundations, and corporate donors—and their priorities are often reflected on a university's board of trustees. Schools are often wary of the media, the worst of which are always poised to stoke controversies or distort disagreements. Faculty can be divided and politicized when they are not anesthetized. Campus managers treasure routine, tranquillity, and studiousness with weekend intervals for sports and parties. Confronting injustice, abuses of power, or other contemporary conflicts, local or national, disrupts this tranquillity.

Nowadays, universities—more so than smaller liberal arts colleges—have become very vocational. The students expect their four years to provide them with a job-producing skill set, whether in accounting, business management, marketing, engineering, or technology, or to prepare them for medicine, the law, or some other graduate program. In such a focused atmosphere, precious little room is left for citizen skills.

Years ago, I decided to challenge students to forgo this trade school environment and start their own nonprofit public interest research groups (PIRGs). Each local PIRG is financed and controlled by students but guided by a professional staff of attorneys, scientists, organizers, and others. Core funding comes from modest annual fees of $5 to $10 automatically billed to all students on campuses that approve a campus PIRG by a majority vote. Refunds are available to students who choose not to support the PIRG. Their student-elected boards (made up of eighteen- to twenty-one-year-old students) would in turn hire twenty-five- to thirty-year-old professionals—attorneys, organizers, canvassers, researchers, and scientists—to help them work to improve their state. Fast-forward forty years, and PIRGs in twenty states have accumulated a record of achievement unparalleled in American higher educational history. Because of the longevity of these institutions, many thousands of students have been trained in civic engagement; these, in turn, have participated in successful environmental and consumer litigation, exposed the standardized test racket, markedly improved mass transit in the New York City subway system, pioneered recycling laws, advanced student and consumer rights, and created many open-government initiatives.

The state PIRGs banded together to create U.S. PIRG, which deals with congressional and federal regulatory agency issues, especially in the environmental field. From California to Massachusetts, Washington State to Florida, PIRGs are helping to fill the vacuum in civic experience at universities nationwide. The students who participate are funding and running their own operations with their own independent nonprofit organizations. Still, of the thousands of higher education institutions—community colleges, four-year colleges, and universities—only about two hundred have allowed this easy fund-raising check-off that makes these PIRGs possible. We can only imagine the positive social impact these PIRGS could have if students at the vast majority of colleges and universities were afforded the same opportunity. (For more information, go to www.uspirg.org and www.environmentamerica.org.)

Another enormous untapped resource for civic engagement is the older alumni of universities and graduate schools. I know this from personal experience. In April 1990, a few months before our thirty-fifth Princeton reunion, my class held a meeting at the Red Cross building in Washington, D.C., on a very rainy Saturday. The class asked me to speak, and I took the occasion to suggest that we create a group to provide civic opportunities for Princeton students. The response was amazing. Classmates stood up to express support and suggested broadening the idea to include activities we could pursue directly. This was exactly what I had hoped for—commitment through public discussion. At the reunion itself, in June, around twenty of my classmates formalized the idea into a 501(c)(3) institution. We called it Princeton Project 55.

Civically-engaged alumni are valuable potential engines for civic engagement because, with their professional lives at or near their peak, they're often primed to turn "success into significance," as one of my classmates put it, by turning their energies toward serious matters in the civic arena. Project 55, for instance, agreed on a charter that stressed our intention to work together to address the needs, injustices, and aspirations of our country. We placed students with groups that focused on removing the structural causes of injustice rather than providing charitable relief. We quickly rented a floor in a building on Princeton's Nassau Street, hired a small staff, and got to work. At first the university fund-raisers saw us as competitive with their alumni fund-raising, but soon—with the approval of the university's president, Harold Shapiro, we developed good, if arm's length, relationships with the school.

Our core organizing group of Fifty-Fivers was representative of our class: surgeons, legal aid and corporate lawyers, business executives, independent consultants, graphic designers, and community organizers. Our work proved to be a constructive, liberating substitute for the usual nostalgic alumni reunion parties, peppered with a few lectures and entreaties from university officials who flattered us into giving money but never really tapped into the intellectual resources we had developed during or since our four years there. Princeton Project 55 became the main placement agency of summer interns and postgraduate fellows for Princeton students. The admissions office even started touting its opportunities for students in their recruiting literature. Two early Princeton fellows who did well in Silicon Valley gave us $2 million to purchase an office building near the campus. Our interns and fellows now number nearly two thousand and encouraged by classmate Kenly Webster, are beginning to form themselves into a PU 55 alumni association. One of our projects, a well-publicized tuberculosis awareness program, has helped interns and fellows who are now working as scientists on infectious diseases. Others are running organizations working on reforms in the industrialized food business and other comparably troubled areas. As interns and fellows spread across the country and now abroad, this Princeton program has become a life-changing experience for many students at this crucial juncture in deciding what to do with their lives.

From early on, Project 55 decided to spread the idea to other colleges and universities through special conferences. We even had a classmate, former stockbroker Chet Safian, work full-time on what we called "diffusion." Other schools have adopted minor projects, though none has yet matched the size of Princeton Project 55 or its ambitions. Princeton has traditionally cultivated class identity: until recently its alumni magazine came out weekly, which is unheard of in university circles. Other schools with comparable class identities, including Yale, Harvard, Oberlin, and Dartmouth, have been approached, but as yet the model has not caught on, largely because the requisite twenty classmates it takes to reach critical mass have not emerged. Yet there's no practical reason that thousands of similar alumni civic organizations couldn't take hold nationwide. It's entirely in our hands. All it requires is a sense of urgency—which shouldn't be difficult, given the state of the nation and the world. With a group of accomplished and motivated alumni well positioned within the halls of power, the opportunity to create such potentially powerful civic groups recalls the words of mathematician-philosopher Alfred North Whitehead: "Duty arises from the power to alter the course of events."

It was that sense of duty that made it possible for a public interest lawyer like me to work with my Harvard Law School classmates—mostly corporate lawyers—to form the Appleseed Network in 1993. Appleseed's objectives were to start centers for law and justice in as many states as possible—and two decades later, seventeen such organizations are up and running, working on problems from the outrageous fees charged to immigrants sending money home to their families abroad, to worker conditions in meatpacking plants.

Imagine if other law school alumni classes around the country were to start similar organizations, working to give average

Americans greater access to justice and to make government and business hew to the rule of fairness and accountability. Such civic organizations can even help older lawyers develop new civic skills, while also strengthening the fabric of our democratic society. And alumni from other fields—medicine, engineering, public health, science, and business—can find similar ways to put their own areas of professional experience to work.

Sure, you may be thinking, *it's easy to build a powerful civic organization when you've got a powerful group of Ivy League lawyers to pave the way.* Whenever I hear this response, I think of Ed and Joyce Koupal and the People's Lobby in California. I've not seen a more impressive example of individuals who went from utter powerlessness to statewide power through careful and determined organization. Ed Koupal, described by reporter Elinor Lenz as "a big roaring avalanche of a man with a face as wide open as a Wyoming range," was a used-car salesman. He had also worked as a boiler tender, restaurateur, chicken farmer, and jazz musician before he and his wife, Joyce, started organizing around various initiatives in California in the late 1960s. As they raised their three children, not so different from millions of other Americans trying to make it through the day, they seized upon the idea of the statewide initiative as a tool of direct democracy that voters could use to bypass the politicians in the legislatures altogether.

To launch this initiative, they had to assemble more than seven hundred thousand signatures in a 160-day period. Collecting so many signatures in a short time was a monumentally difficult job, especially when the Koupals lacked the large amounts of money it would have taken to hire street petitioners. Instead, they recruited a small team of signature gatherers, each member assigned to obtain ten thousand signatures before the filing deadline. They called these stalwarts the "fanatic fifty," and together they brought the initiative process to the people. The Koupals trained their volunteers with a creation of their own: the "table method," which replaced the time-consuming door-to-door method with stationary tables in high-traffic locations, such as campuses and shopping centers. At first, the Koupals failed to get the required number of signatures on a widely publicized petition to recall Ronald Reagan as governor of California. Another anti-pollution initiative suffered a similar fate.

However, the Koupals' efforts succeeded in arousing public interest, and before long regulators started paying attention. They won a case before the California Supreme Court that ruled that citizens could circulate petitions and collect signatures in corporate-owned shopping malls. The oil companies may have defeated the Koupals' Clean Environment Act in 1972, but in defeat the tide against the polluters grew stronger across the country. The Koupals did prevail with Proposition 20, the Coastal Conservation Initiative, and in 1974, Proposition 9, their Political Reform Initiative affecting campaign contributions and disclosure, won by a landslide. They were on a roll. Leading legislators wanted them on their side. The press gave them regular coverage. Even Governor Reagan recognized their power.

One of Ed Koupal's mottos was "Success is failure analyzed. Success is staying power." Through determination and hard work, the Koupals and their determined volunteers grew so skilled at getting signatures that they were able to counter the big corporations' efforts to co-opt the initiative process with their own volunteer-qualified initiatives. The Koupals spent years traveling the country, teaching citizens the many fine points of motivating citizen support. They were working on initiatives to impose a moratorium on nuclear power plant construction when colon cancer struck Ed Koupal, who died in March 1976. Joyce Koupal tried to carry on, but soon she too became ill. If they had lived, they might well have carried organized citizenry to new heights. But their example lives on, a testament to the average citizen's power to bring about positive change, even without any power—and not much more than a piggy bank—to start with. What they did, no one could stop them from doing—and in doing so, they gave a voice, and justice, back to the people of their state.[4]

We should all do the same.

13

Invent New Tools for Reform

On the morning of September 28, 1993, northern Illinois families were greeted by headlines announcing that they'd be receiving $1.3 billion in refunds to their residential electric bills from Commonwealth Edison—the giant utility company not known for such generosity.

No state or federal agency ordered the refund, which would give back an average of $32 per family plus a $339 million rate cut. Nor did any court. It came about because a nonprofit group called the Citizens Utility Board (CUB), with 180,000 dues-paying consumers, had caught Commonwealth Edison red-handed overcharging its customers. The company was billing its customers for an excessive amount of reserve power capacity costs for its nuclear plants. State law requires such excess reserve capacity to be charged to the company (and its owner-investors). CUB enlisted a number of experts, from its own ranks and a couple of other citizen groups, to examine the company's books to document its case. Then the group entered into negotiations on behalf of its members, defending the right of residential consumers not to be defrauded. CUB's case was so strong that Edison didn't even bother to fight it before the public utility commission and the courts.

The Illinois CUB serves a simple function for consumers in return for allowing Edison to be a legal monopoly. In 1989, the

Illinois legislature passed a law that required Edison to insert an envelope periodically with its monthly utility bill inviting Edison's customers to join CUB. The minimum annual dues of $5 would go to hire a staff of consumer advocates—lawyers, economists, and organizers—to defend consumer interests by presenting professionally substantiated concerns before the utility commission regarding rates, conservation policies, and the like. CUB was also empowered to enter into direct negotiations with electric, gas, telephone, or water utilities from a position of technical strength and popular media recognition. Membership in CUB is purely voluntary and comes with a vote for the board of directors, who can be recalled by the members. Within eighteen months after its founding, Illinois CUB had banded together 180,000 consumers—a feat others had tried for decades to accomplish without success. The difference? The simple device of a mailing insert: an inexpensive way to reach consumers at their peak point of interest—when they get their utility bill.

A consumer protection board like the CUB exists for one simple reason: our rights, as citizens and consumers, may be ironclad—but that doesn't mean they are automatically respected. In the course of daily life, these rights can be infringed upon or violated in countless ways—and those violations require remedies, such as going to court to seek damages, injunctions, or penalties from those who violated your rights. But rights and remedies also require *facilities*—that is, convenient ways to pursue those remedies. What good is your right to vote if you have to travel a hundred miles to the nearest precinct, with no transportation and no absentee voting option to do so? A nearby convenient voting precinct is the facility that makes your vote likely.

The Illinois CUB's consumer membership mailing is an example of an effective consumer facility—a service that makes it easy and inexpensive for utility users to band together for common representation by professional advocates. The postage-paid insert (see http://csrl.org/wp-content/uploads/2012/05/

CUB-Insert.pdf) was mandated by Illinois lawmakers, and it came at little or no expense to the corporate carrier, since no added postage was required. (For consumers using electronic billing, the CUB solicitation could be addressed with a simple mouse click.) No tax dollars were involved.

A CUB is one way to build democratic participation in decisions on choices of energy, pollution, pricing, zoning, handling of consumer complaints, billing practices, quality of services, and the overall management of our utilities, which generally enjoy cushy relationships with their state and federal regulators. These regulators, lest we forget, have a statutory responsibility to represent consumers first. The CUB facility provides the regulators with petitions, arguments, evidence, and perspectives needed to do their job—and they can be taken to court if they fail. In regions where these CUBs operate, there are far fewer empty seats marked "consumers" during public hearings or informal meetings between the utilities and their state overseers. (And when consumers aren't represented at such meetings, the results are predictable: the powerful utility companies almost always get their way.)

With a tiny annual budget of just over $1 million, the Illinois CUB has saved state consumers $10 billion over the past twenty-five years. In 2006, the group dug up evidence that People's Energy used an illegal profit-sharing arrangement with the notorious Enron Corporation to overcharge customers during the winter of 2000–1. Result: a $196 million refund for consumers.

Whether it is securing more open procedures, divulging contents of the various utilities' books, pressing for energy efficiency, or preparing consumer satisfaction surveys, CUBs are there representing consumers.

Imagine if We the People could use the mailings of comparable companies across the entire economy—companies that have a legal monopoly privilege, or that receive substantial taxpayer subsidies or bailouts, or that theoretically operate under regulatory frameworks—to solicit customer involvement in a consumer protection group. An example: What if, whenever you receive your health, auto, or home insurance premium bill, in the mail or online, it came with a free option inviting you, for a few dollars a year, to band together to defend your interests and represent your complaints? Or in your monthly bank statement? Or in monthly statements from your landlord, brokerage firm, mutual fund, credit card company, or other sectors of the economy where your voice could be joined with those of other consumers?

We need to use such facilities to band together and defend our rights— to stop being taken advantage of, start asserting our consumer sovereignty, and help ourselves shape a fairer economy. We must start using technology to serve us, rather than control us.

The idea of soliciting consumer membership works for governmental agencies as well. Why shouldn't your motor vehicle registration renewal notice come with a notice for a new group formed to champion auto safety and fuel economy? Or your form 1040 tax return and its state counterpart come with an invitation to join a group defending tax fairness and efficiency? Or your Social Security payment come with a notice for a group whose mission is to protect Social Security and monitor its administration? If this became widespread practice, before you know it tens of millions of Americans, with thousands of full-time advocates, could be linked together in consumer protection groups, keeping an eye on corporations and government agencies that previously held free rein over their wallets.

People must have an organized voice if justice is to be served through a fairer balance of power.

On a much smaller scale, environmental, consumer, and children advocacy groups that have raised private donations from individuals and foundations have demonstrated that they can have value far beyond their budgets. These groups have been responsible for creating public support for many of today's basic air, water, and toxic control laws; for auto, food, and household product safety laws; and for the all-important freedom of information laws at both federal and state levels. But the relentless expansion of corporate power, changing technology, and the burgeoning of our credit economy have now far outpaced these traditional groups. We're long overdue to start a new movement for consumer and taxpayer power. Such simple facilities, at the point of payment or sale, can turn a movement of dozens into tens of thousands—and magnify the bargaining power of the many who have to pay the few.

As you might imagine, the CUB idea has not been welcomed by everyone.

In 1983, California's public utility commission issued a ruling allowing an existing nonprofit consumer group called the Utility Reform Network (TURN) to insert a solicitation envelope four times a year inside the billing envelopes of the giant Pacific Gas and Electric Company. PG&E took exception and filed suit against the regulation, losing in the state courts before finally appealing to the U.S. Supreme Court. In defending its position, TURN noted that for many years PG&E distributed a newsletter in its monthly statements containing practical information for the company's customers—including political editorials and news stories. TURN had argued before the Public Utility Commission that ratepayers should not be forced to bear the expense of PG&E's political speech and urged the commission to ban political editorials from billing envelopes. The commission chose a different remedy: permitting TURN to insert its own clearly labeled materials into PG&E's mailings to raise funds and communicate with ratepayers—based on the principle that the envelope space used to disseminate the newsletter was the property of the ratepayers.

Then came a blow: by a 5–3 vote, the U.S. Supreme Court—speaking through Justice Lewis Powell, a former corporate utility lawyer from Richmond, Virginia—rejected the California Supreme Court's decision not to hear PG&E's complaint and declared that the monopoly electric company had a First Amendment right not to respond to TURN's insert. Specifically, the court found that PG&E should not "be forced either to appear to agree with TURN's views or to respond." In the most extreme extension yet of the doctrine of corporate personhood, the court applied the "freedom of conscience" rationale to corporations. Justice William Rehnquist, a leading conservative, registered a powerful dissent: "Extension of the individual freedom of conscience decisions to business corporations," he wrote, "strains the rationale of these cases beyond the breaking point. To ascribe to such artificial entities an 'intellect' or 'mind' for freedom of conscience purposes is to confuse metaphor with reality." Rehnquist believed that the commission's decision had been a proper exercise of a state's regulatory authority over utility companies.

Having first proposed the CUB model in a syndicated column on October 25, 1974, I have long believed the idea is an indispensable tool to help build the institutions the consumer movement needs. If the CUB framework were applied nationwide, tens of millions of consumers could be connected and independently represented by skilled advocates, organizers, and thinkers. The balance of power, so tilted in favor of corporate giants and their largely captive regulatory agencies, would be redressed in unprecedented ways.

Unfortunately, the Powell decision broke the back of these initiatives. Wisconsin CUB reverted to a small private consumer group, having been stripped of the right to reach all residential ratepayers through the utility company's mailings. Illinois CUB tried to adjust by getting a state law passed requiring state agency mailings larger than fifty thousand—such as those from the motor vehicle department—to carry the insert. That was helpful, but it wasn't the same as reaching people in their utility bill payment. The Powell decision dissuaded consumer groups from pursuing other similar strategies. In 1991, New York governor Mario Cuomo issued an executive order opening up New York State DMV mailings to such inserts. Mailings with inserts were sent out in July and the fall of 1994. But Cuomo's successor, George Pataki, rescinded the order, leading to the shredding of tens of thousands of inserts stored in a warehouse.

There is *no doubt* that using existing or special government mailings for such consumer protection groups passes constitutional muster. Congress should be requiring that any subsidies or tax breaks for a given industry come with the stipulation that the industry agree to allow such mailings in order to give their consumers a voice in their regulation. The same conditions should apply to government contracts. There are many ways to set up CUBs that would not violate the Powell opinion.

But to legislators looking for excuses not to pursue consumer rights, however, *Pacific Gas & Electric Co. v. Public Utilities Commission of California* continues its devastating impact on the people's right to associate and petition their government under the First Amendment. This is the price of corporate personhood: its application costs people their money, time, health, and safety, and makes a mockery of equal justice under law.

It's time to launch voter initiatives in states where they are permitted, to put CUBs back on the table. It's time to petition governors like Andrew Cuomo, Mario's son and current governor of New York, to issue executive orders like his father's. It's time for our state legislatures to stand for the people for a change. In the wake of the recent economic meltdown, the U.S. Congress declined an opportunity to protect consumer rights. After the largest bailout in American history—that of the Wall Street financial giants—the Dodd-Frank Wall Street Reform and Consumer Protection Act, the modest reform legislation that passed Congress, did not include Senator Charles Schumer's amendment SA 3772, the Financial Consumers Association Act of 2010. Millions of people offended by credit card abuses, subprime mortgage deceptions, and other contractual fine-print schemes were denied a visible opportunity to fund and run their own consumer advocacy groups through piggy-back inserts in bills or solicitations from the pampered banks and brokerage firms that their tax dollars saved from oblivion in 2008–9.

A similar effort failed to gain traction during the passage of the health insurance legislation signed by President Obama in 2010—legislation that was loaded with taxpayer subsidies for health insurance giants like Aetna and United Healthcare and drug companies such as Pfizer and Merck. Again, these companies' patients and policyholders could have been invited to become members of a consumer protection group—and millions of them likely would have, after reading of the widespread denials, exclusions, and exemptions these companies routinely issue when their consumers get sick or injured. It didn't help to see that the press couldn't care less about reporting these proposals.

The CUB idea should be revived throughout the nation. Trade unions emerged to build the middle class from the depths of raw industrialization. Given access to democratic facilities to band together, citizens can join hands in their various roles to further advance our society. We the people deserve this facility to join together into powerful forces—that can fight for our rights and those of our nation's children.

14

Organize Congressional Watchdog Groups

It's a pleasant early June evening and you've settled down to watch some TV. The front doorbell rings and you rise to see who's there.

"Hello," says the visitor. "I'm your new neighbor and just wanted to introduce myself."

"Nice to meet you," you say. "What do you do for a living?"

"Well, funny you should ask. I have quite a job. I spend twenty-two percent of your income. I can raise or lower your taxes, send your children off to foreign wars, give your tax dollars in subsidies and bailouts to rich corporations, allow lots of wasteful spending by the executive branch to benefit corporate contractors, limit law enforcement budgets against violations by corporations, and give away your public airwaves and your public lands. And I'm so busy doing all those things that I just never get around to all the important things *you* think I should be doing. Here's a brochure on the many public policies I'm supposed to oversee, including Medicare, Social Security, and the minimum wage. See you later!"

As the new neighbor turns and walks away, you have two choices. You can get angry that he decided to interrupt the finale of *American Idol* you were watching, just to tell you how he's selling the American people down the river. Or you can call him back, saying, "Listen, you mean a lot to me. Come back, because I better mean a lot to you."

This new neighbor is your representative in Congress. In the context of our republic, we have given him enormous amounts of *our power*, to use to promote and protect our rights. And our one remaining direct voice in our government—our vote—has been weakened by the very authority we've given to Congress. And what authority it has! Congress has the power to tax, the power to spend, the power to make war, the power to subpoena witnesses, the power to investigate almost without limits, the power to oversee the immense executive branch of government, the power (in the Senate) to confirm all high-level cabinet nominees and members of the federal judiciary, and the power to impeach any federal official or judge from the president to the Supreme Court on down. Then there's the power Congress has assumed, which is to delegate more and more of its own authority to federal departments and agencies, or has simply abdicated, such as its constitutional authority to either the White House or the federal courts. This latter abdication has slowly been eroding the system of divided powers, established by the framers in 1791, that is supposed to limit the excessive exercise of authority by those who govern We the People.

It was not always thus. Back in the early days of our republic, when most Americans were farmers, the major work of the federal government was delivering the mail; Washington was a sleepy national capital. Some people today pine for those days. But those days are over and they aren't coming back. The life of our society is immensely more complicated and intrusive, and the ways of its most powerful entities more fully obscured from public view, regardless of the ubiquitous mass media and the internet. People everywhere are affected by events and actions that are beyond their control and even their understanding.

Until, that is, We the People start taking this control back. Which we can, if we want.

After all, as the most powerful branch of government, Congress should be our most powerful ally, the most responsive branch of government to our rights and needs. In spite of its staff, which numbers at more than 30,000, Congress comes down to 535 people. And yet roughly 1,500 corporations consistently get their way with a majority of these 535 people to whom we have given so much of our power. These corporations— ExxonMobil, General Motors, DuPont, Pfizer, Aetna, Bank of America, Goldman Sachs, McDonald's, Walmart, Weyerhaeuser, Monsanto, Procter and Gamble, AT&T, Verizon, Boeing, Lockheed Martin, General Electric, United Technologies, Microsoft, Google, FedEx, American Electric Power, and so on—do not have a single vote. They have money and influence. But only we have the votes that send these 535 men and women to Congress.

So if we hold the reins, then, why is it that the corporations control the horses? Because they know what the horses like to eat. Because they are there day after day, plying the corridors of Capitol Hill. Because they fund, socialize, play, drink, and vacation with these lawmakers. Because they have nice, cushy, high-paying jobs waiting for these legislators (as well as their assistants and their relatives) when they retire from their seats. Because they can apply a lot of pressure when these carrots don't work. Because if a legislator doesn't serve their interests, they can run someone more accommodating against him or her. Because they can make these legislators look bad—or undeservedly good—through deceptive advertisements and other seedy slanders or puffery.

Still, they don't have a single vote. And you do.

Only We the People have the vote. Of course, half of us (or more) give it up by not voting. And many of the other half are "hereditary voters," meaning that they vote for the same party as their grandparents and parents, regardless of current conditions. Politicians know that, for the most part, they can take such votes for granted; most party-line voters are too disengaged from the process to break away.

A two-party system like ours amounts to a shared monopoly over the government. And competition between the two parties is reduced further in many states through the practice of redrawing districts known as gerrymandering. With remarkable accuracy, the party in charge of state governments can use gerrymandering to transform natural districts into bizarrely shaped districts that sharply increase one party's domination over the region. At present, a large majority of House districts are noncompetitive—dominated by either the Republican or the Democratic Party. The winner takes 60 percent or more of the vote, with the challenger running a nominal campaign with nominal funds. This discourages voter turnout while diminishing the competitive power of discerning or swing voters. In 2002, only fourteen House incumbents were defeated (and some of these were because of redistricting). In 2004, nine incumbents were defeated. More seats were up for competition in 2006, 2008, and 2010, but still, more than 80 percent of incumbents enjoy slam-dunk reelections in their one-party-controlled districts.

Over the decades, the League of Women Voters has cataloged the many ways voters are obstructed from voting. These tactics include difficult registration requirements, miscounting votes, discrimination, removing candidates from primary ballots, and obstructing third-party and independent candidates from getting on the ballot. Many older obstructions have been eliminated through civil rights laws, but new ones seem to emerge all the time. The obstruction du jour in some states is requiring onerous voter ID cards, which are a burden on lower-income voters. No country in the Western world comes close to the many ways that our state governments obstruct and harass voters from voting and dissenting candidates from running. Some states make it extremely difficult for a primary challenger, even for one of the major parties, to make it onto the ballot in the first place by establishing unnecessarily burdensome petition requirements.[1]

Elections should involve choice. Gerrymandering makes it too easy for elections to become coronations. Multiparty candidates with multiparty debates are the norm in dozens of other Western countries. Their election seasons are marked by more political and economic debate, more discussion of a wider range of ideas. This is one reason that voter turnout tends to be significantly higher in those societies compared with our dismal turnout levels.

The more we keep voters in a weakened state, the more we nullify their votes in favor of the agendas of the corporate players. Their commercial interests are increasingly overriding our civic interests. Congress has forgotten the warnings of its better forebears, its wisest presidents, and its prescient jurists, who could see the incompatibility between limitless corporate power and a deliberative democratic society. As Thomas Jefferson observed, the purpose of representative government is to curb "the excesses of the monied interests." Today, sadly, its primary role is to *serve* those interests.

Far from resisting this influence, most members of Congress have become small businesses—fund-raising businesses unto themselves. In 2010, the average member of the House spent $1.4 million per election, and the average U.S. senator $7 million.[2] They raise this money phone call by phone call, fund-raiser by fund-raiser, week after week. That's what it takes when you're a small business trying to keep your enterprise afloat—and to keep a steady flow of income from friendly suppliers.

All this may seem like reason for despair. But it's not. Why? Because, for as much influence as these companies may have, we still have the one thing they lack: the vote.

Each congressional district has about 650,000 men, women,

and children. At least two-thirds of them are eligible voters. A large majority of Americans think our country is going in the wrong direction and that corporations have too much control over their lives. On many, if not most, of the solutions we've discussed in this book, there is already a majority consensus, in some cases overwhelming. But there are no organizations that are focused specifically on lobbying congressional representatives to pursue these historically overdue changes of direction for our nation.

It's not that our country doesn't already have groups dedicated to positive change. There are thousands of such groups trying to address broader needs and abuses in their communities. But many of them are poorly funded, and they're fighting great odds. They perform valuable charitable services, and most of them score enough victories to keep the flame of democracy alive. Still, Congress feels little pressure from these good people—and, when they do, most representatives have learned how to give them the kind of polite brush-off that can feel like friendship.

Of course, there are also examples of real changes arising from citizen demands back home. How else did Congress respond to the civil rights, nuclear arms control, environmental, consumer, women's rights, and worker safety movements, as well as the enactment of Medicare? Today, however, there is an ominous and deepening trend on Capitol Hill. As corporate outrages become worse and more brazen—witness the recent corporate crime wave, the corporate speculative binge that collapsed the economy, the immense contracting raids on the taxpayers, and the prevailing attitude that some corporations are simply too big to fail—our lawmakers have failed to provide the resources and penalties to bring these outlaws to justice. It's no longer a matter of intense external lobbying. More and more, the corporations are our government. Their officials become high government officials; they perform governmental, even military and national security, functions under contracts; they finance political careers; and they feed public cynicism by lowering our expectations for what government can achieve for the people. The democracy gap is widening as Washington meets more and more problems with poor decisions or inaction. Urged to contact their congressional representatives, more and more people reply, "Why bother? It won't do any good." Cynicism leads to withdrawal—just as the powerbrokers want.

Skepticism is a more positive alternative to cynicism, because skepticism leaves a door open to the possibility of resurgence. Despite how profoundly the decisions of our Congress affect us all, how many people do you know spend as much time watching Congress in the course of a year as they spend working for one day? Or even one hour? The corporate oligarchy has knocked the instinct for rebellion—worse yet, any real sense of engagement—out of the American people. The continual decline in living standards, the increase in absolute and relative poverty, the outsourcing of jobs to serf labor dictatorships, the explosion in home foreclosures, the tens of millions without health insurance, the widespread decline in wages, the growing hostility toward unions, the bailouts rewarding corporate greed and recklessness, the growing feeling that our lives are being treated unfairly—all provide fertile ground for skepticism to spark a new movement for fairness in American life. All that must happen is for Americans to reach their breaking point and to organize and commit to make a difference in the society they want to hand to their descendants. That's how the Occupy movement got started; its long-term fortunes remain to be seen, but its message—born of deep skepticism about income inequality in America—lives on as the seed corn for resurgence.

Imagine this: Two football teams meet in a huge stadium. There are a hundred thousand screaming fans backing Team A, but only a thousand fans rooting for Team B. Team B comes onto the field first, all eleven of them ready for battle. Three minutes later, Team A comes out of the walkway—but it has only one athlete who has to play all eleven positions at once. Impossible, right? No contest! A massive blowout results.

Team A represents the citizens who stand up for what most Americans want—fairness and justice. Team A is on the side of the angels—but it has nowhere near enough players to make an impact on the opposing team.

What does it take to make a difference in Congress? Whatever side you're on, the energy of a new civic movement can do it—especially when it's the only pulse around. In 1980, it was the Moral Majority, led by the Reverend Jerry Falwell. In 2009, it was the Tea Party—largely a revolt by the conservative wing of the Republican Party against all things Washington, including the performance of both major parties. Both movements received major media attention, despite the fact that neither one had more than a few hundred thousand members who were willing to join marches, attend congressional town meetings, or even protest loudly in a local public forum. The *Washington Post* tried tallying the members of the various Tea Party groups nationwide, but it could find little more than three hundred thousand members. Still, both the Moral Majority and the Tea Party shook up Congress and shifted its orientation to a more right-wing view of politics.

We are long overdue for a progressive movement that can reverse that trend.

One way to bring this about is to organize congressional watchdog groups (CWDs) to monitor each of the 435 districts across the country—to lobby all members of Congress on behalf of their constituents, on behalf of an agenda supported by a majority of Americans. It needs to be and is consistent with the rhythms of our society's expectations for our country: expectations that consider them overdue, necessary, ordinary, attainable, and pertinent to peoples' needs and sense of justice. This agenda should include full Medicare for all; a decent living wage; strong law enforcement on corporate crime and fraud; taxing socially damaging phenomena—such as pollution or Wall Street speculation—before workers' income; and so on.

The agenda can be expressed in a pledge to be signed by one thousand people per district—people who support these changes, who raise or give two hundred dollars a year to the cause, and who volunteer two hundred hours per year to support the group. This thousand-person base will be a seed group, who will work in turn to reach a second one thousand people making the same commitment. The first thousand would use their donations and local connections to secure two offices per district, operated by two full-time advocate/organizers in each office, plus the work of the committed volunteers. All these groups would work closely with others across the country on this common agenda.

The first thousand members of each CWD will be interviewed to ensure their seriousness, sincerity, and commitment to volunteer time. The CWDs should follow flexible criteria for admission, to account for differing levels of experience, knowledge, temperament, and openness to self-education. The most important thing is that the members all enter into the group in general agreement with the agenda; that should reduce the likelihood of any major policy conflict, leaving only interpersonal friction as a potential distraction. Experience shows that personality conflicts can be minimized by keeping all eyes on external hurdles and shared goals.

The CWDs would direct their energies toward three goals: (1) enlisting other citizens and groups in each district; (2) coordinating with other districts in joint campaigns; and, most important, (3) getting the 535 members of Congress to review and adopt their agenda.

Many of the avenues available today to citizens who want to influence elected politicians are stagnant and amateurish. To be

sure, there are cases throughout history when populist movements have secured footholds in key positions in the House and
Senate. However, times have changed for the worse. Most of
the health and safety breakthroughs of the 1960s and 1970s—
from auto safety legislation, to regulatory frameworks for air and
water pollution, to product and job safety codes—would not receive a serious public hearing today, much less get to the Senate
or House floor for a vote. The deterioration of our corporatized
Congress has been that profound.

The CWDs would familiarize themselves with their congressional representatives and with the circles—lobbying, ideological, even social—that influence their performance. They would
know their district's makeup, its needs, its conflicts, its potential
for coalition building, its talent, its media outlets, its best venues
for communicating to citizens at large for the common good.
They would establish a process of regular public meetings with
their representative and (less frequently) with their senators.
The CWD advocates and members should be fully informed
about the issues—and their legislators—to make it clear that
they're here to stay, that they plan on increasing their supporters and influence, and that, from the local congressional offices
to Capitol Hill, they'll be making their agenda a daily subject of
attention.

When it comes to the potential seriousness and longevity of
dustups and protests in their home territory, lawmakers have
their antennae exquisitely tuned to detect the first signs of weakness or flagging interest. The CWDs should be sure that every
campaign it launches sends a strenuously determined signal—a
signal that the movement is in it for the duration, building in-
exorably toward victory. As the CWDs start seeing their congressional members begin to listen, to grapple with their issues,
to introduce legislation supporting elements of the agenda, more
people will join as volunteers, canvassers, and fund-raisers. A vibrant online network should keep neighboring CWDs informed

about their progress, learning from and stimulating one another in both a collaborative and competitive manner. Once any people's movement starts using facts, reason, and reality to respond to the felt necessities of a society, within a broad public philosophy of compassion and fair play, a dynamism catches on to replace resigned cynicism with excitement and engagement. Unexpected skills and insights are offered. The least likely people come forward, having shucked their frustrations about what is happening to their beloved country. All kinds of serendipities flower—to nourish the feeling that it can happen!

The prime movers in any CWD would be its four full-time staff members—let's call them the CWD dynamos. Their goal, backed by thousands of committed volunteer hours, would be to build a vibrant problem-solving and results-oriented civic culture. They would serve as community educators, constantly speaking with small groups, service clubs, students, and senior citizen centers about the agenda. They would send petitions and endorsements of the agenda to members of Congress, with copies to the White House. They would raise money from individual donors and recruit more volunteers to donate time and effort to the cause. They would make themselves accessible to the people on a regular basis, to share their insights on issues of importance to the district—from successful projects that deserve to be celebrated to wrongdoing that needs to be corrected. They would manage summer projects for high school, college, and graduate students. And they would focus relentlessly on public accountability, holding well-publicized sessions with representatives during their visits home. In these visits, the CWD dynamos and their members should challenge their representatives to answer certain fundamental questions—from "How are you going to help us become more powerful as citizens?" to "Why should we vote for you?"

The dynamos best qualified to draft legislation would form working committees to turn the agenda into workable law. Other inter-CWD committees would focus on districts represented by key members of Congress considering specific bills and would respond actively to the floor debates on these bills in the House and Senate. Tailored to the need, many dynamos would travel to Washington on an as-needed basis to lobby their members during the final stages of action on any pressing new bill as a long-overdue counterweight to established corporate lobbyists.

The CWD groups will have to be prepared to field a backlash by corporate interests. These will include Washington trade associations, corporate law firms, PACs, public relations propagandists, and their dealers, agents, and other allies back in the districts. Keeping the agenda very concrete will help to keep the opponents at bay. The focus of the pressure should be from the grassroots to Washington without being distracted by local controversies. The agenda needs to be placed on a fast track; for example, universal health care insurance was proposed by President Harry Truman, but it has dragged on as an issue to this day.

Democracy can never be a reality in our daily lives until citizens strive daily to meet the responsibilities it involves. The vast imbalance between the rampaging power of commercial interests and the pitiful, fitful amount of power exercised by citizens is driving our country into the ground.

To those who would question whether such CWD groups can ever succeed, given the present complexion of the corporate Congress, it's worth looking back to a success story from the 1960s. In those days, Senator Warren Magnuson (D-WA) was the powerful chairman of the Senate Commerce Committee. He was the darling of the business lobbies and for good reason: he delivered for them. Then, starting in the mid-1960s, the rumble of public discontent began to travel from Seattle across the country to the District of Columbia. We the People raised our voices in protest against the Vietnam War; against discrimination, sexism, consumer fraud, and environmental contamination. To make a grand story short, Senator Magnuson hired a new, enlightened staff, and in the decade from 1965 to 1975, he passed a historic string of consumer protection legislation, starting with auto and tire safety legislation in 1966. Try as they might, the corporate lobbies could not get to Magnuson. Why? Because he'd heard the rumblings of an awakened populace. The public mood had turned decisively. Senator Magnuson read the tea leaves; his successful 1968 reelection campaign carried the slogan "Keep the Big Boys Honest."

Similar but less dramatic transformations occurred throughout the Senate and the House in those uplifting days. The auto safety bill passed the House unanimously with Republicans and Democrats voting alike. Bill after bill passed in similar fashion, helping to protect and advance the rights of ordinary people in their environment and in the marketplace—many of them signed by President Richard Nixon. It led one advocate to quip, "If the people are mobilized back home and make their demands known, I don't care who is in Congress, just so long as they can read and write."

That must be the feeling that the American Israel Public Affairs Committee (AIPAC) has absorbed from its extraordinary ability to routinely and quickly get more than 90 percent of the Senate and House to sign on to its resolutions backing any number of Israeli government positions vis-à-vis the occupied and repressed Palestinian people and its neighboring states. When Prime Minister Benjamin Netanyahu addressed a joint session of Congress in June 2011, he received from both party faithfuls fifty-nine ovations, of which twenty-nine were standing hoorahs—a historic record in Congress. No president has ever come close to such aerobic unanimity. The lawmakers were jumping up and down in response to the organized forces back home led by AIPAC, complete with money from PACs, pressure, and persistence. There was a time when AIPAC and its predecessors had very little political or media power. Right into World War II, the *New York Times*, Congress, and the White House declined to heed the pleas of those Americans who knew of the ongoing slaughter of European Jews. The civic, political, and economic power of the pro-Israeli government lobbies came from constant hard work and peer pressure driven by those horrible memories. Now neither the oil companies nor the Pentagon nor the State Department can stand up to AIPAC and its demonizing and retaliatory tactics. They have lost so often that they hardly even try in recent years. To be sure, each episode of civic influence over Congress happens under unique characteristics of time, place, and substance that cannot provide uniformly comparable lessons to be emulated. But case studies of lobbyist influence— whether by the NRA, the AARP, the NAACP, MADD, or consumer protection groups—can reveal strategies and tactics that can be useful to the CWDs.

Mark Green, author of the book *Who Runs Congress?*, wrote in 1972:

> Some citizens, peering into the chasm between congressional potential and congressional failure, may understandably shrug their shoulders in indifference. "But mixed among all the cases of sloth, corruption, insensitivity to injustice, and massive lobbying are remarkable instances of citizen power." Congress has been moved by men and women with no special wealth or influence, little or no political experience, and no uncommon genius, but with the modest combination of commitment to a cause and the facts to make a case. Not often, but enough to show the way, citizen advocates have taken on industrial giants, bureaucratic inertia, public indifference, antipathy to "troublemakers"—and they have won, or at least made a difference.[3]

True enough, but these successes were episodic, unable to follow through after legislative enactment to the all-important stage of enforcement or implementation. Moreover their experience and energy did not accumulate into ever better state-of-the-art civic effectiveness or, perchance, institutionalization. Citizen lobbying today—apart from the internet—is pretty much about as advanced as it was fifty years ago. We still await the internet's use to actually get people *acting* together in addition to knowing what is going on in the world.

Congress had a long tradition of shielding corporate misbehavior from the rule of law and turning Congress and the executive branch into a bustling bazaar of tax subsidies, tax privileges, protection from competition, inflated government contracts, and other assorted windfalls.

Congress constantly disregards evidence in its own committee hearings, as well as damning reports by its nonpartisan investigator, the Government Accountability Office (GAO), and often declines to take action—or perversely enacts laws to weaken protections or facilitate boondoggles. As I noted nearly thirty years ago: "Congress as a whole has managed to avoid passage of responsive legislation to meet the problems of energy, taxes, health insurance, inflation, and unemployment. It has not faced up to the relentless concentration of multinational corporate power over the economy. . . ."

Sound familiar? The same is true today. The corporate world is always searching for ways to tighten its grip over the public authority of Congress. It stands to reason, then, that We the People must find ways to intensify our own grip on our future. If we want to continue to enjoy the (relative) freedom and security of our private lives, we must exercise our rights as public citizens, whether by helping to end poverty or by fostering an economy based on the idea that people matter first.

In a presumed democratic republic like the United States, the ultimate governmental power is supposed to reside in the people. In the interest of practicality and expertise, the people

delegate much of the daily exercise of this power to elected legislatures, which on the national level means Congress. But this
delegation of authority shouldn't mean disengagement from the
responsibilities of citizenship. Our system can only work if our
citizens are organized and vigilant in monitoring the ways our
535 representatives, who each year speak for larger and larger
populations, are using the power we grant them. Otherwise delegation *will* become abdication—first by the people, and then
inevitably by Congress, until it falls conclusively into the hands
of the corporate supremacists.

Most Americans don't spend much time trying to correct
this disengagement from Congress. They tend to spend time
worrying about much more immediate concerns: health care,
unemployment, schools, taxes, fraud, housing, prices, crime,
traffic, pollution, injustice, poverty. Yet these are the problems
that Congress is supposed to be working to solve. Since Congress is the branch of our government that should be most responsive to democratic demands, shifting its priorities should be
the CWDs' most immediate priority. This task should become
part of daily life for all Americans—from mothers fighting for
safety rights to college students arguing for student loan reform
and there could be community and four-year colleges in every
congressional district—studying and regularly publicizing the
performance of their representatives and senators for political
science credits. We all need to take responsibility for a more as-
sertive form of self-government.

It's up to us—our sense of justice, our faith in people, and our
sense of commitment to making ours a better society and world.
Every major improvement starts small, with a conversation, a
gathering, a local action. Activity begets activity. Two centuries
of delegation have run their course. Let us not delay today what
should have been launched decades ago: a new system that gives
the people oversight over their own representatives. It can, and
should, be the start of an American renaissance.

15

Get Congress to Have Skin
in the Game

The gap between Congress and We the People—the gap in wealth, power, privilege, and accountability—has never been wider. The people who came to rallies all over the country during my presidential campaigns made this point again and again. They expressed outrage, to be sure, at the Washington scandals of the day. But the most instant and passionate applause came when I made two simple suggestions, two simple one-paragraph bills that would prevent a lot of problems:

First: Before the Washington politicians plunge our country into another undeclared or declared war overseas, they should be informed that all their able-bodied and qualified children and grandchildren will be drafted into the armed services. That should make them think twice about making war. Even as Congress acceded to the lies and deceptions of the imperial Bush presidency and countenanced the invasion of Iraq, only six elected representatives had children in the military.[1]

Second: The members of Congress can have no benefits unless the American people all share in those benefits universally. There would be no health insurance, no life insurance, no lush pensions, and no accessible gym facilities for the 535 members of Congress unless they saw fit to provide these benefits for all.

Why did these two ideas get such overwhelming support?

Because, whatever their political differences, what the American people value most is fair play.

So how can these two proposals gain headway in the very national legislature that has to enact them? The first step is to start a public conversation about the growing gaps between the supposed people's representatives and those who sent them there. In a front-page article titled "Economic Downturn Took a Detour at Capitol Hill," the *New York Times* reported:

> Nearly half of all members of Congress—250 in all—[are millionaires,] and the wealth gap between lawmakers and their constituents appears to be growing quickly, even as Congress debates unemployment benefits, possible cuts in food stamps and a "millionaire's tax." . . .
>
> With millionaire status now the norm, the rarefied air in the Capitol these days is $100 million. That lofty level appears to have been surpassed by at least 10 members, led by Representative Darrell Issa, a California Republican and former auto alarm magnate who is worth somewhere between $195 million and $700 million.[2]

And yet consider: even as the gap between our wealthiest citizens (including our representatives) and average Americans rises, worker productivity has been on a constant rise during this period—and the federal minimum wage, adjusted for inflation, has fallen well below its 1968 level! Working Americans are working longer for less money, and their representatives are pocketing the difference.

Congress has always been skittish about giving itself the pay increases it would love to have. In 1989, to avoid certain backlash from public hearings and public debate on their pay, the lawmakers put their salaries on an automatic cost-of-living adjustment (COLA). This meant that their annual pay would increase every year unless they acted to reverse the provision. From 2000 through 2010, the members' pay increased nine times.

All this attention and reward cannot but go to the heads of the congressionally anointed lawmakers, and they respond accordingly. The members of Congress enjoy many unique arrangements. They get to police their own ethics; they arrange for their own multiple freebies; and they imperially exempt themselves from a wide array of major laws—including the Freedom of Information Act, the Privacy Act, the Whistleblower Protection Act of 1989, and until recently the Insider Trading Act, which is under revision after recent exposés. Members of Congress are even exempt from state and municipal taxes.

Another, more dangerous exemption came to light when the workers who operate the steam pipe network deep beneath the congressional buildings in D.C. rose in protest over serious asbestos and excessive heat conditions in the tunnels. These catacombs were so dangerous that members of Congress were prohibited by the Capitol Police from going down there—and yet tunnel workers were forced to toil there for years as the conditions went uncorrected. As my sister Dr. Claire Nader (who administers the Joe A. Callaway Award for Civic Courage) said, "The Architect of the Capitol callously disregarded the health consequences of asbestos exposure that tunnel crew members endured and the risk of major injuries, including death, from collapsing concrete tunnel sections, as well as inadequate emergency communications and escape exits."

In the past four decades, Congress has become less productive and more self-rewarding than ever. More than thirty years ago, when Congress actually enacted useful legislation and conducted oversight hearings, Missouri congressman Richard Bolling said that "more and more people are coming to understand that the Congress doesn't work," and California congressman Ron Dellums called senators and representatives "mediocre prima donnas who pass legislation that has nothing to do with the reality of misery in this country." If they thought their fellow legislators were bad, imagine how they would feel about today's gerrymandered and gridlocked and callous Congress.

It's all well and good for citizens back home to present their legislators with calls for reform. But these proposals, without the laser focus of congressional watchdog groups, will fall on deaf ears.

What will get their attention? The fastest way to get a re-action from your representative may be by making an in per-sonam demand—a gesture that speaks directly to the welfare of the representative and his or her family. For instance, a demand to reduce congressional pay to match that of the av-erage worker in their district would certainly get a representa-tive's attention—especially if accompanied by a bill drafted and signed by thousands of constituents, and promoted in a well-publicized ceremony. This is the cry for equality to replace the widening imbalance between the lawmakers and the taxpayers. We can make similar demands to remove all exemptions from laws that Congress enjoys. We should do so, out of respect for the principle of equality under the law. The moral authority to govern, so debased, would begin to recover with each such level-ing gesture—especially when the less high-minded senators and representatives start retiring under such pressure and retreat to the wildly enriching prospect of becoming a lobbyist down on Washington's K Street to the reward of more than half a million dollars a year.

The most personal of in personam demands are those I in-voked at the start of this chapter. Lest it seem extreme to de-mand that our elected representatives send their children and grandchildren into battle if Congress and the White House plunges our country into another war, recall that FDR had four sons in the armed forces during World War II and Dwight D. Eisenhower's son John was a career army officer. In the years since the end of World War II, our wars have been wars of choice, undeclared by Congress despite the requirements of Article I, Section 8 of the Constitution. Our representatives should have this kind of skin in the game; if they did, it would surely make the members more wary of warmongering propaganda and more willing to deliberate seriously rather than easily give in to the White House. If this provision had been in place in 2003, for instance, we would have never invaded Iraq, for the lies and deceptions behind the invasion would have been exposed by the public hearings and the dissenters.

We need a grassroots drive under the slogan "If it's good for you, it's good for us." A majority of Americans favor Medicare for all, with free choice of physician and hospital. If asked, they would likely favor the same kind of pension plans that Congress has given itself.

The privileges accorded to members of Congress by the Constitution do not extend to normal criminal laws. Although observers believe that these laws have not been adequately enforced when applied to members of Congress, there have been close to one hundred criminal prosecutions of senators and representatives since 1945. Members of Congress have been jailed for bribery, tax evasion, kickback schemes, perjury, using campaign funds for personal expense, conspiracy to defraud government, extortion, and obstruction of justice. Yet no member has ever been prosecuted for violating the oath of office, with its promise to abide by the Constitution—despite the fact that appropriating funds for undeclared wars amounts to just such a violation. Such violations in principle by members of Congress do not trigger criminal or civil laws.

At what point is a campaign contribution a bribe and at what point is it, as the longtime news anchor David Brinkley called it, "legalized bribery"? It depends on the facts of each case, especially whether the tendered money is disclosed as campaign contributions or goes personally to the legislator under the table. The widespread practice of corporations funding the campaigns of key committee members and other influential lawmakers who are directly in charge of supervising the corporations' commercial interests has somehow escaped being interpreted as bribery. Thus, when corporations that want to protect sugar quotas, oil company tax breaks, deferred air pollution rules, the granting of pipeline or broadcast licenses, or the procurement of bailouts target key lawmakers for contributions, these exchanges are not considered bribes—even though everyone knows that the contributions are being tendered in exchange for legislative services rendered.

Such institutionalized corruption among members of Congress affects how this branch of government exercises its constitutionally prescribed role to act as a check on the president and the executive branch. What Congress would be willing to initiate impeachment proceedings against a sitting president when the Justice Department and the media might well turn to Capitol Hill and ask, "What about you?"

Over the years, our presidents have also managed to square off an ever-broadening zone of immunity for behavior that should be impeachable or actionable under federal criminal laws. This is especially true in the area of military/foreign affairs, but it's equally true of such matters as secret unilateral Wall Street bailouts, for example. Yet, except for their exposure to the normal criminal and civil laws for personal misbehavior, the risk of prosecution for official duties is controlled by the impeachment clause of the Constitution. In cases of "high crimes and misdemeanors," the president's grand jury and courtroom are the House of Representative and the U.S. Senate, respectively. Congress has viewed the impeachment power as a rarely used tool for presidential accountability. It is invoked even more rarely in areas where Congress has abdicated its constitutional authority or responsibility to the president. Without the exercise of the impeachment power, presidents would face no repercussions for their official actions, as it is very unlikely that presidents would be pursued under criminal laws after leaving office. The only recent exception was the special Watergate task force in the Justice Department that was preparing to have a grand jury indict Richard Nixon for Watergate-related crimes when Gerald Ford pardoned him in 1974. President Obama echoed Ford's gesture when he declared that George W. Bush and Dick Cheney would be subject to no special investigation under his watch.

So holding the president accountable is a responsibility Congress can abdicate at will, abandoning its fundamental oversight roles and allowing the executive branch to do its work in an unconstitutional and illegal manner. The Bush administration was so arrogant in its attitude toward executive privilege that it greeted a series of detailed American Bar Association White Papers outlining his unconstitutional behavior on three counts (signing statements, illegal surveillance, and an unprecedented presidential power grab that threatened the separation of powers) with a contemptuous silence.

But it's the war-making behavior of both Presidents Bush and Obama that truly defy belief. These presidents' escalating military operations, the product of a "unitary presidency," in the words of their apologists—others might call it an imperial presidency—have escaped the reach of law, court, Congress, and the American public.

President Obama—a former lecturer in constitutional law at the University of Chicago—seems determined to explore the outer reaches of his power. He initiated a war against Libya, together with NATO allies and the endorsement of the Arab League and a UN resolution. Exceeding even George W. Bush, he was attacking a government that presented no imminent threat to the United States with neither a war declaration nor even an evasive war resolution from Congress. Nor did he ask for congressional authorization or appropriation for use in overthrowing the Libyan dictatorship. Instead, President Obama himself authorized and appropriated funds from the Pentagon and Central Intelligence budgets under his control. The U.S. Supreme Court has ruled that even U.S. actions taken under the authority of a UN resolution must still conform with the U.S. Constitution. In the case of President Obama's Libyan war, there was no conformity and were no challengers. Indeed, short of calling for the president's impeachment, no individual member of Congress or private citizen could raise any formal challenge to the president's war-making action without having the attempt dismissed because the complainants had no standing to sue. Moreover, the courts would declare any judicial challenge to be "political" and thus a matter not for them but for the legislative and executive branches to resolve.

The zone of executive immunity was further enlarged by the latest Obama doctrine, described as follows by constitutional lawyer Bruce Fein:

Through the National Defense Authorization Act of 2012 and acquiescence in repeated executive usurpations, Congress has empowered President Obama to kill any person anywhere in the world who is secretly listed as an enemy on a list that's reminiscent of the Lord High Executioner's "Little List" in *The Mikado*. The putative "battlefield" is boundless. The standards for listing are secret. The evidence justifying a listing is secret. The legal justification for the assassinations is secret. The secrecy persists after the alleged enemy target is vaporized. No proof is proffered that the corpse had conspired or attempted or had actually engaged in hostilities against the United States; or, that capturing the victim for criminal prosecution or detention would have been unfeasible. Instead, the White House summons into being as its defense a counter-constitutional divine doctrine of presidential infallibility when it comes to killing suspected enemies. Due process is buried in the detritus of "collateral damage."[3]

An amendment to the National Defense Authorization Act of 2012, following repeated congressional inaction toward such executive overreaches, only affirmed the complicity of Congress, not the constitutionality of the actions authorized by this legislation. A democratic society committed to "the rule of law," not the rule of men, cannot exist if it allows its president to be above and beyond the law, able to usurp otherwise lawful instruments of enforcement and defense for unlawful means and ends.

Where are the first responders to this expanding dictatorial behavior by the White House—the one million lawyers who are officers of the court, the hundreds of law professors, and the scores of law school deans? Except for a very noble few, they have remained silent, preoccupied with their daily professional obligations. How can we expect uninformed citizens to be alarmed when our own attorneys at law see no reason to challenge a wide array of executive malfeasance—including arrests without charges, indefinite imprisonment in military prisons, illegal wiretapping, state secrets that terminate judicial remedies, extraordinary rendition, and torture? All of these illegal acts have now been gathered under the umbrella of presidential powers. Indeed, illegal wiretapping—once a felony under the FISA Act—is now allowed. As the ACLU has noted, "In 2001 . . . President Bush authorized the National Security Agency (NSA) to launch a warrantless wiretapping program, and in 2008 Congress ratified and expanded that program, giving the NSA almost unchecked power to monitor Americans' international phone calls and emails."[4]

By definition, a democracy governed by the rule of law cannot be a "trust the leader" system. It cannot tolerate an executive power that acts as secret prosecutor, judge, jury, prison warden, and executioner. A Congress that allows such violations of the Constitution, of statutes, of international treaties, and of procedural due process—by funding them and looking the other way as the action continues—is betraying the republic it purports to serve.

The separation of powers that is at the heart of the American governmental system with its checks and balances has been abandoned by the limitless, anywhere "war on terror." The American public has been blocked from even contesting this breakdown in court on the grounds that we have no standing to sue. All these modes of congressional and presidential waywardness combine in a seamless web of immunities. We must correct this imbalance by reminding our elected representatives that they are not beyond the law. That they must reclaim their constitutional responsibility to oversee the conduct of the executive branch. And that they can no longer stand by in silent assent as our government becomes a growing zone of dictatorial overreach and social injustice. We must challenge them to fight for a better system—a system that involves accepting the same risks of law enforcement that apply to their constituents.

16

Enlist the Enlightened Super-Rich

Progressives tend to assume that the wealthiest among us are all cut from the same cloth: politically reactionary, rapacious in business, personally self-indulgent. But those who buy into that stereotype are doing so to the detriment of their causes. We all want justice to be advanced in our society. But justice is obstructed unless its advocates have the resources to pursue it. Year after year, popular agendas to improve our country stall because of a lack of resources. Progressives are constantly complaining about all the money pouring into the coffers of their opponents. But they spend precious little time cultivating the more enlightened super-rich for their own causes—when the support of even one or two of these successful businesspeople could make all the difference.

The right-wing super-rich have contributed billions of dollars to establish lobbying organizations and corporate think tanks in Washington, D.C., and in the state capitals. From the American Enterprise Institute to the Heritage Foundation, the Hoover Institution, the Hudson Institute, the Manhattan Institute, and the Cato Institute (to name some of the better-known organizations), wealthy benefactors such as David and Charles Koch, Richard Scaife, and the Bradley family have filled the conservative tanks with fuel. These institutes also harbor hundreds of former government officials and others who accept a good salary and berth from which to spew forth their ideologies of corporatism, commercialism, and militarism.

To date, the resources available to promote these interests—enlarging the military budget, weakening or blocking health and safety regulations, limiting corporate crime enforcement, and turning government into an accounts-receivable for industry and commerce—tower over the financial support available to progressive causes. The progressive/liberal pundits are right to growl about the amount of corporate money that gets poured into conservative campaign budgets during election seasons. But they have not devoted enough attention to the fact that their own cause needs similar financial support just to reach critical mass and become part of the electoral and political debate.

History tells us that the great civil rights struggles in American history have been sparked or bankrolled by wealthy contributors. The abolitionist movement against slavery in the first half of the nineteenth century was accelerated by wealthy benefactors, who often became actively engaged with the cause above and beyond just giving money. Gerrit Smith, Joshua Bowen Smith, and Arthur and Lewis Tappan courageously placed their wealth squarely behind the very uphill drive to rid this country of the scourge of slavery. In 1831, Arthur Tappan started the Anti-Slavery Society. In 1840, James G. Birney, who came from a wealthy Kentucky family, pressed for the formation of the Liberty Party—an independent antislavery third party that ran Birney for president in 1840 and 1844. William Henry and Frances Seward funded Frederick Douglass's *North Star* newspapers. The opposition and organized hatred that confronted these wealthy supporters of freedom for black people make today's controversies appear restrained by comparison.

Another bitter controversy was the pre– and post–Civil War movement to give women the right to vote. Many early industrialists despised the brave women who fought for their voting rights—in part because they were also fighting against child labor, cruel working conditions in dungeonlike factories, and consumer price gouging by monopolies. Ida Tarbell wrote the book that exposed the powerful Standard Oil Company of John D. Rockefeller and its predatory, monopolistic practices. Taking on both abusive corporate bosses and snarling misogynists, these women marched, petitioned, picketed, went door-to-door, and were roughly treated every step of the way. Women picketing the White House were arrested by police and dragged down to the local jails. But the women's suffrage movement received little traction, scraping along on "the nickels and dimes of housewives and laundresses,"[1] as one account put it—until the end of the nineteenth century, when wealthy benefactors like New Yorkers Louisine Waldron Elder Havemeyer, Carrie Chapman Catt, Alva Belmont, and Julia Ward Howe contributed resources that one commentator said "turned a stalled movement into an avalanche of pressure." Catt, the wife of a wealthy engineer, contributed a million dollars to the final push in 1917–1918, sending masses of materials to newspapers, magazines, and activists. (That million dollars would amount to $25 million today.)

While the modern civil rights and environmental movements received support from wealthy families, even their generous contributions could not keep up with the demand or the needs of the full-time fighters and champions for these missions. Throughout the last half century—and especially since the 1980s—the economy has created more and more megamillionaires and billionaires. Fueled by the stock market, Silicon Valley, and the real estate booms, billionaires and megabillionaires are replicating by the dozens each year in the United States. It's time to enlist open-minded, politically progressive benefactors to take their concern over conditions in their country and turn it into action. I believe there has been no more auspicious time than now to recruit some of the super-wealthy to join our cause.

In 2010, the media began reporting on an ambitious project by Warren Buffett and Bill Gates Jr., whose combined financial wealth is nearing $100 billion. Together they prepared what they called the Giving Pledge, inviting "the wealthiest American families and individuals to commit to giving more than half of their wealth to philanthropy or charitable causes either during their lifetime or after their death. . . . The Giving Pledge is specifically focused on billionaires or those who would be billionaires if not for their giving."[2] So far, more than eighty-one such figures have signed the pledge—and the growing group is meeting once or twice a year to exchange ideas about giving and how to make such giving produce results.

Warren Buffett is known for his candor. He has told me and others that businesspeople like him "know how to make a lot of money, but we don't have a clue about what to do with it, including me." At breakfast with Buffett in his hometown of Omaha, Nebraska, he told me that giving to "good works" requires knowing how to define "good works" most effectively. Perhaps his highest priority so far has been assuring nonproliferation of nuclear weapons and materials, and he has given millions of dollars to the cause. Most notable was his pledge to give a total of some $35 billion, over time, to the Gates Foundation, which has chosen as its causes infectious disease prevention and treatment and improving education in our schools. As one of four members of the foundation's board of directors (along with Bill and Melinda Gates), Buffett is certainly positioned to direct further contributions toward additional missions.

In 2005, Bill Gates's father, William Gates Sr., teamed up with economic expert Chuck Collins and gathered about one thousand rich people to oppose the repeal of the estate tax. This move was a rare example of successful businesspeople taking a stand that ran against their own economic interest—simply because they believed it was the right thing to do. Gates Sr. and Collins wrote a little book titled *Wealth and Our Commonwealth: Why America Should Tax Accumulated Fortunes* about the responsibility to pay an estate tax as payback for all the help that rich people like them have received over their lifetimes, from public programs like the GI Bill of Rights and education, to public services. Having observed directly how close the Republicans, under George W. Bush, came to ending this estate tax—which less than 2 percent of the estates actually have to pay—the organization Responsible Wealth (part of the larger group United for a Fair Economy) spent millions of dollars on a three-year effort to ensure its preservation.

As a case study, let's contemplate how the Bush-Cheney invasion of Iraq in March 2003, with all its attendant costs in blood, treasure, and international goodwill, could have been prevented. Recall that Bush and Cheney made their false case for war on highly dubious grounds: that Saddam Hussein had weapons of mass destruction; that he was aligned with al-Qaeda; that he was a threat to his Middle East neighbors; even that he was a long-distance threat to the United States. It was also implied, though not expressly stated, that Saddam had had a hand in the 9/11 attack. All this false propaganda went essentially unchallenged by the commercial media and Congress, including the Democratic Party leadership. Yet the strategic basis for war was challenged by hundreds of retired military, diplomatic, and national security officials who had served under both Republican and Democratic administrations—including James Baker and Brent Scowcroft, national security and diplomatic advisers to George H. W. Bush, the president's own father. Other opponents included retired general William Odom, who ran the NSA; retired general Anthony Zinni, a former commander in chief of the U.S. Central Command; and retired vice admiral Jack Shanahan, former head of the Second Fleet. Zinni ridiculed Bush's promises to "stay the course," saying that the course was "headed over Niagara Falls,"[3] and added that he blamed the civilian leadership of the Pentagon directly, calling for resignations from Defense Secretary Donald Rumsfeld and his deputy Paul Wolfowitz. Retired general Merrill McPeak, former air force chief of staff, said that Rumsfeld had "done more damage to the country than we will recover from in 50 years." These and many other high-ranking retirees knew that many other U.S. Army generals and other military officials actively serving in the Pentagon were also opposed to the war but were muted from speaking in public.

The problem with all these expressions of opposition was that they were never coordinated, directed at Congress, or broadcast strategically enough to fuel the legitimate doubts of the public. One by one, these patriotic Americans were over-powered by the media-intense relay of daily White House propaganda repeated by a compliant press. They spoke out, wrote, were interviewed—and then nothing happened, because there was no infrastructure to transform their objections into a genuine movement with sustained visibility and momentum.

There was one voice among the opposition who could have made a more substantial difference in that moment: George Soros, the wealthy philanthropist and supporter of progressive causes.

Soros was certainly on the right side of the argument. He spoke out against the prospect of war repeatedly, citing an array of reasons and predicting that the United States would descend into a quagmire as a result. He did receive some media coverage for his own statements. But that coverage was easily drowned out by the White House's months-long campaign of lies, deceptions, and propaganda, capped by Bush's decision to send the armed forces to Iraq without letting the UN inspectors finish their job there.

But Soros could have done more. In the nine months before the invasion, he could have turned the tide and more than tripled the three hundred or so retired officials openly against the war. How? By recruiting other influential objectors and working together to build a mass media campaign, coordinate their opposition, and enlist full-time organizers in key congressional districts to call for public hearings and challenge the abdicating Congress to assert its constitutional duties.

How much would it have cost? Perhaps as much as $200 million. But that would have been nothing to Soros, one of the world's most successful financial speculators. Soros, whose reported income in recent years is between $2 billion and $3 billion, spends a lot on what he calls "political philanthropy," helping to build democratic institutions in the United States and many other countries. In 2004, he contributed about $35 million to the Democratic Party's campaign on behalf of John Kerry. Both before and after the Iraq sociocide commenced, I tried to call Soros and suggest that putting big money behind these stalwart patriots could avert a very big disaster. He did not call back.

This exercise in "what if" thinking is something anyone who is serious about change should use to spark his or her imagination. Any culture's definition of charitable giving is liable to change over time. Up to the late nineteenth century, America's wealthy tended to give to their churches and to fund some basic needs of the poor—following the biblical definition of Christian charity. When the first wave of wealthy industrialists reached an advanced age, their giving became more institutional. In his 1889 book *The Gospel of Wealth*, the steel magnate Andrew Carnegie observed that "the man who dies thus rich, dies disgraced." The Scotch immigrant established scientific institutions, a university, a foundation, and paid for the construction of five thousand libraries all over his adopted country. John D. Rockefeller founded Rockefeller University and other institutions advancing science and public health. Philanthropy moved toward investment in enduring institutions in addition to traditional, immediate relief for the poor, sick, and orphaned.

Wealthy benefactors in my small hometown in Connecticut built the local high school, the local hospital, the local library—all around 1900. This was the pattern for early twentieth-century philanthropy in many cities and towns. Foundations were established to support existing civic institutions in the arts, sports, and, most ambitiously, prep schools, colleges, and universities. The Ford Foundation figured prominently in these grants, along with many of the very wealthy who funded libraries, dormitories, laboratories, museums, and other buildings for their alma maters.

To whatever extent the wealthy felt about certain political ideologies, public policies, or candidates for office in the second half of the twentieth century, their response was to make campaign contributions. After the tumultuous 1960s, the Ford Foundation broke new ground in philanthropy by providing substantial seed money for several public interest law groups. In doing so, Ford was financing the very practice of advocacy, mostly in the form of litigation in the civil rights, environmental, and consumer arenas. These and other public interest law organizations brought many successful cases that shifted some power from the perpetrators to the aggrieved classes, as did the reform laws passed during that period of American history. These relatively large grants gave these groups a head start, allowing them to solicit a broader base of funding through smaller donations from a larger number of citizens. These efforts demonstrated that organized, focused citizen action could counter corporately-compromised politicians and their commercial allies. Yet in recent decades, this kind of action has not translated into larger and more established funding for civic campaigns pushing for major redirections of our political economy and major curbs on the entrenched corporate government.

But it's not just a matter of scale—rising from a few millions of dollars to billions of dollars for redirections. It's also a matter of distinguishing between charity and justice. As the peace activist Colman McCarthy wrote in the *National Catholic Reporter*: "a difference exists between charity and justice. Money to charity eases the problem; money to justice destroys the problem. Charity money intervenes after the problem. Justice money goes to prevention."[4] There are many talented Americans working in charitable services dealing with issues such as hunger, homelessness, and adult illiteracy who would rather work to *prevent* these problems than to treat their effects. But the money to fund this work just isn't there. The supply of talent vastly exceeds the supply of payroll.

The demand for justice far exceeds the supply of payroll. Yet the potential supply of private wealth that could be applied to bridge the gap between the promise and the realities of our society is truly enormous. Half of the estimated wealth of the Forbes 400 in 2009 amounted to $600 billion. Most of that wealth can be considered "dead money"—that is, idle money earning interest, dividends, or capital gains from treasuries or the impersonal market, not live money being invested toward active, constructive, socially beneficial ends. Only a very few super-rich citizens have been willing to step into potentially controversial arenas to support the principles of justice and fair play.

Let's take the wondrous case of Warren Buffett, America's second-richest person after Bill Gates Jr., who has called on Congress to "stop coddling the super-rich" so that "billionaires like me pay more taxes." He has pursued this argument from meetings with senators to the opinion pages of the *New York Times*. He has called on Congress to raise rates on capital gains and dividends, which are mostly taxed at 15 percent. He has mocked the theory that higher taxes on capitals gains and dividends discourage investment and reduce job creation. Despite his wealth, Buffett says that he paid 17.4 percent in taxes on his multimillion dollars of taxable income—a lower rate than any of the other twenty people in his office paid, including his secretary. Buffett has said that his calls for tax reform are about more than getting revenue numbers up to reduce the deficit. They're about fairness. "Our leaders have asked for 'shared sacrifice.' But when they did the asking, they spared me. I checked with my mega-rich friends to learn what pain they were expecting. They, too, were left untouched. . . . It's time for our government to get serious about shared sacrifice."[5]

Commenting on Buffett's widely noticed op-ed, *Times* columnist James B. Stewart reminded us that President Ronald Reagan treated ordinary income and capital gains the same and "made it a centerpiece of his successful 1986 tax reform law,"[6] which lasted for eleven years before Newt Gingrich and Bill Clinton lowered the rates on capital gains and dividends.

So how could Warren Buffett proceed if he truly wanted Congress to turn his idea into law? First, he could make a sizable first-stage investment—say, $50 million—to fund a lobbying campaign and ask dozens of his close mega-rich friends to contribute at a similar level. Their objective would be to get a super-majority of the Senate and House to agree to a specific tax reform bill inspired by the idea of shared sacrifice. My guess is that this group—call it Billionaires for Shared Sacrifice—would start with about 30 percent of the 535 members of Congress already in agreement. Their task would then be to convince roughly 190 more legislators to come on board. The moment the group's existence is announced, it would become big news for the mass media—with interviews, profiles, running commentary, and spirited reactions from the affluent opponents and their ideological apologists. All this and more would doubtless keep the issue in the news—ensuring that emerging political candidates would have to debate the issue on the campaign trail and take a stand for or against the group and its principles.

The real question is: Why hasn't Buffett turned his eloquent calls for reform into a drive for concrete legislative change? Well, he is running a huge conglomerate business. Time is his most precious commodity—so much so that a major part of his success over sixty years has been his recruitment of capable managers, holding them to specific standards and objectives and delegating authority and responsibility to them. But this management style would suit the organization of a lobbying drive on Congress equally well. Buffett himself could serve as the serious, congenial, jovial, gregarious, brainy maestro who knows how to get along with his peer group and who knows how to find the people with experience, energy, and judgment to bring those additional 190 lawmakers home. From his retail experience, he knows that the victory starts and finishes back home in the lawmakers' districts, but that the real battle will be fought on Capitol Hill. Are the times auspicious for such tax reform? They could hardly be better. Greed and incompetence at the top, especially on Wall Street, have given rise to extraordinary anger on Main Street. For them it is no longer a question of what and who, only a question of when and how.

For a society such as ours—which puts price tags on just about everything, from the asset value of a corporate logo to the rental premium for a penthouse apartment view—isn't it time that we start paying a price for justice? How much would it cost to get single-payer health insurance, prison and drug policy reform, a living wage, severe reductions in corporate crime and fraud, voluntary public funding of public campaigns, and organized consumer watchdog groups? How much would it cost to place our country on a sure path to replacing fossil fuels and nuclear power with renewable energies and massive energy efficiency technology? How much would it cost to implement electoral reforms, such as ending the practice of gerrymandering or removing ballot access obstructions to give voters a choice of many candidates with varied agendas? How much would it cost to enact a sales tax on Wall Street trading transactions, which would bring in hundreds of billions of dollars a year to salvage budgets and lighten up taxes on workers? How much would it take to enact the kind of carbon tax that's been favored even by ExxonMobil, as well as sustainable pioneers like the late Ray Anderson, former CEO of the environmentally responsible corporation Interface Inc.? I authored a work of realistic political fiction—"*Only the Super-Rich Can Save Us!*"—about what it takes to make these changes.

Unlike most major social changes—which rely on the kinds of behavioral change that's almost impossible to mandate—these popular proposals need only to go through Congress and the president to take effect—and they already have solid intellectual, empirical, and public support. The only question is how much money it will take to organize a successful campaign to get them enacted.

As for who will provide these funds, the answer should be clear. The enlightened super-rich—those who are interested not just in money but in justice—are diverse in background, experience, temperament, age, interests, and priorities. Our society, sadly, suffers from plenty of low-hanging problems from which they're free to pick and choose. For example one with a legal background could bankroll campaigns to break down the barriers that keep most Americans from having access to justice—in the courts or before government agencies—without the delays, costs, and needless obstacles that currently stand in the way of equal justice under law.

To be sure, this is a call for a plutocratic cultural revolution—which may strike some as a quixotic goal. But never before in human history has it been so clearly within reach. One successful breakthrough by a progressive-minded wealthy American will only encourage others into action, just as the early grand donors to city symphonies encouraged others to give. Of course, starting city symphonies is much easier than enacting major reforms, but then the gratifications of improving our country are also much greater. Consider the goal of abolishing poverty in the United States, which exists at a level that has been unknown in Western Europe for more than half a century. Enacting safety nets, as these war-torn countries did in a democratic fashion after World War II, should be well within our reach. There is no reason that our nation, with its unimaginable wealth, should not enjoy the world's highest overall standard of living.

Some of the enlightened wealthy have found a role for themselves by investing in better management of advocacy groups, trying to help them connect more effectively with one another through broader umbrella groups advancing a progressive agenda. One such effort is the Democracy Alliance (DA), launched in 2005. Though the DA has made some strides, as yet it has operated within existing parameters and has not yet become the kind of transforming presence the movement needs. A truly galvanizing new group would focus on speed of mobilization, a critical mass of human and material resources, and a sharp, smart focus on a specific objective. That's the best recipe for substantial and effective change. We need singular pioneers, people who seek to make history and use their fortunes to fuel historic achievements. A wonderful experience awaits them if they should devote themselves not just to charity but to justice—and to establishing a modern tradition of responsibility for their posterity.

Of course, there are changes that don't necessarily require legislative action. There are direct ways to make major changes if the money is there. One example is establishing a string of citizen laboratories where people can take samples of water, air, food, soil, and other materials suspected of contamination and have them reliably tested for free. Such labs would encourage the further growth of citizen scientists and would be an early alert network that could catch potential hazards years before they spread any further. Or a super-rich group might establish a network of after-school good citizenship clubs, where youngsters could learn about their community—past and present—and study how to correct harmful, wasteful, or otherwise undesirable conditions in their communities. These developing civic skills would stay with them into adulthood, making for more socially responsible future generations. In our video-saturated society of virtual reality and rote education, giving youngsters a civic life experience would open up a whole new world—the world of reality—and prepare them to be public citizens with the power to change circumstances rather than withdrawing into themselves.

Some of the initiatives are already under way. One such project has been launched by the Gates Foundation and a group of hedge fund investors, who have been purchasing millions of mosquito nets for free distribution to afflicted African regions. Malaria takes nearly 1 million lives a year, mostly children and pregnant mothers; for endangered families, a mosquito net is not a panacea but a measurable fix. I have a personal stake in this cause: as a child I contracted malaria overseas, and as an adult I have long urged officials in Washington to reduce malaria fatalities in just this and other ways. During the Clinton administration, I spoke with several White House special assistants, urging them to persuade the president to give a major speech on infectious diseases, including malaria. Hillary Clinton's special assistant told me that whenever the First Lady traveled to Asia and Africa, the fear of getting infected was always on their minds. But when President Clinton was invited to address the annual convention of the American Society of Tropical Medicine and Hygiene Conference in Washington, D.C., in 1999, he declined to appear.

Obviously there are some very rich people, besides Bill Gates, who have decided not to wait forever for the government to take action. One leveraged-buyout investor, Ray Chambers, has used not only his own money but, more important, his organizational and convening skills to raise money, awareness, and action on the malaria issue. Alex Perry's book *Lifeblood: How to Change the World One Dead Mosquito at a Time* describes how Chambers focused on seven African countries hardest hit by malaria. According to the *New York Times Book Review*: "It's hard to say which was tougher: herding thousands of bureaucrats toward a single goal or getting all those nets into the hands of so many of the poor, especially in remote areas of Congo, Nigeria and what is now South Sudan." Millions of nets were distributed and in some areas with astounding though not surprising results. Chambers was so effective that he was named a United Nations special envoy for malaria eradication. Notice the word "eradication," which means prevention, not "cure," which means treatment after the parasite enters the bloodstream. What Chambers did any motivated peer of his could do, combining major financial investment with real management savvy, to make real headway in a longstanding problem.

It's customary for futurists to emphasize how fast society is changing from year to year. Technologically they're correct, though the changes aren't always positive—as the rapid proliferation of weapons of mass destruction teaches us. But when it comes to changes that address our widely recognized social problems, we are more paralyzed than ever before. Think of how quickly our fractious forebears made this country into what they thought it should be: from the Declaration of Independence in 1776, to the Constitution in 1789, to a host of other social revolutions: enacting codes to curb the danger of fire in the cities; establishing a universal postal system; founding a network of lending libraries; bolstering a homestead small-farm economy and agricultural extension services; investing in massive yet essential public works; establishing scores of land grant universities; creating a network of national parks and national forests—all with far fewer tools than we now possess.

We must unlock our gridlocked nation. Paralysis has become our trademark—except when it comes to unleashing our war machine. We were once a nation that built highways and libraries, industries and schools. Today we have become a nation that failed to rescue or assist hundreds of thousands of victims from the largely preventable disaster of Hurricane Katrina. We are better than that.

But we cannot bring about any solutions to our nation's problems without making a serious commitment to civic engagement—the kind of commitment that can be jump-started by major investments from our wealthiest Americans. Every community has its exceptionally well-to-do members. Bill Gates estimates that about 15 percent of the wealthy currently give away a substantial part of their money. They could all be giving more—and they would if their communities explicitly looked to them for concrete inspiration and if more of their peers led by example. As Daniel Webster once said, "Justice, sir, is the great interest of man on earth." Without justice there can be no freedom and no liberty. "Philanthropy" means "love of mankind." Collective love is at the core of justice. The wealthiest among us, those who have the broadest horizons to put forces in motion, should embrace that work as their own highest calling.

17

Get Back on the Field—Literally

What in the world could sports be a *solution* for? Sports are about entertainment, recreation, fun, competition, wish fulfillment, or diversion, depending on your mind-set. For many people they're part of everyday life, not civic or professional life. What problem could sports possibly solve?

Would it surprise you to hear that sports could be a surprising solution not just to our epidemic of obesity but to our society's lack of civic engagement, to our younger generation's passive, sedentary lifestyle, and even to the explosion of health care costs that are crippling our economy?

Sports are as old as society itself. In every known culture, no matter its size, anthropologists have found evidence that *play* was part of its social fiber. And one major form of play has been physical sport—that is, playful physical activity that follows a basic set of rules and exists to test its players' skills and endurance. In early tribal societies, sport was unorganized, with players generally outnumbering spectators. By the time organized sports emerged, as in the original Olympic Games in Athens, spectators had come to far outnumber the athletes. But the spectators were allowed to watch for free.

Fast-forward to twenty-first-century America. When most people hear the word "sports," they generally think of organized team sports, both amateur and professional. The drive to set and break new performance records, and the growth of 24/7 media coverage, has widened the gap between player and spectator. Those who make it to the games themselves are often the true devotees who have dedicated decades to obsessing over arcane statistics and who have often portioned a significant amount of their personal budget each year to pay the stiff ticket, food, and parking prices that come with regular attendance. And, for the far larger number of spectators who watch the games on television, organized sports is one-way entertainment.

This was not always the way. Decades ago, before professional leagues and big-time college divisions came to dominate our sports culture, the focus was on local, informal sports. Through the first half of the twentieth century, games were just as likely to start up in a backyard as in a stadium. Teenagers played stickball or touch football; younger kids played hopscotch or kick the can. Grandparents would mix it up with their ten-year-old grandchildren. With no TVs or computers to keep the kids inside, all the fun was happening outdoors.

At school, physical education was a requirement. It was conducted so that all could participate as long as they were mobile. There really were no organized teams until high school, and then only three sports at the most. Most youngsters engaged in informal intramural sports, picking up a glove or grabbing a basketball. Baseball was by far the dominant sport in America, from the sandlots to the major leagues. The Olympics were strictly amateur with no corporate sponsorships, logos, advertisements, or any participation by paid professional athletes. It recalled the ancient Athenian ideal of physical and mental fitness.

How different the scene is today! The missions of professional sports today are victory (at all costs) and profit (at all costs). The sports industry relies on a massive, and passive, fan base that watches countless games at home (in 2011, there were five NBA games on Christmas Day) while scarfing down the junk food, beer, and soft drinks they see advertised between play. The results are the troubling escalation of obesity among Americans of all ages and especially among the young. Ironically, the more professional sports absorb our time, the more we fall into a sedentary lifestyle that compromises our overall physical fitness.

Students who aren't engaging in sports are spending their time sitting before computers at school and at home. They are being bused to school instead of walking or biking, living in isolated suburban enclaves where street life, public spaces, and even sidewalks are a rarity. All these trends point in one direction: fewer youngsters getting active. The schools themselves are feeding into the trend, cutting physical education classes and intramural sports programs, whether because of budget limitations, overemphasis on testing, or a lack of interest from their pupils. And yet studies show that students receiving daily physical education are not only healthier but perform better academically as well.[1]

By the time boys and girls reach the age of thirteen, most are done participating in competitive sports. We no longer expect them to maintain a lifetime engagement with sports, whether in the backyard or in the public arenas. Granted, our national and local fitness associations have rightly dedicated much more attention to trying to reverse the rise of obesity. But these challenges should go hand in hand: the more we encourage children to get involved with community-based sports, the more we're leading them to view athletic activity as a permanent and rewarding part of their lives.

One continual problem is the increasing connection between the high-stakes business of professional sports and the aspirations of our young athletes.

The alluring spectacle of professional sports has replaced neighborhood games as the primary way youngsters learn about athletics today. And the mirage of potential stardom works its way into the consciousness of countless middle school students every year. Whether because they're mimicking the behavior of their elders or because they're desperate to secure an athletic scholarship and put themselves on the road to the pros, more youngsters are starting to specialize in particular sports at younger and younger ages. At the same time, the pressure on varsity athletes to perform—often under tyrannical coaches, themselves pressured by parents and alumni to win—has led to a growing use of steroids and other performance-enhancing drugs among high school students.

The anything-to-win drift of sports culture, with its attendant calculus of adult and peer pressure, testosterone, and violence, has led to a long-ignored epidemic of concussions on our playing fields, often involving brain trauma with devastating long-term effects. The recent investigations of such injuries among young players illustrate how fully the business of sports has obliterated any semblance of public accountability for its excesses, as encouraged by the professional sports leagues—the National Football League, the National Basketball Association, Major League Baseball, and the National Hockey League—along with the Division 1 NCAA big-money college teams.

As a society, we must take immediate action to dial down the violent, high-stakes world of professional sports—and replace it with a rebirth of local, community-based athletics.

To promote the growth of safe and reasonable sports participation for all ages, we need to shift our focus from the concentrated, profit-based orientation of professional or quasi-professional sports and replace it with something that has already taken hold in many countries, especially in the West: a National Sports Commission (NSC).

Significant sports reform in our country would be difficult without a more democratic change in the way we, as a society, set our sporting priorities. The NSC, chartered by Congress to represent all sports stakeholders, would offer everyday citizens a forum to suggest, discuss, and debate potential changes to the status quo. Among those invited to join would be players, coaches, fans, students, teachers, administrators, the media, local civic and municipal groups, philanthropists, sports physicians, and parents.

The NSC would position itself to set a new national sports policy, one that respects all stakeholders, including taxpayers, and the goals of a physically fit citizenry. It would conduct research and analysis on contemporary sports issues, serve as an arbitrator and regulator in clearly defined areas, and be a clearinghouse for all sports stakeholders in the country. The commission would not shy away from serious abuses, from health and safety issues in all age groups to the seizure of taxpayer money away from community sports facilities to subsidize professional stadiums, ballparks, and arenas.

In any major reform initiative, there are many more people who favor potential changes than there are actively engaged citizens who are willing to organize and push for those changes. Decades ago, a young lawyer/reporter named Peter Gruenstein and I started a group called FANS to foster a new debate about sports in our society, but the group never got traction because even fans who agreed with us about issues like ticket prices and television blackouts by teams of games in their hometowns, were reluctant to band together to fight for changes. We recently revived the effort under the banner of League of Fans (leagueoffans.org), and in the process we're learning even more about what millions of Americans want to change about today's sports culture:

First, they would like to see their sports tax dollars used to build recreational facilities for all ages in their communities or neighborhoods. Public opinion has largely been against tax dollars building corporately owned professional sports facilities. That is why billionaire sports owners do not like referendums on such taxpayer-funded structures. Much better, they believe, to cut a private deal with local politicians, who desire box-seat season tickets and face time with the celebrity athletes.

Second, they want physical education reinstated in schools and tailored to the needs of different children. Even parents who are overweight and out of shape themselves don't want their children to follow in their footsteps, obsessed with their mobile phones and computer screens and rarely getting off the couch.

Third, fans and parents alike want more attention paid to the safety and health of the players. It is ironic that sports are producing so many injuries—concussions and substance-related injury and disease—when sports should be enhancing health and physical strength.

Fourth, they want equal opportunity in sports for all Americans. Although conditions have improved in the last half century, women and people with disabilities are still discriminated against in the world of sports. Female athletes continue to lag significantly behind their male counterparts in participation opportunities, number of scholarships, and prospects for advancement in athletic administration. With more than 50 million people in the United States who have documented disabilities, the opportunities for athletes with disabilities are not keeping up with the marvelous expectations generated by the Special Olympics.

Fifth, many people are turned off by the win-at-any-cost attitude that's so prevalent in today's sports culture—from overbearing pressure from coaches and parents, to schools that let athletes skimp on their education as long as they keep winning. The frenzy for revenue and wins has damaged two critical goals for college sports: (1) enhanced academic integrity in college athletics, and (2) fair, ethical, and safe treatment of college athletes. Coaches who treat their athletes inhumanely, using force and fear to motivate them, should not be rewarded with lucrative employment contracts. Humanistic coaches, such as the legendary John Wooden of UCLA and John Gagliardi of St. John's

University, have been among the winningest coaches of all time in basketball and football, respectively. The common belief that coaches must be abusive to be successful is a myth. Research shows that if you find a task fun, you'll perform better. If more coaches took, in the philosophy of Gagliardi, a Golden Rule approach to coaching, treating their players the way they themselves would like to be treated, fewer athletes would drop out of sports in their teens, and more athletes at every level would be happier and more satisfied.

Moreover, especially in first-rank college sports, where yearly athletic scholarships are contingent on athletic performance, athletes are under the extreme domination of the coach and the athletic department. If education is truly a university's first priority—as it should be—then athletes, like the rest of the student body, should be under the direction of the academic department.

Big-time college sports is filled with hypocrisy. NCAA administrators, college and university presidents, athletic directors, and coaches are constantly bragging about their educational values and the importance of "student-athletes" getting an education. But their actions speak louder than their words. They have resisted even simple reforms that would reflect their commitment to education, such as offering only four- or five-year athletic scholarships, structured so that only a student's academic performance, not his or her athletic record, can affect whether their financial aid is renewed. The Drake Group, a panel of college teachers, has promoted this reform as one of numerous changes to restore education as the primary motive for all schools offering athletic scholarships. Yet commercialism keeps spreading throughout the college system—as with the emergence of the lucrative Bowl Championship Series (BCS) football cartel, which blocks non-BCS schools from competing. It may be necessary to remove the nonprofit, tax-exempt status of the big-time, highly commercialized college athletic departments that they currently enjoy at the expense of their college athletes.

But all these reforms are just that—attempts to correct deeply entrenched problems in our professional and collegiate sports culture. How can sports be a solution to some of society's larger problems?

The truth is restoring informal sports as a regular part of American life is far more important than the considerable task of reforming organized sports. We need to bring the heart of American sports back to the neighborhood—to the millions of baseball diamonds, soccer fields, and home driveway basketball hoops across the country. Such simple facilities can afford millions of people a little exercise, either alone or together with friends and neighbors for a few minutes of friendly competition. We need more of such simple, cheap facilities in residential areas where people live and work. Some larger white-collar companies provide their workers with exercise rooms laden with modern exercise equipment. That is not sport, though it does address the need for physical fitness in workplaces dominated by fingers and eyes operating computers. Sport should be defined as fun, competitive, socially bonding, and enjoyably recallable enough for repeat engagements.

More community gyms, playscapes, ball fields, and tracks (including smaller versions) easily accessible from home or work and on weekends would have a measureable effect on obese or overweight, out-of-shape Americans. Shedding pounds means shedding risks of diseases such as diabetes and high blood pressure, which in turn sheds big money from our collective huge health care bills and allows life to be more pleasurable. The more available, affordable, and accessible these facilities are, the more the culture of sports returns to its amateur origins where the players outnumbered the spectators.

———

We're at a point in this country where two-thirds of adults and one-third of children are overweight or obese. Those figures have doubled for adults and *tripled* for children and teens over the last three decades.

Moreover, those percentages continue to be on the rise, with some research economists predicting that 42 percent of Americans may be obese by 2030. To look at it another way, the U.S. health care system could be burdened with 32 million more obese people within two decades. These upward trends could be disastrous, not only for our health and well-being but also in terms of the country's health care costs and our productivity as a nation.

The obesity epidemic even has a negative impact on airline costs. Due to the extra weight Americans gained over the last decade, the airline industry spends an additional $275 million each year on jet fuel.

Rising health care costs could be especially damaging for the United States. Health economists warn us that we have little hope of controlling our rising health care costs until we effectively address obesity. Consider this: if we could just keep obesity rates at today's (unacceptable) levels, we could save nearly $550 billion in medical expenditures over the next two decades, according to health economist Eric Finkelstein. Obesity-related medical costs are nearly 60 percent more than the expenses for all types of cancer. And the situation will get much worse without a significant major public health intervention.

To that end, developing more community sports and recreation facilities, and creating more sports opportunities for Americans of all ages, should be a major part of a significant physical activity prescription for the nation.

While the adult obesity problem we're dealing with is an ugly situation, what's even uglier is that our children are on pace to be significantly fatter than we are by the time they reach adulthood. Until recently, type 2 diabetes was considered an adult disease, often called "adult-onset diabetes." Yet in recent years, the incidence of the disease has increased dramatically in children and adolescents because of more children being overweight and inactive. "Children today have a shorter life expectancy than their parents for the first time in 100 years," according to Dr. William J. Klish, professor of pediatrics at Baylor College of Medicine. Isn't that stunning?

Making this health challenge even more confounding is the fact that, while the physical fitness and health of our young people has been steadily declining, the number of physical education classes, intramural sports programs, and lower-level varsity sports squads is also steadily declining in our schools. This despite an array of experts stressing more physical activity is crucial if children are to avoid obesity and achieve optimal health.

Schools from the junior high school level through college have put more resources into sports programs for elite varsity athletes at the expense of participation opportunities for all students. The focus on top-level athletes is especially troublesome when considering that more than 75 percent of U.S. children are not active for even twenty minutes a day, the minimum daily activity requirement. A combination of bad junk food and sugary drinks with a sedentary lifestyle of staring at screens is a deadly concoction for both physical and mental health.

Dr. Kenneth Cooper, known as the "father of aerobics," agrees that the state of our kids' physical fitness has never been worse than it is today. He has called for quality, daily, fitness-based physical education in schools across the nation.

Undoubtedly, sports can be a big part of the solution to our dual inactivity and obesity epidemics—for children and adults. The United States lags behind other industrialized nations when it comes to lifelong sports participation. A small percentage of us play; the rest of us are spectators. There is a huge gap between the sports resources for top-level athletes and the resources available for everyone else. We continue to build sparkling stadiums and arenas for wealthy professional sports team owners, yet cut physical education classes and sports programs for our children . . . all while we're in the midst of a childhood obesity crisis!

A good model for adult sports participation is the European system. In most European countries, there's a sports club for everyone, regardless of age or ability. Whether you're a premier adult athlete or athletically challenged youngster, everyone can find a sports club. The United States needs a club system that allows citizens to keep playing sports well into adulthood. Sports clubs in Europe will often have an A team, a B team, a C team, etc., so that everyone who wants to play is accommodated.

Here, in contrast, the move to spectating starts early. Our youth sports programs are set up to weed out marginal athletes by the age of thirteen, when the focus turns to developing top-level competitive, travel teams.

Unfortunately, the teen years are a time when sports can have the most positive impact on young people. Multiple studies show that teenagers who participate in sports are less likely to smoke, consume illegal drugs or alcohol, suffer from anxiety or depression, become pregnant, miss classes, and drop out of school. Research also reveals that fit children perform better academically. In addition, for those who regularly participate in sports, self-esteem tends to rise, and the ability to solve problems, handle adversity, and be creative improves.

Most of these benefits apply to adults as well. Of particular note is the fact that cardiovascular exercise, of the kind required in most sports, is especially good for brain health. Dr. John Ratey, a Harvard psychiatrist and an expert on exercise's impact on the brain, says that exercise acts like Miracle-Gro for the brain because it grows neurons and increases brain function during cognitively challenging tasks.

Cutting physical education classes and intramural sports

programs for our children, despite the numerous benefits of sports participation, is simply unconscionable. Moreover, the fact that we don't have more lifelong sports opportunities and facilities for adults, especially in this era of skyrocketing health care costs, is irrational.

A national sports policy, incorporating many of these programs and principles, would have an impressive impact on daunting challenges facing our country today.

For centuries, sports have been part of the fabric of communities. Stickball and sandlot baseball are popular examples from the last century. In early America, sports were frequently part of camp meetings, farm festivals, and community feasts. Popular competitions included footraces, wrestling, horse racing, and rifle shooting. Sports were a matter of neighbors, young and old, getting together for fun and competition. These highly social games helped create community harmony.

The industrial revolution led to new forms of sport, and while informal sport remained a mainstay of communities, this era also fostered the beginning of organized sport. Prizefighting gained popularity, but the first large-scale spectator sport was horse racing. Baseball was primarily an informal game played in neighborhoods by children and adults.

While organized sport, some of the commercial variety, became more prevalent in the nineteenth and twentieth centuries in the United States, informal sports—engaged in primarily for the enjoyment of community participants—remained a key part of community life up to the middle of the twentieth century. The rules were generally informal, mutually agreed to by the participants and not by an organizing, private regulatory body. Games were local and friendly.

Today, "community sports" can run the gamut from informal to highly organized. But what should distinguish community sports is the lack of professionalization and commercialization. Community sports organizations have codified rules and regulations, but they largely manage to avoid the win-at-all-costs, profit-at-all-costs attitudes of modern-day big-time sports organizations—or highly competitive youth sports programs. The purpose of community sports should honor its original intentions: fun, recreation, exercise, socialization, and widespread participation.

Today, too many youth and high school sports programs are based on an elite athlete philosophy: a few athletes play on "varsity"-level teams, while the vast majority of young people are left to become spectators. They should be refocused away from sports spectating (including video gaming) to more of an intramural participation model, with sports programs that promote participation, fun, exercise, and social interaction, rather than just excellence in athletic skill.

A proper community sports program is one where control is democratized and humanized. It should offer adequate sports facilities and equipment to all who would like to participate—and offer citizens of all ages an opportunity to stay healthy. Its goals should be maximizing participation and social interplay rather than winning alone. And certainly profit should have nothing to do with it—beyond the human ways each athlete can profit from the experience.

And finally, as a larger society, We the People need to develop a national sports policy—a movement we've started talking about online with League of Fans. As the league's policy director, Ken Reed, has written, it should be one that cultivates community sports opportunities; that removes barriers of sex, race, and age; that encourages local organizers to grow programs from the bottom up; that offers disadvantaged kids positive models of cooperative behavior and social harmony; and that includes a campaign to draw spectators out of the bleachers and down onto the field to play.

It's hard to think of a better metaphor for what our country needs.

"Commencement"

When students graduate from a college or university, their ceremony is called a "commencement," another word for "beginning." As we come to the end of this book, I'd like to strike the same tone—to call upon readers to make this ending a new beginning.

Whether you're already civically engaged or you're wondering what you can start doing to make a difference, in this book I've offered a host of ideas for action—ideas that might catch fire in your imagination, whatever your experience or temperament, wherever you live, and however much time you have available. All focus on empowerment and on the potential to take actions that can bring about justice and a finer quality of life for human beings.

Throughout history, change has started with conversations between two or more people, growing into community discussions that continue to widen and deepen into breakthrough social justice movements. If there's one important thing we've lost sight of in our culture today, it's the importance of *gathering*—of a group of people getting together in one place, in real time, to turn their shared ideas into a call for action. Get enough people together—three to four hundred will often do it—and you can persuade a member of Congress or state legislator to attend a public town meeting exclusively devoted to your cause, whether it's calling for a tax on Wall Street speculation, advancing peace, cutting corporate welfare, cracking down on corporate crime, raising the minimum wage, or expanding Medicare for all.

Such gatherings can get your agenda on the front burner and generate media coverage. They can lead to wider community calls for lawmakers to press for public hearings or pursue legislative action. All of this can start by leveraging just a few people, and then a small community. It's a good way to catapult an issue to a larger stage, and it's remarkable what a significant number of people showing up on a decision-maker's doorstep can accomplish.

The kinds of people who traditionally launch such efforts are those who have self-confidence as active citizens. They don't shy away from reaching out to their inactive friends and neighbors and inviting them to join the cause. And they're always looking for ideas and solutions to seemingly intractable problems. They're the "influentials"—people who blend a skepticism about corporate government or propaganda with an unrelenting optimism about the potential for change.

How can you reach good people in your community who seem resigned to doing nothing? One idea is to invite people who already want to join a cause, say, saving a post office branch or shoring up Medicare, to a civic skills gathering, where they can become engaged with their fellow citizens and take the opportunity to learn about successful social movements throughout American history. Such movements have often begun with a few stalwarts—ordinary people who did extraordinary things. And the activists who changed our history had far fewer tools than we have today—from the internet, with its massive ability to track and share information, to cell phones and video, which allow activists to coordinate while on the move. And there are plenty of free ways to get messages across—such as dialing local or regional talk radio shows—and broaden the available pool of interested citizens.

It's important to remember that no movement gets very far without taking the occasional step backward. There will be points when opposition starts appearing on the horizon—but by then, if your own efforts have been successful, you'll have amassed a good team of allies, and momentum will be on your side.

Of course, one challenge is that activism takes time and dedication—and these things can be hard to come by if you're working harder than ever to make ends meet, as many of our most motivated citizens are. But civic activities are usually far less onerous than the work most people have to do to pay the rent—and the rewards can be transcendent. One of the least burdensome civic activities is simply to spend more of your money in local economic communities. Prudently patronizing local credit unions, farmers' markets, local wind, solar, and other renewable energy sources, and community health clinics strengthens the vendors of these goods and services, which are rooted where you live and work. These local enterprises, unlike multinational corporations, aren't going to threaten to quit the country. Nor will they inflict the kinds of penalties that often straitjacket consumers who are trying to grapple with faceless corporate bureaucrats. The more we divert our consumer dollars away from these absentee global corporations and toward our local economic communities, the better chance we give those communities to remain stable and self-reliant for the long term.

As you gradually devote more consistent time and energy to the civic life, the more you'll come to see yourself as a public citizen. And you'll probably be pleasantly surprised at how your talents and skills start to have a positive effect on your community—and our nation. Public citizens become watchdogs who prevent harms directed at private citizens by standing up for the rights of consumers, workers, and taxpayers. Public citizens look forward to enlisting younger generations, including elementary-school children, in civic projects. They create community events that can become traditions— like Earth Day,

Food Day, or Taxpayer Day. They start enlivening existing institutions to become better and more productive. And public citizens encourage service clubs and schools to share civic knowledge and experiences with youngsters.

None of the Seventeen Solutions are beyond the range of the cultural rhythms of our society. None of them are contrary to America's historic traditions and values of democratic practice and fair play. None of them would require exorbitant amounts of time or many millions of active participants. Just think of the anguish, the turmoil, the expense, and the time needed to deal with the casualties, diseases, and trauma that stem from preventable wars and toxic environments. Imagine the painful anxieties that are associated with poverty, crushing debt, and political disenfranchisement.

Of all the ideas presented in *The Seventeen Solutions*, none is more important, more ignored, and less expensive than the need to shift power back to the people, to give every American the tools of democracy and access to justice. Injustice strips people of control over their lives. Any nation suffering from an imbalance of power will be plagued by chronic injustice; new ideas will never get heard in such a regime, much less get put into daily practice.

Until we manage to shift power away from the few and back to the many, our country is sure to continue its current decline, dragging our lives and livelihoods down with it. But once we start taking back the powers granted to us in the Constitution, our potential for civic enrichment, for a better society, is limited only by our resurgent ability to imagine new possibilities and new realities. There is no reason for us to fear or exaggerate the obstacles before us.

Our problems are clear and urgent. But We the People can always find better solutions.

Let us begin by looking at ourselves in this refreshing and invigorating way.

Resources

American Antitrust Institute
antitrustinstitute.org
Center for American Progress
AmericanProgress.org
Center for Corporate Policy
corporatepolicy.org
Center for Health, Environment and Justice
chej.org
Center for Justice and Democracy
centerjd.org
The Center for a New American Dream
NewDream.org
Center for Science in the Public Interest
cspinct.org
Center for the Study of Responsive Law
csrl.org
Citizen Scientists League
citizenscientistsleague.com
Citizens for Tax Justice
ctj.org
Citizen Works
citizenworks.org
Commercial Alert
CommercialAlert.org
The Community Environmental Legal Defense Fund
celdf.org
Corporate Crime Reporter
corporatecrimereporter.com

Corp Watch
  CorpWatch.org
Crocodyl
  crocodyl.org
Economic Policy Institute
  epi.org
Edge of Sports
  edgeofsports.com
Electronic Privacy Information Center
  epic.org
Environment America
  environmentamerica.org
Essential Information
  essential.org
Fair Contracts
  Faircontracts.org
The Giving Pledge
  givingpledge.org
International Center for Technology Assessment
  icta.org
International Corporate Accountability Roundtable
  accountabilityroundtable.org
Institute for Local Self-Reliance
  lsr.org
Institute for Policy Studies
  ips-dc.org
Knowledge Ecology International
  keionline.org
League of Fans
  leagueoffans.org
Ralph Nader's Website
  nader.org
Open Debates
  opendebates.org
Project on Government Oversight
  POGO.org
Physicians for Social Responsibility
  psr.org
Public Citizen
  citizen.org
Renewable Energy World
  RenewableEnergyWorld.com
Science and Environmental Health Network
  sehn.org
Taming the Giant Corporation
  TameTheCorporation.org

Tax Justice Network, USA
  tjn-usa.org
Taxpayers for Common Sense
  Taxpayer.net
Too Much: A Commentary on Excess and Inequality
  toomuchonline.org
US PIRG
  uspirg.org

BOOKS

Alinsky, Saul D. *Rules for Radicals: A Practical Primer for Realistic Radicals.* New York: Random House, 1971.

Alperovitz, Gar. *America Beyond Capitalism: Reclaiming Our Wealth, Our Liberty, and Our Democracy.* Washington, DC: Democracy Collaborative Press and Dollars and Sense, 2011.

Amato, Theresa. *Grand Illusion: The Myth of Voter Choice in a Two-Party Tyranny.* New York: The New Press, 2009.

Angell, Marcia. *The Truth About the Drug Companies: How They Deceive Us and What To Do About It.* New York: Random House, 2004.

Ashford, Nicholas A., and Ralph P. Hall. *Technology, Globalization, and Sustainable Development: Transforming the Industrial State.* New Haven: Yale University Press, 2011.

Bakan, Joel. *Childhood Under Siege: How Big Business Targets Children.* New York: Free Press, 2011.

———. *The Corporation: The Pathological Pursuit of Profit and Power.* New York: Free Press, 2004.

Black, Charles L. Jr. *A New Birth of Freedom: Human Rights, Named and Unnamed.* New York: Grosset/Putnam, 1997.

Blake, Casey Nelson, ed. *The Arts of Democracy: Art, Public Culture, and the State.* Washington, DC: Woodrow Wilson Center Press, 2007.

Blum, William. *Killing Hope: U.S. Military and CIA Interventions Since World War II.* Monroe, ME: Common Courage, 1995.

Bogus, Carl T. *Why Lawsuits Are Good for America: Disciplined Democracy, Big Business, and the Common Law.* New York: New York University Press, 2001.

Bollier, David. *Silent Theft: The Private Plunder of Our Common Wealth.* New York: Routledge, 2002.

Bollier, David, and Joan Claybrook. *Freedom from Harm: The Civilizing Influence of Health, Safety and Environmental Regulation.* Washington, DC: Public Citizen, 1986.

Brown, Jerry, and Rinaldo Brutoco. *Profiles in Power: The Antinuclear Movement and the Dawn of the Solar Age.* Farmington Hills, MI: Twayne Publishers, 1997.

Byrne, Janet, ed. *The Occupy Handbook.* New York: Back Bay Books, 2012.

Cahn, Edgar S. *No More Throw-Away People: The Co-Production Imperative.* Warner, NH: Essential Books, 2000.

Chomsky, Noam. *Necessary Illusions: Thought Control in Democratic Societies.* Cambridge, MA: Southend Press, 1989.

Clements, Jeffrey D. *Corporations Are Not People: Why They Have More Rights Than You Do and What You Can Do About It.* San Francisco, CA: Berrett-Koehler, 2011.

Clinard, Marshall, and Peter Yeager. *Corporate Crime.* Piscataway, NJ: Transaction Publishers, 2005.

Collins, Chuck. *99 to 1: How Wealth Inequality Is Wrecking the World and What We Can Do About It.* San Francisco, CA: Berrett-Koehler: 2012.

Commoner, Barry. *Making Peace with the Planet.* New York: Pantheon, 1990.

Court, Jamie. *Corporateering: How Corporate Power Steals Your Personal Freedom . . . and What You Can Do About It.* New York: Putnam, 2003.

Derickson, Alan. *Black Lung: Anatomy of a Public Health Disaster.* Ithaca, NY: Cornell University Press, 1998.

Drutman, Lee, and Charlie Cray. *The People's Business Controlling Corporations and Restoring Democracy.* San Francisco, CA: Berrett-Koehler, 1996.

Estes, Ralph W. *Taking Back the Corporation: A "Mad as Hell" Guide.* New York: Nation Books, 2005.

Farah, George. *No Debate: How the Two Major Parties Secretly Ruin the Presidential Debates.* New York: Seven Stories Press, 2004.

Fox, John O. *If Americans Really Understood the Income Tax.* New York: Basic Books, 2004.

Gardner, John W. *On Leadership.* New York: Free Press, 1993.

Geoghegan, Thomas. *Which Side Are You On? Trying to Be for Labor When It's Flat on Its Back.* New York: Plume, 1992.

Goodwyn, Lawrence. *The Populist Moment: A Short History of Agrarian Revolt in America.* New York: Oxford University Press, 1978.

Green, Mark. *Selling Out: How Big Corporate Money Buys Elections, Rams Through Legislation, and Betrays Our Democracy.* Darby, PA: Diane Publishing Company, 2002.

Greenwald, Glenn. *With Liberty and Justice for Some: How the Law Is Used to Destroy Equality and Protect the Powerful.* New York: Metropolitan Books, 2011.

Greider, William. *Who Will Tell the People: The Betrayal of American Democracy.* New York: Touchstone, 1993.

Hartmann, Thom. *Unequal Protection: How Corporations Became "People" and How You Can Fight Back.* San Francisco, CA: Berrett-Koehler, 2011.

Hawken, Paul, Amory Lovins, and Hunter L. Lovins. *Natural Capitalism: Creating the Next Industrial Revolution.* Boston: Back Bay Books, 2000.

Hedges, Chris. *Death of the Liberal Class.* New York: Nation Books, 2010.

Hightower, Jim. *Thieves in High Places: They've Stolen Our Country and It's Time to Take It Back.* New York: Viking, 2003.

Hochschild, Arlie Russell. *The Commercialization of Intimate Life: Notes from Home and Work.* Berkeley, CA: University of California Press, 2003.

Hock, Dee. *The Chaordic Organization.* San Francisco, CA: Berrett-Koehler, 2000.

Holtzman, Elizabeth, with Cynthia Cooper. *Cheating Justice: How Bush and Cheney Attacked the Rule of Law, Plotted to Avoid Prosecution, and What We Can Do About It.* Boston: Beacon Press, 2012.

Hunn, Dwayne, and Doris Ober. *Ordinary People Doing the Extraordinary: The Story of Ed and Joyce Koupal and the Initiative Process.* Mill Valley, CA: People's Lobby, 2001.

Isaac, Katherine. *Civics for Democracy: A Journey for Teachers and Students.* Warner, NH: Essential Books, 1992.

Jacobson, Michael F. *Marketing Madness: A Survival Guide for a Consumer Society.* Boulder, CO: Westview Press, 1995.

Johnson, Chalmers. *The Sorrows of Empire: Militarism, Secrecy and the End of the Republic.* New York: Metropolitan Books, 2004.

Johnston, David Cay. *Free Lunch: How the Wealthiest Americans Enrich Themselves at Government Expense (and Stick You with the Bill).* New York: Portfolio Hardcover, 2007.

———. *Perfectly Legal: The Covert Campaign to Rig Our Tax System to Benefit the Super Rich—and Cheat Everybody Else.* New York: Portfolio, 2003.

Jones, Van. *Rebuild the Dream.* New York: Nation Books, 2012.

Korten, David. *When Corporations Rule the World.* San Francisco, CA: Berrett-Koehler, 1995.

Krimsky, Sheldon. *Science in the Private Interest: Has the Lure of Profits Corrupted Biomedical Research?* Lanham, MD: Rowman & Littlefield Publishers, Inc. 2003.

Krimsky, Sheldon, and Peter Shorett, ed. *Rights and Liberties in the Biotech Age: Why We Need a Genetic Bill of Rights.* Lanham, MD: Rowman & Littlefield Publishers, 2005.

Leonard, Annie. *The Story of Stuff: How Our Obsession with Stuff is Trashing the Planet, Our Communities, and Our Health—and a Vision for Change.* New York: Free Press, 2010.

LeRoy, Greg. *The Great American Jobs Scam.* San Francisco, CA: Berrett-Koehler, 2005.

Levine, Bruce E. *Get Up, Stand Up: Uniting Populists, Energizing the Defeated, and Battling the Corporate Elite.* White River Junction, VT: Chelsea Green Publishing, 2011.

Levy, Stuart B. *The Antibiotic Paradox: How the Misuse of Antibiotics Destroys Their Curative Powers.* New York: Perseus Books, 2002.

Lewis, Charles. *The Buying of the Congress: How Special Interests Have Stolen Your Right to Life, Liberty, and the Pursuit of Happiness.* New York: Avon Books, 1998.

Linn, Susan. *The Case for Make Believe: Saving Play in a Commercialized World*. New York: New Press, 2009.

———. *Consuming Kids: Protecting Our Children from the Onslaught of Marketing and Advertising*. New York: Anchor Books, 2004.

Mattei, Ugo, and Laura Nader. *Plunder: When the Rule of Law is Illegal*. New York: Wiley-Blackwell, 2008.

McKibben, Bill. *Deep Economy: The Wealth of Communities and the Durable Future*. New York: Times Books, 2007.

Mitchell, Stacy. *Big-Box Swindle: The True Cost of Mega-Retailers and the Fight for America's Independent Businesses*. Boston: Beacon Press, 2006.

Mokhiber, Russell. *Corporate Crime and Violence: Big Business Power and the Abuse of Public Trust*. San Francisco, CA: Sierra Club Books, 1988.

Monks, Robert. *Corpocracy: How CEOs and the Business Roundtable Hijacked the World's Greatest Wealth Machine—and How to Get It Back*. New York: John Wiley & Sons, 2008.

Nace, Ted. *Gangs of America: The Rise of Corporate Power and the Disabling of Democracy*. San Francisco, CA: Berrett-Koehler, 2003.

Nader, Ralph. *Cutting Corporate Welfare*. New York: Seven Stories Press, 2000.

———. *Getting Steamed to Overcome Corporatism: Build It Together to Win*. Monroe, ME: Common Courage Press, 2011.

———. *"Only the Super-Rich Can Save Us!"* New York: Seven Stories Press, 2009.

Nader, Ralph, Mark Green, and Joel Seligman. *Taming the Giant Corporation: How the Larger Corporations Control Our Lives*. New York: W.W. Norton & Co., 1976.

Noble, David. *America by Design. Science, Technology, and the Rise of Corporate Capitalism*. New York: Oxford University Press, 1979.

Piven, Frances, and Richard A. Cloward. *Poor People's Movements: Why They Succeed, How They Fail*. New York: Random House, 1977.

Ridgeway, James. *It's All for Sale: The Control for Global Resources*. Durham, NC: Duke University Press, 2004.

Ritz, Dean, ed. *Defying Corporations, Defining Democracy: A Book of History and Strategy*. New York: Apex Press, 2001.

Roseland, Mark. *Toward Sustainable Communities: Resources for Citizens and their Governments*. Gabriola Island, BC, Canada: New Society Publishers, 1998.

Rosenfield, Harvey. *Silent Violence, Silent Death: The Hidden Epidemic of Medical Malpractice: A Consumer Guide to the Medical Malpractice Epidemic*. New York: Essential Books, 1994.

Rushkoff, Douglas. *Life, Inc.: How the World Became a Corporation and How to Take It Back*. New York: Random House, 2009.

Schlosser, Eric. *Fast Food Nation*. New York: Houghton Mifflin, 2001.

Schmidt, David. *Citizen Lawmakers: The Ballot Initiative Resolution*. Philadelphia, PA: Temple University Press, 1989.

Schor, Juliet. *Born to Buy: The Commercialized Child and the New Consumer Culture.* New York: Anchor, 2005.

Schultz, Ellen E. *Retirement Heist: How Companies Plunder and Profit from the Nest Eggs of American Workers.* New York: Portfolio/Penguin Hardcover, 2011.

Schumacher, E. F. *Small Is Beautiful: Economics as if People Mattered.* New York: HarperCollins, 1991.

Shaw, Christopher W. *Preserving the People's Post Office.* New York: Essential Books, 2006.

Sheinbaum, Stanley K., and William Meis Jr. *Stanley K. Sheinbaum: A 20th Century Knight's Quest for Peace, Civil Liberties and Economic Justice.* Los Angeles: Fairtree, 2011.

Shiva, Vandana. *Biopiracy: The Plunder of Nature and Knowledge.* Cambridge, MA: South End Press, 1997.

Shuman, Michael. *Local Dollars, Local Sense: How to Shift Your Money from Wall Street to Main Street and Achieve Real Prosperity: A Community Resilience Guide.* White River Junction, VT: Chelsea Green Publishing, 2012.

Smiley, Tavis, and Cornel West. *The Rich and the Rest of Us: A Poverty Manifesto.* New York: Smiley Books, 2012.

Sparrow, Malcolm K. *License to Steal: How Fraud Bleeds America's Health Care System.* Boulder, CO: Westview Press, 2000.

Sudetic, Chuck. *The Philanthropy of George Soros: Building Open Societies.* New York: Public Affairs, 2011.

Sullivan, Bob. *Stop Getting Ripped Off: Why Consumers Get Screwed, and How You Can Always Get a Fair Deal.* New York: Ballantine Books, 2009.

Taibbi, Matt. *Griftopia: A Story of Bankers, Politicians, and the Most Audacious Power Grab in American History.* New York: Spiegel & Grau, 2011.

Van Gelder, Sarah, ed. *This Changes Everything: Occupy Wall Street and the 99% Movement.* San Francisco, CA: Berrett-Koehler Publisher, Inc., 2011.

Walljasper, Jay. *All That We Share: A Field Guide to the Commons.* New York: The New Press, 2010.

Washburn, Jennifer. *University Inc. The Corporate Corruption of Higher Education.* New York: Basic Books, 2005.

Washington, Harriet A. *Deadly Monopolies: The Shocking Corporate Takeover of Life Itself—and the Consequences for Your Health and Our Medical Future.* New York: Doubleday, 2011.

Wenk, Edward. *Making Waves: Engineering, Politics and the Social Management of Technology.* Urbana-Champaign, IL: University of Illinois Press, 1995.

West, Cornel. *Race Matters.* Boston, MA: Beacon Press, 2003.

Woolhandler, Steffie, Ida Hellander, and David Himmelstein, M.D. *Bleeding the Patient: The Consequences of Corporate Healthcare.* Monroe, ME: Common Courage Press, 2001.

Worldwatch Institute. *State of the World 2012: Moving Toward Sustainable Prosperity.* Washington, DC: Island Press, 2012.

Wylie, Jeanie. *Poletown: Community Betrayed.* Urbana-Champaign, IL: University of Illinois Press, 1989.

Zinn, Howard. *A People's History of the United States.* New York: Harper-Collins, 1995.

Zirin, Dave. *People's History of Sports in the United States: 250 Years of Politics, Protest, People, and Play:* New York: New Press, 2009.

Zunz, Olivier. *Philanthropy in America: A History (Politics and Society in Twentieth-Century America).* Princeton, NJ: Princeton University Press, 2011.

Notes

1: FUNDAMENTAL TAX REFORM

1. Beutler, Brian, "Chart of the Day: The '47 Percent' Pay Their Fair Share," *Talking Points Memo*, Oct. 21, 2011, http://tpmdc.talking pointsmemo.com/2011/10/chart-of-the-day-the-47-percent-pay -their-fair-share.php.
2. Talking Points Memo.com, Brian Beutler, personal interview, June 11, 2012.
3. Collins, Chuck, "Pay Up, Corporate Tax Dodgers: We're Chumps unless We Force Congress to Stop Tax Haven Abuse," *Other Words*, Feb. 28, 2011, www.otherwords.org/articles/pay_up_corporate_tax _dodgers.
4. Ibid.
5. "Frequently Asked Questions and Answers about Carbon Taxes and the Carbon Tax Center," Carbon Tax Center, www.carbontax.org/ faq/ (accessed Oct. 7, 2011).
6. Institute on Taxation and Economic Policy, "Basic Principles and Terms," *The ITEP Guide to Fair State and Local Taxes* (Washington, D.C., March 2011), p. 3. Accessible online at www.itepnet.org/pdf/ guide2.pdf.
7. National Taxpayers Union 1988. "History of Federal Individual Income Bottom and Top Bracket Rates," http://ntu.org/tax-basics/ history-of-federal-individual-1.html.
8. World Wealth Report. 2011. Merrill Lynch. P.6. www.ml.com/me dia/114235.pdf.
9. Johnston, David, *Perfectly Legal: The Covert Campaign to Rig Our Tax System to Benefit the Super Rich—and Cheat Everybody Else* (New York: Portfolio, 2003), p. 183.
10. Barlett, Donald L., and James B. Steele, *America: Who Really Pays the Taxes?* (New York: Simon and Schuster, 1994).

2: MAKE OUR COMMUNITIES MORE SELF-RELIANT

1. Alperovitz, Gar, Steve Dubb, and Ted Howard, "7 Cool Companies: The Best Alternatives to Corporate Power," *Yes! Magazine*, July 29, 2007, www.yesmagazine.org/issues/stand-up-to-corporate-power/7-cool-companies.
2. Miller, Ethan, "Independence from the Corporate Global Economy," *Yes! Magazine*, Oct. 31, 2006, www.yesmagazine.org/issues/go-local/independence-from-the-corporate-global-economy.
3. Farrell, John, "New York City's Solar Windfall Illuminates America's Clean Energy Future," RenewableEnergyWorld.com, Sept. 20, 2011, www.renewableenergyworld.com/rea/blog/post/2011/09new-york-citys-solar-windfall-illuminates-americas-clean-energy-future.
4. Barringer, Felicity, "White Roofs Catch On as Energy Cost Cutters," *New York Times*, July 29, 2009, www.nytimes.com/2009/07/30/science/earth/30degrees.html.
5. Davidson, Greg, and Paul Davidson, *Economics for a Civilized Society*, rev. ed. (Armonk, NY: M. E. Sharpe, 1996), p. 214.
6. Van Gelder, Sarah, "Pete Seeger: How Can I Keep from Singing?" *Yes! Magazine*, Feb. 1, 2008, www.yesmagazine.org/issues/climate-solutions/pete-seeger-how-can-i-keep-from-singing.
7. Alperovitz, Gar, "The New-Economy Movement," *Nation*, June 13, 2011, www.thenation.com/article/160949/new-economy-movement.
8. Bollier, David, "The Marginalization of the Commons and What to Do About It," Thirteenth Biennial Conference of the International Association for the Study of the Commons, Hyderabad, India, Jan. 12, 2011. Available online at http://bollier.org/marginalization-commons-and-what-to-do-about-it.
9. Row, Jonathan, "How Commerce Consumed the Commons," *YES! Magazine*, Nov. 30, 2006, www.yesmagazine.org/issues/go-local/how-commerce-consumed-the-commons.
10. Schorr, Lisbeth B., *Common Purpose: Strengthening Families and Neighborhoods to Rebuild America* (New York: Anchor Books, Doubleday, 1997), p. 49.
11. Ibid., p. 1.

3: GIVE SCIENCE AND TECHNOLOGY BACK TO THE PEOPLE

1. Shiva, Vandana, *Biopiracy: The Plunder of Nature and Knowledge* (Boston: South End Press, 1997), p. 17.
2. Levy, Stuart B., *The Antibiotic Paradox: How the Misuse of Antibiotics Destroys Their Curative Powers* (Cambridge, MA: Perseus, 2002), pp. 276–7.
3. *New Developments in Biotechnology: U.S. Investment in Biotechnology— Special Report*, Office of Technology Assessment (Washington, DC: U.S. Government Printing Office, July 1988), p. 114. Available at

www.scribd.com/doc/4100898/New-Developments-in-Biotechnology
-US-Investment-in-Biotechnology.

4. Naik, Gautam, "Mistakes in Scientific Studies Surge," *Wall Street Journal*, Aug. 10, 2011, http://online.wsj.com/article/SB100014240 52702303627104576411850666582080.html.

5. Visvanathan, Shiv, "A Celebration of Difference: Science and Democracy in India," *Science* 280, no. 5360 (Apr. 3, 1998), 42–3.

6. Zwarenstein, Carlyn, "Here Comes Everybody," *Canadian Geographic* 130, no. 3 (June 2010).

7. Hayes, Denis, "A Plan for the Solar Revolution," *Mother Earth News*, Apr./May 2009, www.motherearthnews.com/Renewable-Energy/ Solar-Power-Green-Jobs.aspx?page=2.

8. Lovins, Amory B. *Soft Energy Paths: Toward a Durable Peace* (New York: Harper and Row, 1977).

9. Hayes, "Plan for the Solar Revolution."

4: PROTECT THE FAMILY UNIT

1. Grossman, Dave, and Gloria DeGaetano, *Stop Teaching Our Kids to Kill: A Call to Action Against TV, Movie and Video Game Violence* (New York: Crown Publishers, 1999).

2. Huesmann, L. Rowell, et al. "Longitudinal Relations between Children's Exposure to TV Violence and Their Aggressive and Violent Behavior in Young Adulthood: 1977–1992," *Developmental Psychology* 39, no. 2 (Mar. 2003), 201–21.

3. Rodriguez, Richard, "The Coming Mayhem: Pre-Teens Today Are More Violent than Ever Before," *Los Angeles Times*, Jan. 21, 1996, http://articles.latimes.com/1996-01-21/opinion/op-27205_1_adult-responsibility.

4. Klaassen, Abbey, "Why Google Sees Cellphones as the 'Ultimate Ad Vehicle,'" *Advertising Age*, Sept. 8, 2008, http://adage.com/article/ print-edition/google-sees-cellphones-ultimate-ad-vehicle/130697/.

5. Griffith, Erin, "Facebook's Holy Grail of Branding: 'Sponsored Stories' Get 50 Million 'Likes' a Day," *Adweek*, May 24, 2011.

5: GET CORPORATIONS OFF WELFARE

1. Barlett, Donald L., and James B. Steele, "Corporate Welfare," *Time*, Nov. 9, 1998.

2. *Unnecessary Business Subsidies*, Committee on the Budget (Washington, DC: U.S. Government Printing Office, 1999).

6: CRACK DOWN ON CORPORATE CRIME

1. "Injury and Illness Prevention Program," OSHA White Paper, Jan. 2012, p. 4. Accessible online at www.osha.gov/dsg/topics/safety health/OSHAwhite-paper-january2012sm.pdf.

2. "Key Facts about Air Pollution," American Lung Association, www
.lung.org/assets/documents/key_air.pdf.
3. "100,000 Lives Campaign Objectives, December 2004–June 2006,"
Institute for Healthcare Improvement, www.ihi.org/offerings/Ini
tiatives/PastStrategicInitiatives/5MillionLivesCampaign/Docu
ments/100000%20Lives%20Campaign%20Scorecard.pdf.
4. Wilper, Andrew, et al., "Health Insurance and Mortality in U.S.
Adults," *American Journal of Public Health* 99, no. 12 (Dec. 2009).
Available at http://pnhp.org/excessdeaths/.
5. Easterbrook, Frank H., and Daniel R. Fischel, "Antitrust Suits by Targets of Tender Offers," *Michigan Law Review* 80, no. 6 (May 1982): 1157.
6. Ferner, Mike, "Taken for a Ride on the Interstate Highway System,"
CounterPunch, June 28, 2006, www.counterpunch.org/2006/06/28/
taken-for-a-ride-on-the-interstate-highway-system/print.
7. Braithwaite, John, and Brent Fisse, *The Impact of Publicity on Corporate Offenders* (Albany: State University of New York Press, 1983),
p. 246.
8. Braithwaite, John, *Crime, Shame and Reintegration* (New York: Cambridge University Press, 1989), p. 143.
9. Geis, Gilbert, "Deterring Corporate Crime," in *The Consumer and
Corporate Accountability*, ed. Ralph Nader (New York: Harcourt
Brace Jovanovich, 1973), p. 343.
10. Green, Mark J., *Selling Out: How Big Corporate Money Buys Elections,
Rams through Legislation, and Betrays Our Democracy* (New York:
ReganBooks, 2002).
11. Eaton, Joe, "Lobbyists Swarm Capitol to Influence Health Reform," *iWatch News*, Center for Public Integrity, Feb. 24, 2010,
www.iwatchnews.org/2010/02/24/2725/lobbyists-swarm-capitol-
influence-health-reform.
12. www.taf.org/DoJ-fraud-stats-FY2011.pdf. $11 billion estimate given
and confirmed by Patrick Burns, director of communications at Taxpayers Against Fraud.
13. Geis, Gilbert. 2006. *White-Collar Criminal: The Offender in Business
and the Professions*, pp. 114–15.
14. Mokhiber, Russell, "Twenty Things You Should Know about Corporate Crime," *Corporate Crime Reporter* 25, June 12, 2007, http://
corporatecrimereporter.com/twenty061207.htm.

7: CREATE NATIONAL CHARTERS FOR LARGE CORPORATIONS

1. Nader, Ralph, and Mark Green. *Corporate Power in America*, Fore-
word. (New York: Grossman Publishers, 1973).
2. William Gossett, in *Corporate Power in America*.
3. Henry Simons, *Politico Credo* (self-published, 1947), p. 59.
4. *Houston, We Still Have a Problem: An Alternative Annual Report on
Halliburton, May 2005*, CorpWatch, www.halliburtonwatch.org/
about_hal/houston.2005.pdf.

5. Hinkley, Robert, "28 Words to Redefine Corporate Duties: The Proposal for a Code for Corporate Citizenship," *Multinational Monitor* 23, nos. 7–8 (July/Aug. 2002). Available at http://multinationalmon itor.org/mm2002/02july-aug/july-aug02corp4.html.

8: RESTORE OUR CIVIL LIBERTIES

1. "Issues 2012: The Candidate's Briefing Book—Middle East," Heritage Foundation, www.candidatebriefing.com/middle-east/.
2. Dahl, Erik, "The Plots That Failed: Intelligence Lessons Learned from Unsuccessful Terrorist Attacks against the United States," *Studies in Conflict and Terrorism* 34, no. 8 (Aug. 2011), pp. 621–48.
3. "A New Presidency: How Bush Should Spend His Windfall of Political Capital," editorial, *Wall Street Journal*, September 2001.
4. Clarke, Richard A., *Against All Enemies: Inside America's War on Terror* (New York: Free Press, 2004), p. 246.
5. Tribe, Laurence, and Patrick O. Gudridge, "The Anti-Emergency Constitution," *Yale Law Journal* 113 (2004).
6. Will, George F., "No Checks, Many Imbalances," *Washington Post*, Feb. 16, 2006.
7. ABA Task Force on Presidential Signing Statements and the Separation of Powers Doctrine, "Recommendation Adopted by the House of Delegates, August 7–8, 2006," American Bar Association, 2006, www.americanbar.org/content/dam/aba/migrated/leadership/2006/annual/dailyjournal/20060823144113.authcheckdam.pdf.
8. Jonathan Turley (http://jonathanturley.org/about/), Michael Ratner and Bill Goodman (www.globalpolitician.com/23523-bush), Bruce Fein (http://blog.sfgate.com/chroncast/2007/07/28/conservative-law yer-bruce-fein-argues-for-the-impeachment-of-bush-and-cheney/), and Elizabeth Holtzman (www.truthdig.com/report/item/20060912 _elizabeth_holtzman_impeachment_bush/).

9: USE GOVERNMENT PROCUREMENT TO SPUR INNOVATION

1. Carmen, Gerald. 1988. Panel on "The Automobile Airbag: Case Study of a Stimulative Procurement," p. 59.
2. *2011 Agency Financial Report*, General Services Administration, www.gsa.gov/graphics/staffoffices/GSA_FY2011_AFR.pdf.
3. Lovins, Amory B., and L. Hunter Lovins, "Energy Forever," *American Prospect* 13, no. 3 (Feb. 11, 2002), pp. 30–4.
4. "1603 Treasury Program," Solar Energy Industries Association, www.seia.org/cs/solar_policies/1603_treasury_program.
5. Paglia, Todd, "At the White House Copier Paper Summit," *Washington Post*, Jan. 18, 1998.
6. Mick, Jason, "Office 2010 to Launch Today, Microsoft Owns 94 Percent of the Market," *DailyTech*, May 12, 2010, www.dailytech.com/

Office+2010+to+Launch+Today+Microsoft+Owns+94+Percent+of +the+Market/article18360.htm.

7. "Gartner Says Worldwide Operating System Software Market Grew to $30.4 Billion in 2010," press release, Gartner, Apr. 27, 2011, www .gartner.com/it/page.jsp?id=1654914.

8. Ashford, Nicholas A., and Ralph P. Hall, *Technology, Globalization, and Sustainable Development: Transforming the Industrial State* (New Haven, CT: Yale University Press, 2011), p. 12.

10: REINVEST IN PUBLIC WORKS

1. *Lessons Learned: A National Report*, Healthy Schools Network, Apr. 2006, www.healthyschools.org/documents/Lessons_Learned_Rpt .pdf.

2. "Table 242. Public Elementary and Secondary Schools—Summary: 1980 to 2009," *Statistical Abstract of the United States*, U.S. Census Bureau, 2012, www.census.gov/compendia/statab/2012/tables/ 12s0243.pdf.

3. "Schools in Need," Rebuild America's Schools, http://rebuildamer icasschools.org/Need.html.

4. Duhigg, Charles, "Millions in U.S. Drink Dirty Water, Records Show," *New York Times*, Dec. 7, 2009, www.nytimes.com/2009/12/08/ business/energy-environment/08water.html?pagewanted=all.

5. ———, "That Tap Water Is Legal but May Be Unhealthy," *New York Times*, Dec. 17, 2009, www.nytimes.com/2009/12/17/us/17water. html?_r=1.

6. *Drinking Water Infrastructure Needs Survey and Assessment, First Report to Congress*, Environmental Protection Agency, Jan. 1997.

7. "Local Government Investment in Municipal Water and Sewer Infrastructure: Adding Value to the National Economy," Mayors Water Council, U.S. Conference of Mayors, Washington, D.C., Aug. 14, 2008, www.usmayors.org/urbanwater/documents/LocalGovt%20 InvtInMunicipalWaterandSewerInfrastructure.pdf.

8. "New Report Shows Failing to Invest in Transportation Will Cause Job Losses, Shrink Household Incomes," press release, American Society of Civil Engineers, Aug. 3, 2011, www.asce.org/Press-Releases/2011/ New-Report-Shows-Failing-to-Invest-in-Transportation-Will-Cause-Job-Losses,-Shrink-Household-Incomes/.

9. *Status of the Nations Surface Transportation System—Condition and Performance: Report to Congress*, Department of Transportation, Washington, DC, 1997.

10. Alvarez, Mila, *The State of America's Forests*, Society of American Foresters, Bethesda, MD, 2007, www.safnet.org/publications/ameri canforests/StateOfAmericasForests.pdf.

11. Hansen, Matthew C., Stephen V. Stehman, and Peter V. Potapov, "Quantification of Global Gross Forest Cover Loss," *Proceedings of*

the National Academy of Sciences of the United States of America 107, no. 19 (May 11, 2010): 8650–55. Available at www.pnas.org/con tent/107/19/8650.full.

11: REDUCE OUR BLOATED MILITARY BUDGET

1. Adams, Gordon and Matthew Leatherman. 2011. "A Leaner and Meaner Defense: How to Cut the Pentagon's Budget While Improving Its Performance." *Foreign Affairs.* www.foreignaffairs.com/articles/67145/gordon-adams-and-matthew-leatherman/a-leaner-and-meaner-defense.

2. Jarecki, Eugene, *The American Way of War: Guided Missiles, Misguided Men, and a Republic in Peril* (New York: Free Press, 2008), pp. 149–54.

3. Ibid., p. 144.

4. Bacevich, Andrew J., *The New American Militarism: How Americans Are Seduced by War* (New York: Oxford University Press, 2005), p. 2.

5. "Pentagon Releases Sexual Harassment Data," Associated Press, Mar. 14, 2008, www.msnbc.msn.com/id/23636487/ns/us_news-military/t/pentagon-releases-sexual-harassment-data/.

6. "The Department of Waste," Taxpayers for Common Sense, June 10, 2005, www.taxpayer.net/projects.php?action=view&category=&type=Project&proj_id=479.

7. Interview with Shane Ratliff, former driver for KBR, in *Iraq for Sale: The War Profiteers*, directed by Robert Greenwald, Brave New Films, 2006.

8. Since the U.S. invasion of Iraq, reports of wasteful spending and excessive charges under these contracts have multiplied. Former Halliburton employees have provided information to Congress that the company charged $45 for cases of soda and billed $100 to clean fifteen-pound bags of laundry. *Halliburton's Questioned and Unsupported Costs in Iraq Exceed $1.4 Billion*, Committee on Government Reform, Minority Staff, Special Investigations Division, June 27, 2005, p. 2. Available at http://dpc.senate.gov/hearings/hearing22/jointreport.pdf.

9. *Recommended Budget Cuts for the 112th Congress*, Taxpayers for Common Sense, Jan. 2011, www.taxpayer.net/uscr_uploads/file/FederalBudget/BudgetReform/BudgetCuts/TCS_cut_list_112th_Congress.pdf.

10. Korb, Lawrence J., Laura Conley, and Alex Rothman, "Sensible Defense Cuts: How to Save $400 Billion through 2015," Center for American Progress, July 6, 2011, www.americanprogress.org/issues/2011/07/defense_cuts.html.

11. *Defense Acquisitions: Assessments of Selected Major Weapon Programs*," Government Accountability Office, Mar. 2006, p. 8. Available at www.gao.gov/new.items/d06391.pdf.

12. *Defense Acquisitions: Assessments of Selected Major Weapon Programs,"* Government Accountability Office, Mar. 2011, p. 140. Available at www.gao.gov/assets/320/317081.pdf.
13. Galbraith, John Kenneth, *The Good Society: The Humane Agenda* (Boston: Houghton Mifflin, 1996), p. 99.
14. Ibid., p. 100.
15. Ibid., p. 102.
16. Korb, Lawrence, and Miriam Pemberton, *Report of the Task Force on a Unified Security Budget for the United States,* June 30, 2011, www.fpif.org/reports/unified_security_budget_fy2012.
17. Gerencser, Mark, "Re-imagining Infrastructure," *American Interest* 6, no. 4 (March/April 2011). Available at www.the-american-interest.com/article.cfm?piece=926.
18. Bacevich, *New American Militarism,* p. 225.
19. Ibid., p. 7.

12: REENGAGE WITH CIVIC LIFE

1. King, Martin Luther, Jr. 1955. "Alabama City Speech."
2. You can read more about Gibbs at http://chej.org/about/our-story/about-lois/.
3. Kahn, Si, *Creative Community Organizing: A Guide for Rabble-Rousers, Activists, and Quiet Lovers of Justice* (San Francisco: Berrett-Koehler, 2010). Reprinted with author's permission.
4. Hunn, Dwayne, and Doris Ober, "Ordinary People Doing the Extraordinary: The Story of Ed and Joyce Koupal and the Initiative Process," People's Lobby, 2001, http://old.ni4d.us/library/koupals.pdf.

14: ORGANIZE CONGRESSIONAL WATCHDOG GROUPS

1. Nader, Ralph, and Theresa Amato, "So You Want to Run for President? Ha!: Barriers to Third-Party Entry," *National Civic Review* 90, no. 2 (Summer 2001), p. 163.
2. "The Fair Elections Now Act Is a Declaration of Independence for Congress: Public Citizen Enthusiastically Endorses S. 750 and H.R. 1404," Public Citizen, Apr. 12, 2011, www.citizen.org/documents/FENA-Statement-20110412.pdf.
3. Green, Mark J., et al., *Who Runs Congress?* 4th ed. (New York: Dell, 1984).

15: GET CONGRESS TO HAVE SKIN IN THE GAME

1. "Lawmakers Share Parents' Fear," Associated Press, Mar. 14, 2005, http://web.archive.org/web/20050316042350/www.cnn.com/2005/ALLPOLITICS/03/14/congress.kidsatwar.ap/index.html.
2. Lichtblau, Eric, "Economic Downturn Took a Detour at Capitol Hill," *New York Times,* Dec. 26, 2011, www.nytimes.com/2011/12/27/us/

politics/economic-slide-took-a-detour-at-capitol-hill.html?pagewanted
=all.

3. Fein, Bruce, "God Is Alive, Due Process Is Dead," *Daily Caller*, Jan. 5, 2012, http://dailycaller.com/2012/01/05/god-is-alive-due-process-is-dead/#ixzz1ivVzkyFs.

4. "Fix FISA—End Warrantless Wiretapping," ACLU, Feb. 17, 2012, www.aclu.org/national-security/fix-fisa-end-warrantless-wire tapping.

16: ENLIST THE ENLIGHTENED SUPER-RICH

1. Firestone, Shulamith, "The Women's Rights Movement in the U.S.A.: New View," in *Notes from the First Year* (New York: New York Radical Women, 1968). Available at www.marxists.org/subject/women/authors/firestone-shulamith/womens-rights-movement.htm.

2. "Giving Pledge FAQ," Giving Pledge, http://givingpledge.org/Con tent/media/GivingPledge_FAQ.pdf.

3. Bacevich, *New American Militarism*, p. 66.

4. McCarthy, Colman, "There's a Difference between Charity and Justice," *National Catholic Reporter*, Sept. 2, 2010, http://ncronline.org/news/justice/theres-difference-between-charity-and-justice.

5. Buffett, Warren E., "Stop Coddling the Super-Rich," *New York Times*, Aug. 14, 2011, www.nytimes.com/2011/08/15/opinion/stop-coddling-the-super-rich.html.

6. Stewart, James B., "Questioning the Dogma of Tax Rates," *New York Times*, Aug. 19, 2011, www.nytimes.com/2011/08/20/business/ques tioning-the-dogma-of-lower-taxes-on-capital-gains.html?pagewanted
=all.

17: GET BACK ON THE FIELD—LITERALLY

1. Coe, Dawn Podulka, et al. "Effect of Physical Education and Activity Levels on Academic Achievement in Children," *Medicine and Science in Sports and Exercise* 38, no. 8 (Aug. 2006), pp. 1515–9. Available at www.kapoleims.k12.hi.us/campuslife/depts/electives/dance/Ef fects%20of%20Physical%20Education%20and%20Activity%20lev els%20on%20Academic%20Achievement%20in%20Children.pdf.

BOOKS BY RALPH NADER

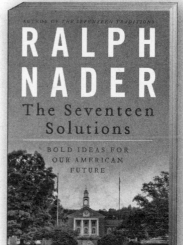

THE SEVENTEEN SOLUTIONS
Bold Ideas for Our American Future
ISBN 978-0-06-208353-1 (paperback)

From one of the most important and provocative progressive voices in American history comes a new and uplifting program to rescue America from its social doldrums. In *The Seventeen Solutions*, Ralph Nader surveys the stark, concrete contrasts between the kind of society and economy America can and should have, and the unjust conditions under which so many people actually live today.

THE SEVENTEEN TRADITIONS
Lessons from an American Childhood
ISBN 978-0-06-221064-7 (paperback)

Activist and humanitarian Ralph Nader looks back on his small-town American childhood and the traditions that shaped his worldview. Weaving memoir with thoughtful inspiration, Nader reawakens our own memories of a simpler time and celebrates the enduring values that informed his perspective on politics and gave him the courage to spend decades crusading for change.

"*The Seventeen Traditions* brings us back to what's important in life—and what makes America truly great."
—Jim Hightower, *Illinois Times*